THE ENCYCLOPEDIA OF
EXPLORERS AND
ADVENTURERS

THE ENCYCLOPEDIA OF EXPLORERS AND ADVENTURERS

WRITTEN BY
JUSTINE
CIOVACCO

Franklin Watts
A Division of Scholastic Inc.
New York Toronto London Auckland Sydney
Mexico City New Delhi Hong Kong
Danbury, Connecticut

CREATED IN ASSOCIATION WITH MEDIA PROJECTS, INCORPORATED
Carter Smith, *Managing Editor*
Karen Covington, *Project Editor*
Laura Smyth, *Designer*
Anthony Galante, *Production Editor*
Oxygen Design: Sherry Williams, Tilman Reitzle, *Cover Design*
Athena Angelos, *Picture Researcher*
Ron Toelke Associates, *Cartographer*
Marilyn Flaig, *Indexer*

FRANKLIN WATTS STAFF
Phil Friedman, *Publisher*
Kate Nunn, *Editor-in-Chief*
Andrew Hudak, *Editor*
Marie O'Neill, *Art Director*

Picture Credits
TITLE PAGE: Álvar Núñez Cabeza de Vaca, Library of Congress.
TABLE OF CONTENTS: Upper left: Delia Akeley, The American Museum of Natural History.
Lower right: Roald Amundsen, The London Illustrated News.
INTRODUCTION (PAGE 6, FROM TOP TO BOTTOM): Sebastian Cabot, Library of Congress; Amerigo
Vespucci, Media Projects Archives; Annie Smith Peck, Library of Congress; Vasco Nuñez de Balboa,
Media Projects Archives; Sacagawea, Library of Congress.

Every endeavor has been made to obtain permission to use copyrighted material. The publishers would
appreciate errors or omissions brought to their attention.

Library of Congress Cataloging-in-Publication Data

Ciovacco, Justine
   The encyclopedia of explorers and adventurers / Justine Ciovacco
     p. cm.
   Summary: Briefly describes the life and accomplishments of men and women who have made significant contributions as explorers and adventurers throughout the world and throughout history.
   Includes bibliographical references (p.).
   ISBN 0-531-14664-2
    1. Explorers—Encyclopedias, Juvenile. 2. Discoveries in geography—Encyclopedias, Juvenile. 3. Adventure and adventurers—Encyclopedias, Juvenile. 4. Explorers—Biography—Juvenile literature. 5. Discoveries in geography—Juvenile literature. 6. Adventures and adventurers—Biography—Juvenile literature. [1. Explorers—Encyclopedias. 2. Discoveries in geography—Encyclopedias. 3. Adventure and adventurers—Encyclopedias.] I. Title.

G200 .C56 2003
910'.92'2—dc21
[B]   2002027004

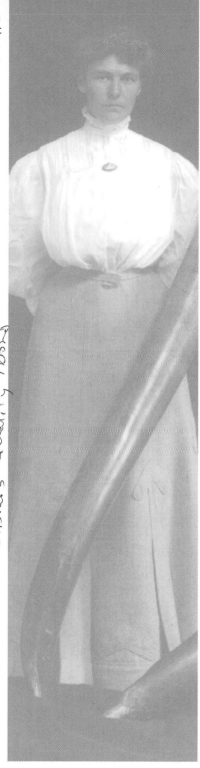

Contents

Introduction

THE SEED OF SUCCESS

The mix of world travelers, missionaries, explorers of the deep and the sky, conquerors of new lands, and history-making adventurers in this book may seem like a random bunch. That is, until you realize how the goals, struggles, successes, and even failures of each one easily stand up against the others profiled on these pages. Achieving a goal is not just a dream for these explorers and adventurers—it's the driving force in their lives.

Take for example Reinhold Messner, who became the first person to climb all 14 of the world's 26,247-foot-plus (8,000-meter) peaks by 1985. Messner's feat is made more impressive by the fact that he wasn't deterred from climbing when his brother was killed in an avalanche and all of his major climbs have been made without the use of supplemental oxygen. Self-imposed struggles also allowed Simón Bolívar to almost single-handedly change the fate of South America. Angered by Napoleon's rise to fame after the French Revolution, Bolívar vowed he would devote his life to fight for his homeland's independence from France—with or without the help of leaders in other countries.

Some explorers and adventurers are not only prepared for early struggles, but also to give their lives to do what they love. Bessie Coleman, one of 13 children born to a poor, African-American family, worked menial jobs so that she could afford flying lessons and then trained to become America's first and most famous female African-American stunt pilot. Though an early crash shelved her career briefly, she continued flying soon after her broken bones healed only to die later in a second crash. "King of the wild frontier" Davy Crockett literally fought to the death, defending Texas's independence from Mexico. The first American to walk in space, Edward White, is another casualty of adventure. He died, along with astronauts Gus Grissom and Roger Chaffee, when their space-training mission went awry.

GUIDING FORCES

Of course the many explorers and adventurers profiled on these pages could not have succeeded in their actions without the guidance or love of their families, partners, or even a higher force. While missionaries like Father Junipero Serra found drive through a constant yearning to spread God's message, most of the book's daring explorers and adventurers had a family waiting patiently behind the scenes or even helping.

Sometimes family members offer hands-on assistance, as is the case with Delia Akeley, who learned to hunt in order to help her husband create museum exhibits. Other loved ones offer mental and financial support. The first woman to sail around the world alone, Naomi James, found her boat through her husband and received daily support—via radio—from her father-in-law, as her husband was achieving his own goals in yacht racing. Explorer John Franklin's wife showed her greatest strength when guiding search missions to find her husband after he failed to return from an Arctic expedition.

Countless others who helped these explorers and adventurers find their way don't receive a mention in this book. Still, as you read, you may wonder how each person profiled could have dreamed so big and coped with the challenges along the way, and you may end up considering the people that stood behind each man or woman who dared to attempt such unique, difficult, and amazing feats.

You will discover that some of the explorers' stories are intertwined. When a featured explorer is mentioned on another explorer's page his or her name appears in bold print. The majority of places visited by the explorers and adventurers appear in all capital letters to indicate that they may be found on the map pages at the back of the book. Lastly, each profile shows that behind every heroic (or sometimes villainous) exploit is the seed of a dream, and a constant drive to make it happen, and that ultimately success or failure is based on strength of character and sometimes pure luck.

By Justine Ciovacco

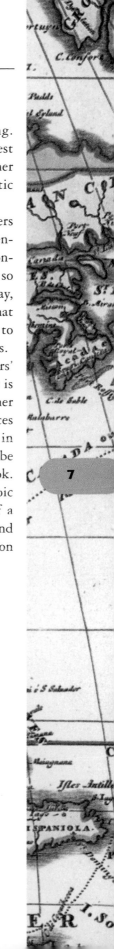

Harriet Chalmers Adams

(1875–1937) WAR CORRESPONDENT·TRAVELER

At age 11, Harriet Chalmers began a life-long quest for adventure. On a chilly day in August 1886, she swam 250 yards (229 m) from the shore of the Pacific Ocean in Santa Cruz, California, to a wooden raft and back to shore. The feat was featured in her hometown newspaper the next day. "That's my girl," her father, Alexander, told her. "You can do anything you want to do."

Three years later, Chalmers and her father explored California's San Joaquin Valley and the SIERRA NEVADA on horseback, making her the first white child to cross several trails in the Sierra Nevada. "I was an explorer when I was too young to realize it," Chalmers later wrote of her early travels.

LATIN AMERICA

Educated at home with tutors, Chalmers's sense of adventure didn't end when she became an adult; the explorations just got more challenging. In 1889, she married fellow traveler Franklin Pierce Adams, and a few years later they began a three-year trip through every country in Central and South America. Traveling by boat and horseback, the pair crossed at least 20 territories where it was noted that Chalmers Adams was the first white woman to set foot on their soil. She was also one of the first to climb EL MISTI, a 19,200-foot-tall (5,852-m) peak in the ANDES.

Chalmers Adams met with danger more than once, most notably when a bridge she was standing on washed out over a steep ravine in Peru and when she came upon a tribe of headhunters in the AMAZON RAINFOREST. Yet, by 1916, Chalmers Adams met her goals of seeing all of the places Christopher Columbus had first visited in the New World and every former Spanish and Portuguese conquest.

WAR CORRESPONDENT

During World War I, Chalmers Adams worked as a war correspondent for *Harper's* and *National Geographic*. The French government allowed her to visit the front-line trenches, making her the only woman to do so.

Chalmers Adams was a lively speaker who loved to share her adventures and thousands of color photographs and slides. In fact, she was the first person in the Western Hemisphere to use color slides for presentations to mass audiences. The pictures allowed many people to view Central and South America's

brightly colored jungle plants, peaks, and wild animals for the first time.

In 1925, after she was denied membership to the then-males-only National Geographic Society, Chalmers Adams began the Society for Women Geographers and was named its first president. "The men, you know, had their hide-bound, exclusive little explorers' and adventurers' clubs for years and years," she told a reporter in 1928. "They have always been afraid that some mere woman might penetrate their sanctums of discussion…(which) might be mutually beneficial."

Still, Chalmers Adams's greatest challenge came in 1926, when she fell off a cliff in Spain. She shattered her back and doctors told her she would never walk again. Chalmers Adams lay in a plaster cast with steel braces for two years. After learning to walk again, she took a 20-month trip around the world.

Carl Ethan Akeley (1864–1926)

HUNTER·TRAVELER·TAXIDERMIST

Carl Akeley spent his youth hunting and working on his family farm near Rochester, New York. At age 17, he became an assistant at Ward's Natural Science Establishment, a company that supplied museums with stuffed and mounted animal specimens. At that time, it was common in taxidermy to fill an animal's dried skin with rags, straw, and wood shavings, but Akeley was unhappy with the preserved animals the establishment produced. He felt their method did not do justice to the animals' true shapes, so he experimented with other ways to display animals. At 19, Akeley was offered a major project: mounting Jumbo, circus impresario P. T. Barnum's famous elephant who had recently died. Akeley constructed a lightweight, yet sturdy bentwood frame over wooden planks, on which he stretched the elephant's hide.

Akeley continued to develop new methods of taxidermy while working at the Museum of Milwaukee (1887–1895) and the Field Museum of Natural History in Chicago (1895–1909). His final method, still used today, consisted of mounting specimens by applying their skin to a hollow, finely contoured plaster cast model.

AFRICAN ADVENTURE

Akeley made the first of many expeditions to British Somaliland (modern SOMALIA) in East Africa in 1896. There, he was a member of a safari expedition with native guides, porters, and scientists. For five months, Akeley hunted, collected specimens, and studied wild animals for museum displays. He became intrigued by African elephants, and began a project that he worked on throughout his life—a full-scale African diorama made to educate the public about the continent and its wildlife.

In later expeditions he had the help of his wife **Delia Akeley** and, on his final trips, second wife Mary Jobe Akeley. They took photographs, made plaster casts of grasses and leaves, and gathered or killed specimens when necessary.

Akeley made his third African trip to UGANDA and KENYA, among other remote areas, in 1906–1907. With wife Delia and a crew, Akeley hunted a family of four elephants for a display at the American Museum of Natural History in New York City. Akeley became so obsessed with finding a large, male "father figure" that he came down with a number of illnesses, including meningitis, during his exhaustive search. With the task still unfinished, museum officials told Akeley they had run out of money for the expedition. Unwilling to give up, he sold his family farm to buy more time.

Twice in his career, Akeley faced a charging elephant. The second time, the elephant attacked most fiercely, scalping Akeley's forehead, smashing his nose, tearing one cheek so that it hung down, breaking many ribs, and puncturing one lung. On a later trip to Africa, Akeley returned to the site to shoot the large male that he needed to finish his collection.

THE FINAL JOURNEY

In 1926, Akeley made his last trip to Africa to study mountain gorillas. Years before, he had noticed the growing rate at which they were being killed by poachers and enlisted the help of the Belgian government to establish the Albert (now Virunga) National Park, Africa's first game reserve. It finally opened a few months after Akeley's death.

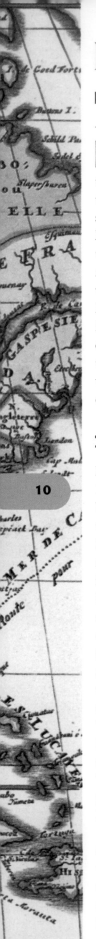

Delia J. Akeley (1875–1970)

HUNTER·TRAVELER

Delia Denning grew up on a Wisconsin farm and had little formal schooling. She met taxidermist **Carl Akeley** when she began working at the Museum of Milwaukee, and soon took an interest in what he loved most: hunting. After traveling with her then-boyfriend on many local hunts, the petite 5-foot, 5-inch (1.6-m) Denning became an expert markswoman, saying later that she did so because "a woman who could not take care of herself could be a handicap."

TRAVELS IN AFRICA

Four years after marrying in 1902, the Akeleys traveled to UGANDA and KENYA, where they spent a year and a half collecting plant and animal specimens and hunting elephants for a museum display. In her book, *All True*, Akeley recalled she was "terribly afraid but fascinated" as she stood 8,000 feet (2,438 m) atop Mt. Kenya and

shot her first elephant. "Scarcely breathing, and with legs trembling so I could hardly stand, I waited for the elephant to move forward," she wrote. "Dimly through the mist the dark shape came slowly from behind the bush, exposing a splendid pair of tusks and a great flapping ear which was my target." The 10-foot, 10-inch (3-m) elephant is still on display today in Chicago's Field Museum of Natural History.

After she divorced her husband in 1923, Akeley remained enamored with the continent and returned to explore it several more times. Her fourth hunting trip, the first without her husband, was arranged to collect

> **In her African adventures, Akeley was able to make the discovery of new species of antelope and bird.**

animals and artifacts for the Brooklyn Museum in New York City. The journey made Akeley the first woman to cross Africa—from the Indian Ocean to the Atlantic—alone, except for her native porters. In her travels, Akeley crossed Kenya's crocodile-infested Tana River by canoe and the then-unexplored desert between the Tana River and ETHIOPIA on camelback.

THE AUTHOR

Akeley put pencil to paper and scrawled all of the sights, sounds, smells, and excitement in a journal, which later yielded books. She traveled in a relatively elegant caravan style with her porters carrying tents, cooking gear, photographic equipment, luggage, a rubber bathtub, and full sets of silver dining utensils on their backs. She rode camels or donkeys or walked.

Some of the people who lived in the places Akeley visited along her route had never seen a white person, let alone a white female. On a visit to the Belgian Congo (modern DEMOCRATIC REPUBLIC OF THE CONGO), she lived with and studied the Pygmy tribe in the Ituri Forest for several months. While she hunted and socialized with them, Akeley also had to fight the curious tribe's efforts to see if the rest of her body was as white as her face and hands.

When she returned to the UNITED STATES, Akeley wrote about her African adventures and the little-seen parts of Africa she visited in the books *Jungle Portraits* (1930) and *J. T. Jr.* (1929), a biography of her pet monkey and constant traveling companion.

10

Afonso de Albuquerque (1453–1515)

EXPLORER · CONQUEROR

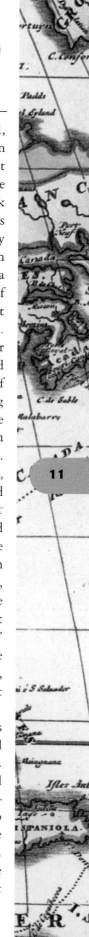

Afonso de Albuquerque was born and raised in Alhandra, Portugal. A relative of the royal family, he received many favors from them. In fact, he served as an attendant to King Alfonso V on his trip to Otranto, ITALY, in 1480. Albuquerque first traveled to INDIA in 1503, commanding a small fleet that built a Portuguese fort at the southern trading center of COCHIN. When Albuquerque returned home, he presented Portuguese King Manuel with a plan to increase Portugal's power by capturing the key ports of the East Indian trading regions that guarded access to it— ADEN, ORMUZ, and MALACCA.

Albuquerque sailed back to India in 1506 with commander Tristão da Cunha to take control from the Viceroy of India, Francisco de Almeida. Their journey took them along the coasts of MADAGASCAR, East Africa, and the island of SOCOTRA (modern SUQUTRA) at the mouth of the GULF OF ADEN. They took control of this gulf region in the name of the Portuguese crown. In Socotra and each city Albuquerque conquered on the rest of his travels, he built churches and forts and set up shipbuilding and other commercial endeavors in an effort to gain control of the sources of spices and the routes on which they were traded.

CONFLICT AHEAD

Albuquerque left Tristão behind to rule, while he sailed along the coast of OMAN to conquer the port city of Ormuz in 1507. When he returned to India, Albuquerque found that Almeida refused to give up command. Almeida briefly imprisoned Albuquerque, but a fleet of Portuguese ships arrived to ensure that Albuquerque was appointed the new viceroy of India. As viceroy, he was annoyed by the constant uprisings in CALICUT (modern KOZHIKODE) and destroyed the city, killing many people, on January 4, 1510.

Free to conquer more lands for Portugal, Albuquerque captured GOA, a major Muslim port in Southern India, in March 1510. The Portuguese lost control of the city soon after, but Albuquerque returned in November to recapture it. He took revenge on those who dared to protest his country's rule by massacring every Muslim man, woman, and child in the city. Albuquerque then set up a new city and made it the center of Portuguese power in Asia—as it remained for the next 450 years.

The very next year Albuquerque further extended Portuguese domination of Southeast Asia by conquering the city of Malacca on the MALAY PENINSULA with a force of 1,400 men and 18 ships. They gained control of the area, breaking down the guard that had been up on the narrow STRAIT OF MALACCA between SUMATRA and MALAYSIA, which served as the main route between the Indian Ocean and the Far East. When Malacca's prince was suspected of treason, Albuquerque publicly executed him and all of the male members of the royal family. He then sent three ships to the MOLUCCAS, or "Spice Islands," making them the first Europeans to travel to the spice source directly. By February 1515, Albuquerque was back in Ormuz, ensuring that it stayed under Portuguese rule.

As Albuquerque sailed from Ormuz to India, his ship was approached by another en route to give word that Lupe Suarez had replaced him as Viceroy of India. Albuquerque was hurt by the king's ingratitude and wrote him a letter explaining his past actions— including the murders—and requested financial help for his young son. Albuquerque died at the entrance to Goa harbor, never able to give the king his letter. Fifty-one years later, Albuquerque's remains were transported to Lisbon where he received a monument at his gravesite.

Alexander the Great (c. 356–323 BC)

KING·CONQUEROR

Alexander was born in Pella, the ancient capital of MACEDONIA, where his father, Philip II, ruled as king and created the Macedonian kingdom from separate tribes and principalities. When Philip was assassinated in June 336 BC, Alexander, only 20, became ruler of the Macedon kingdom.

With tensions running high in tribes and cities around him, Alexander and his army fought against neighboring Greek cities whose people were in a state of rebellion. One of the last of these battles was against the city of THEBES, which had most of its population massacred or enslaved by the Macedon army. At age 21, Alexander became the unopposed leader of the Greek world.

EXPANSION

In the fifth century BC Persian King Darius the Great, and later his son Xerxes, unsuccessfully led an army that attempted to conquer the Greeks and extend their empire into Europe. With the history of that Great Persian War on his mind, Alexander set out to conquer PERSIA (modern IRAN) in 334 BC. At the River Grancicus, near the ancient city of Troy, Alexander and an army of 35,000 Macedonian and Greek troops attacked an army of 40,000 Persians. After Alexander's army won this battle, all of the states of Asia Minor submitted to him.

Continuing south, Alexander and his army encountered the Persian army, commanded by King Darius III, in northeastern SYRIA in 333 BC. Again, Alexander claimed victory, as Darius fled to the north. Alexander's next conquest came a year later in a seven-month struggle with the seaport of Tyre. Gaza was captured next, and soon Alexander had control of the entire eastern Mediterranean coastline. To make his mark, he founded the city of ALEXANDRIA at the mouth of the NILE RIVER in 332

BC. Although Alexander named many cities after himself, this Alexandria became the literary, scientific, and commercial center of the Greek world.

Alexander's control reached into Carthaginian territory when Cyrene, the capital of the ancient North African kingdom of Cyrenaica, submitted to Alexander at the end of 332 BC. After reorganizing his army at Tyre, Alexander crossed the EUPHRATES and TIGRIS RIVERS and headed for BABYLON. Again, he met Darius and defeated his large army in the Battle of Gaugamela on October 1, 331 BC. Alexander continued on to PERSEPOLIS, the Persian capital. After stealing royal treasures in midwinter, Alexander got drunk and ordered his men to burn the city. With this act, Alexander destroyed the ancient Persian Empire. The Greek Empire now stretched from the southern shores of the CASPIAN SEA, including AFGHANISTAN, and northward through Central Asia.

After sailing down the INDUS RIVER to the PERSIAN GULF, Alexander arrived in Babylon in the spring of 323 BC to prepare for further conquests. Within a month, he contracted a deadly case of exhaustion with high fever. Alexander said he left his empire "to the strongest."

> **At the age of 13 or 14, Alexander was sent to study with philosopher Aristotle.**

Roald Amundsen (1872–1928)

EXPLORER

Roald Amundsen came from a family of Norwegian sailors, and by age 15 he knew he wanted to become a polar explorer. To achieve his dream, he conditioned himself by taking long ski trips across the countryside and sleeping with his windows open in the icy Norwegian winters.

After entering the Norwegian navy in 1894, he sailed as a naval officer on an expedition to map the ANTARCTIC coast. Then, between 1903 an 1906, he led a 70-foot (21-m) ship on the first-ever voyage through the Northwest Passage, the ice-filled route through Canadian islands separated by the Atlantic and Pacific oceans. These trips were the ultimate training ground for Amundsen's later work, as he learned how native people of the ARCTIC eat, dress, and move across country—most efficiently, by dogsled.

THE SOUTH POLE

Amundsen hoped that his next expedition would make him the first to reach to the NORTH POLE, but that plan was called off when news spread of Robert Peary's successful journey to the Pole. The heavily in debt Amundsen knew he needed a major triumph to make money, and decided he would become the first to reach the SOUTH POLE. Yet he also knew his contributors were weary of funding adventures to unexplored lands, and his government would be against his trip since GREAT BRITAIN was already funding one for Robert Scott. With these things in mind, Amundsen publicly announced that his next trip would be simply for scientific research—only his brother and his ship's commander knew his real plan.

Amundsen's ship, *Fram*, set sail with a crew of nine in June 1910 for the coast of MOROCCO. There Amundsen told his crew of his plan to find the South Pole. After four months of sailing to the BAY OF WHALES in Antarctica, the crew set up camp and killed seals for meat—always saving some for the dogs they had brought with them for sled-pulling (and later, food). "The dogs are the most important thing for us," Amundsen told his men. "The whole outcome of the expedition depends on them."

On October 18, 1911, Amundsen and his crew set out toward the pole, gliding over chunks of snow and ice on dogsleds and skis. Finally, at 3:00 PM on December 10, 1911, they arrived at the South Pole and planted a Norwegian flag.

BACK NORTH AGAIN

For his next expedition, Amundsen again looked to the North Pole. This time his goal was to become the first to fly over it. After years of unsuccessful attempts, he finally succeeded in May 1926 during a 70-hour blimp flight from SPITSBERGEN, NORWAY, to Teller, ALASKA. Yet the triumph was marred by controversy over which country could claim credit for the flight. The blimp, *Norge*, was designed, built, and co-piloted by Italian Umberto Nobile, who felt that his country should get credit since the Italian government helped finance *Norge*'s construction. Still, Amundsen claimed credit for Norway.

Amundsen later volunteered to search for Nobile when his blimp crashed during another polar flight. Nobile was eventually rescued, but Amundsen died when his search plane crashed into the Arctic Ocean.

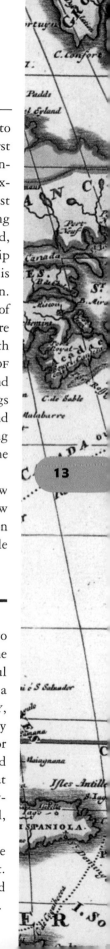

Neil Alden Armstrong (1930–)

ASTRONAUT·WAR VETERAN

At 16 years old, Neil Armstrong began flying as a student pilot. His love of flying continued and in 1950, midway through his education at Purdue University, Armstrong began active duty with the U.S. Navy during the Korean War. For the next two years, he flew fighter planes through 78 combat missions in Korea, until he returned home to earn his degree in aeronautical engineering in 1955.

Upon graduation, Armstrong joined the National Advisory Committee for Aeronautics (NACA), the precursor to NASA. By the end of 1955, he became a test pilot at NACA's Flight Research Center at Edwards Air Force Base in California. There, he flew many of the aircraft used as experiments for future spacecraft.

In 1962, Armstrong joined NASA's second group of astronaut trainees. He became the commanding pilot on *Gemini 8*, which launched on March 16, 1966, along with astronaut David R. Scott. During the mission, the craft docked with an Agena satellite 185 miles (298 km) above Earth. Thirty minutes later, the adjoined craft and satellite began rotating unexpectedly, eventually reaching 60 revolutions a minute. With the help of the ground crew, Armstrong

and Scott found that one of *Gemini 8*'s thruster rockets was open and spewing fuel into space. The two men used 75 percent of *Gemini 8*'s fuel to activate a second set of thrusters to stabilize themselves, leaving them with just enough to safely return to Earth.

Armstrong continued with assignments as part of the backup crew on *Gemini 11* and *Apollo 8*. Then, in 1968, he faced his most famous mission. As commander of *Apollo 11*, he was in charge of the ship's crew—Edwin "Buzz" Aldrin and Michael Allen Collins—whose goal it was to walk on the uncharted territory of the moon.

FIRST MOON WALK

After launching from Cape Canaveral, Florida, on July 16, 1969, *Apollo 11* began to orbit the moon four days later. On its 14th orbit, the lunar module *Eagle*—with Armstrong and Aldrin inside—undocked from *Apollo* and lowered toward the moon. Approximately 5,000 feet (1,500 m) above the moon, Armstrong began piloting to avoid boulders on the moon's surface. Three hours later, *Eagle* touched down and the two astronauts ate a meal, prepared the *Eagle* for liftoff in case of an emergency, and readied themselves for a moonwalk.

On July 21 at 10:56 PM, Armstrong exited the module. As he became the first human to set foot on the moon, he told ground control and millions of TV-viewers, "That's one small step for a man, one giant leap for mankind." Aldrin exited the module 15 minutes later, and the men spent 2-and-a-half hours collecting rock samples and setting up equipment, such as a laser reflector that reflected laser light fired from Earth in order to measure the distance between Earth and the moon. After *Eagle* rejoined *Apollo 11*, the crew returned to Earth on July 24 by splashing down in the Pacific Ocean near HAWAII. They then spent 18 days in biological quarantine to make sure they didn't bring any contaminant back to Earth.

Isabelle Autissier (1957–)

SOLO SAILOR

Isabelle Autissier grew up in a coastal town near Paris, France, where her father taught her to sail. At age 12 she decided that some day she would sail by herself around the world. By 30, she entered her first major competition, the Mini-Transat, a solo race from Brittany across the Atlantic to the French Antilles. Although she came in third, Autissier decided to quit her job as a marine biologist to focus full-time on solo sailing.

AROUND ALONE

Four years later, in 1991, Autissier set sail in Around Alone, a 27,000-mile (43,451-km), four-stop solo journey around the world that begins and ends in Charleston, SOUTH CAROLINA. Near AUSTRALIA, rough seas and high winds ripped the mast on Autissier's 60-foot boat. She fashioned a makeshift mast that enabled her to sail into port for repairs, and went on to finish the race, seventh out of eighteen. Still, Autissier became the first woman ever to complete Around Alone.

In 1994's Around Alone, Autissier had a five-day lead over her competitors in the first leg. However, she lost a mast to high waves in the Indian Ocean. On the way to an island to replace the mast, a huge wave knocked the boat over a full 360 degrees, breaking off its rigging and a chunk of the deck. Autissier had been safely below deck at the time, but she had to stay with the boat for four days until an Australian Navy frigate was able to help her out of the water.

ROUGH SEAS AHEAD

Autissier tried once again to win the Around Alone in 1999. She was second among three boats in the race's third and most difficult phase—a 5,960-mile (9,591-km) journey across the southern Pacific Ocean to PUNTA DEL ESTE, URUGUAY. Thinking she would save time, Autissier took a southern route through an area sailors call "the Screaming 50s" because of its location and rough seas.

After a day full of sail maneuvering on February 15, Autissier was exhausted. She laid down on the navigation bench, turned on autopilot, and took a nap. As she slept, autopilot misread the quickly changing wind speed and the boat jerked violently, throwing Autissier under a table. Within seconds, the boat rolled over. Everything that wasn't bolted down crashed around Autissier. With the glass top of her cabin now below her, Autissier saw the mast and rigging drift toward the bottom of the ocean. At 6:23 AM, she used her Emergency Position Indicating Radio Beacon to alert the race's command center of her trouble. Autissier then pulled on a survival suit, partially made out of titanium, to keep herself warm.

Meanwhile, the command center sent emails to Autissier's two competitors—because of their positions, they would be best able to save her. Giovanni Soldini, an Italian who was 200 miles (322 km) away from Autissier and in last place, used his satellite-tracking system to find Autissier's boat in 14 hours.

Aboard Soldini's boat, the two sailors celebrated with wine and pasta. Soldini, later declared the race's winner, dropped Autissier off in Uruguay. There, she announced she would continue sailing alone—but not around the Screaming 50s.

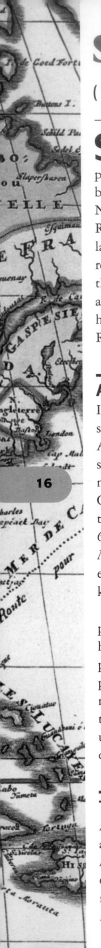

Sergei Petrovich Avdeyev

(1956–) COSMONAUT

Sergei Avdeyev was born and educated in St. Petersburg, RUSSIA. After he received a diploma in physics from the University of St. Petersburg, Avdeyev became a junior researcher at the Joint Institute for Nuclear Research in Dubna, Russia, in 1979. Fourteen years later, he was made a senior researcher at the institute, but that promotion came a year after the job that would make him famous: cosmonaut on the Russian Space Station, *Mir*.

A NEW RECORD

In the course of three trips into space between 1992 and 1999, Avdeyev spent more days in space than any other cosmonaut or astronaut before him. On June 20, 1999, he broke the record for days in space when he marked his 680th. In all, Avdeyev lived 748 days in space aboard *Mir*, orbited Earth 11,968 times, and was transported approximately 321 million miles (517 million km) around the cosmos.

Every minute Avdeyev spent in *Mir* was carefully planned. Days began at 8:00 AM MOSCOW time, when his wristwatch alarm rang. Although the station passed through night and day 16 times in a 24-hour period, Avdeyev was on the go with his fellow astronauts once he awoke. While much of his time was taken up with scientific experiments and station upkeep, Avdeyev also exercised on running and bicycle machines to keep his muscles toned.

THE LAST FAREWELL

Avedeyev's last mission, which ended in 1999, was also 13-year-old *Mir*'s last. The Russians abandoned *Mir* due to financial difficulties and to complete work on the International Space Station. Along with astronauts Viktor Afanasyev and Jean-Pierre Haignere, Avdeyev spent his last few months in space preparing

the station for an unmanned flight on which much of it would burn up in the atmosphere. The men finally left the station and climbed into an escape capsule at 2:17 PM on August 28, 1999.

Yet, back on Earth, Avdeyev felt the effects of his final mission, which lasted more than a year. His stay was double the amount of time he had expected to be in space due to financial problems at Moscow's Star City space headquarters. An astronaut's body goes through many internal changes after only a few weeks in space—because the body is weightless, the heart doesn't need to pump blood upwards so powerfully and its muscles break down or change shape, as do the veins and arteries feeding off it. As a result, Avdeyev was too weak to walk or even sit without slumping forward in a chair when he touched down on Earth. He had to be brought out from the space capsule on a stretcher. A year later his heart rate was back to normal and his body had adjusted to gravity, but doctors did detect slight damage to his vision.

Avdeyev was invited to fly over the remains of *Mir*'s crash site in the Pacific Ocean, and he did so with a heavy heart. "I know every piece of technology has an expiry [expiration] date," he told British newspaper, *The Guardian*, in July 1999. "But as a person I will be sad—sorry to lose the place where I spent more than two years of my life."

Vasco Nuñez de Balboa

(c. 1475–1519) EXPLORER

Born in Jerez de los Caballeros, Spain, Vasco Nuñez de Balboa yearned to explore new lands. He sailed on his first major voyage, from SPAIN to VENEZUELA, with an expedition led by Rodrigo de Bastidas in 1501. The men searched for pearls and gold along the northern coast of South America and the GULF OF URABA, located near San Sebastián (on the coast of modern COLOMBIA). They had little luck, and when their ship began to leak near the island of HISPANIOLA (divided into modern HAITI and the DOMINICAN REPUBLIC), Balboa and Bastidas abandoned it. Balboa, who desperately needed money, tried to make a living as a farmer, but proved unlucky in the field, too.

THE FIRST SETTLEMENT

By 1510 Balboa was ready for more adventure—and he was hiding from creditors. He stowed away with his dog, Leoncico, on a boat going from Santo Domingo to the settlement of San Sebastián. Upon his arrival, Balboa saw that San Sebastián had been completely burned by Native Americans, and persuaded its settlers to move to PANAMA, which he had explored with Bastidas. There, in 1511, Balboa founded the town of Santa Maria de la Antigua del Darien (modern DARIEN), the first European settlement in South America. After he became the town's governor, Balboa sent the expedition's original leader, Martín Fernández de Enciso, back to Spain. In Spain, Enciso complained to King Ferdinand about his treatment by Balboa.

In 1513 Balboa was officially accused of treason for his actions. Knowing the king was upset with his activities, Balboa was determined to make him happy by finding the rumored "great sea" on the other side of Panama. (The Atlantic Ocean had already been discovered.)

After marrying the daughter of Careta, a local Indian chief, Balboa had sufficient influence with the Native Americans. In September 1513, he led 190 Spanish and 100 Native Americans through thick jungles to view a sea no European had seen before. When they finally reached the sea on September 29, Balboa became the first European to see the Pacific Ocean. He named it *Mar del Sur* (South Sea) and claimed it and all the land around it for Spain.

Balboa notified Spain of his discovery and sent gifts of gold and pearls, which he had taken from Native Americans who lived along the Pacific coast. The news did little to appease the king, who sent a new governor, Pedrarias Dávila, to supervise Balboa. The two men became fierce rivals as Dávila was envious of Balboa's success and Balboa refused to be ordered around by the new governor. Dávila finally had Balboa arrested, and convicted of treason. As a result, Balboa was publicly beheaded in Acla, Panama. Later, Panama named its monetary unit, the *balboa*, after the explorer.

Robert Ballard (1956–)

EXPLORER·MARINE SCIENTIST

Growing up in Southern California, Robert Ballard loved to scuba drive and study sea creatures. After receiving undergraduate degrees in geology and chemistry and a postgraduate degree in marine biology from the University of Hawaii, Ballard entered the U.S. Navy in 1967 and was assigned to their Deep Submergence Laboratory, where he worked for the next 30 years.

The early part of his career was spent studying plate tectonics and mapping the Mid-Atlantic Ridge, a mountain range under the Atlantic Ocean. He and his crew made many exciting discoveries using deep-diving submersibles. One of the biggest came in 1977, when Ballard reported on 8-to-10-foot-long (2.5-to-3-m) tubeworms living around hot water springs in the waters near the Galapagos Islands, at depths well beyond those at which scientists had thought life could sustain itself.

LOST UNDER THE SEA

In 1983, Ballard was commissioned to study two nuclear submarines that the UNITED STATES had lost at sea. Amazed at how well preserved the subs were, Ballard began to focus his expeditions on lost historic vessels. "I've come to realize that the deep sea is a preserver of human history," he told news magazine, *Insight on the News*.

Two years later, Ballard made his most famous discovery, the cruise ship *Titanic*, which sank in 1912 and was buried 12,000 feet (3,658 m) below sea level.

With the help of his colleagues, Ballard developed a new underwater exploration technology called telepresence. In it, remote-controlled robotic cameras explore the deep sea and relay information to scientists above the surface through fiber optic wires. The first robot's mission, to photograph *Titanic*'s interior, was successful. Ballard continued to use this technology to explore other sunken vessels, including the German battleship *Bismark*, which sank 16,000 feet (4,877 m) down to the seafloor during World War II.

Yet, Ballard has said he felt his May 1998 search for the American aircraft carrier, *Yorktown*, which sank in 1942, was one of the hardest. Working 17,400 feet (5,304 m) down in the Pacific Ocean, Ballard first tried to use a deep-submergence explorer. When that blew-up in the water, he switched to sonar to locate the ship among the ocean's tall volcanic mountains. "An aircraft carrier is big, but so are the features at the bottom of the sea," Ballard explained to *Insight*. "There are places it could have gone down where we would have never found it." But he did.

BLACK SEA DISCOVERY

On another expedition in 1999, Ballard sailed from Sinap, TURKEY to the BLACK SEA to prove a theory that suggested an epic flood moved over the region 7,500 years ago—an event that might have led to the biblical story of "Noah's Ark." Using sonar, Ballard found the shoreline of an ancient lake and evidence of a shift from fresh to salt water 500 feet (150 m) beneath the Black Sea. In a quest to explore deeper, Ballard dropped a robotic camera more than a thousand feet (300 m) below sea level. On his monitor, he saw an upright ship with a 35-foot-tall (11-m) mast. After exploring the wreck, Ballard determined that it was a late Roman or early Byzantine vessel dating back to 410–520 AD. Ballard's Black Sea discovery was the best preserved wooden ship ever seen from the classical world.

In May 2002 Ballard led a National Geographic Expedition and found what is thought to be the remains of John F. Kennedy's PT-109. The patrol boat sank in the Solomon Islands when a Japanese destroyer sliced through it during World War II.

Jean Gardner Batten (1909–1982)

AVIATOR

New Zealand-born Jean Batten became fascinated with flying when, at age 19, she flew with Australian Charles Kingsford Smith. Smith had become a national hero a year earlier when he made the first solo flight from ENGLAND to AUSTRALIA. "Cruising about high above the Blue Mountains, I...felt completely at home in the air," Batten wrote in her autobiography, *Alone in the Sky* (English version, 1979), "and decided that here indeed was my element."

Batten traveled to England to earn a pilot's license in 1930. Although her father disapproved of her flying and the activity was expensive, Batten was set on making her own flight from England to Australia. Unable to find sufficient funding from sponsors in NEW ZEALAND, Batten returned to LONDON to earn a commercial pilot's license in 1932, believing that more experience would encourage more sponsors.

ENGLAND TO AUSTRALIA

After a failed attempt with a borrowed Gypsy Moth plane, Batten found funding to buy another Gypsy Moth in April 1934. At this point in history, planes did not have the control panels that help modern pilots fly. Instead, Batten and other pilots used a compass, landmarks, and a map to chart their course. On her first attempt in the new aircraft, Batten's plane suffered from engine trouble over INDIA. In a second attempt, Batten almost crashed trying to make a stop in ROME, ITALY.

On May 8, 1934, Batten attempted to reach Australia again. Flying at 80 miles per hour with an open cockpit, Batten was exposed to the elements— extreme cold over the ENGLISH CHANNEL, dust storms over the Syrian Desert, and monsoons over Southeast Asia that were so heavy Batten's cockpit filled with water. Yet, on May 23, she landed in Darwin, setting a new women's record of 14 days, 22 hours, and 30 minutes to fly from England to Australia. Batten spent the next year in New Zealand and Australia trying to earn money for future flights by lecturing, making product advertisements, and giving passenger flights.

NEW RECORDS

Her next adventure was a round-trip flight from England to Australia in April 1935. While flying over the shark-infested TIMOR SEA, Batten's plane had temporary engine failure. Batten recovered and completed the flight, becoming the first woman to make the round-trip journey. In the process, she set a record for the fastest crossing of the Timor Sea.

With her past successes, Batten finally had enough money to buy a closed-cabin Percival Gull for a flight from West Africa to BRAZIL. Leaving London for CASABLANCA on November 11, Batten reached the city in a record time of 9 hours, nonstop, and then continued on to Brazil. Only pilot Jim Mollison had made the flight previously, and Batten beat his time by almost 4 hours.

In October 1936, Batten began the first ever flight from England to New Zealand. With brief refueling stops, she made it to Australia in a record eight days. After a rest, she took off for New Zealand, flying through heavy rain. Ten hours later, she reached AUCKLAND, where her father and a crowd of thousands awaited to celebrate her historic flight.

James Pierson Beckwourth

(c. 1798–1866) PIONEER·FUR TRAPPER

Born in Fredrick County, VIRGINIA, to an African American slave mother and a British father, Jim Beckwourth was legally considered a slave. But, his father, Sir Jennings Beckwourth, bestowed a Deed of Emancipation to him in his youth.

Beckwourth moved with his family to MISSOURI in the early 1800s, and later became an apprentice to a blacksmith in ST. LOUIS. After a dispute with his boss, Beckwourth left to work in the lead mines. In the summer of 1824 he joined the American Fur Company on an expedition to the ROCKY MOUNTAINS.

ALLIANCE WITH THE CROW

Around 1828, while on a trapping expedition for the Rocky Mountain Fur Company, Beckwourth began living with the Crow nation of Native Americans. In his autobiography, which mixes facts with exaggerations, Beckwourth claimed he was mistaken for the long-lost son of Big Bowl, one of the tribe's chiefs, and adopted into the tribe. However, other accounts recall that his stay was prearranged by the fur company to establish a trading relationship. Either way, Beckwourth spent the next six to eight years with the Crow, and gained enough influence to become their War Chief.

By the summer of 1836, Beckwourth grew tired of fur trapping. "I had encountered savage beasts and wild men," he recalled in his autobiography, "…and what had I to show for so much wasted energy, and such a catalogue of ruthless deeds?" He went back to St. Louis in the fall of 1837 and heard that the government was recruiting mountain men to serve in the Seminole War in FLORIDA. When his friend, William Sublette, told Beckwourth there was opportunity for fame, Beckwourth decided to go.

On October 26, 1837, Beckwourth and others set out for TAMPA BAY by boat. After ten months with little activity, Beckwourth became restless. He went back to St. Louis in 1838 and found work with another trading company. Beckwourth set out on the Santa Fe Trail for Fort Vasquez in what is now COLORADO, and quickly built a trading relationship with the Cheyenne, enemies of the Crow.

SIERRA NEVADA TRAIL

After establishing a hotel in SANTA FE, NEW MEXICO, Beckwourth headed for CALIFORNIA. In early 1850, while on a gold prospecting expedition, Beckwourth saw a low-lying mountain pass. The next day he ventured toward the pass, which went through the SIERRA NEVADA. He told friends that he thought it might be "the best wagon-road into the American Valley (modern Quincy, California) approaching from the east…." Beckwourth explored and cleared a trail from modern-day Reno, NEVADA, up north, west, and then south to Marysville, California, in 1850 and 1851. In late summer of 1851, the first wagon train of settlers rode the trail. It was heavily used until 1855, when the railroad became the preferred method of transportation. Parts of the trail were later turned into highways.

In 1854–1855, Beckwourth dictated his autobiography to Thomas D. Bonner, a Justice of the Peace. *The Life and Adventures of James P. Beckwourth, Mountaineer, Scout, and Pioneer, and Chief of the Crow Nation of Indians* (1856) was printed twice in the UNITED STATES, and even had a French translation.

William Charles Beebe (1877–1962)

SCIENTIST·OCEAN EXPLORER

William Beebe's first passion was the study of birds. His interest led him to become curator of ornithology at the New York Zoological Society in 1899, and then director of the society's Department of Tropical Research in 1916. His fascination with the unexplored inspired him to establish a research facility in what were once yellow fever quarantine buildings on Nonsuch Island in Bermuda. From there, he sailed in a tugboat to collect plant and animal specimens with a net. On more adventurous days, he put on a bathing suit, rubber-soled sneakers, and a copper helmet with glass in front to swim down as far as 40 feet (12 m) to get a better look at his studies.

Still, Beebe was frustrated that he wasn't seeing all that the sea had to offer. "Personal exploration under the sea is really unearthly," he said. "We are penetrating a new world." Beebe knew that a mile from shore the sea bottom dropped at least a mile down—he just needed the proper equipment to explore there.

THE BATHYSPHERE

By 1929, American inventor Otis Barton designed and produced a deep-sea diving vessel. The 5,000-pound (2,268-kg) steel sphere measured 4-feet, 9-inches (1.4 m) in diameter. On its surface were two round windows and a 400-pound (181-kg) lid that fit over the sphere's 14-inch (36-cm) opening. Barton donated the sphere to the Zoological Society, where Beebe welcomed its possibilities.

Beebe arranged to have the sphere brought to Bermuda, where it could be lowered into the sea by a steel cable. Inside the cable were two wires for telephone communication and two wires for lighting. Oxygen tanks and trays with carbon dioxide and moisture-absorbing chemicals were placed inside the sphere. Beebe named the vessel "bathysphere," noting that *bathy* was the Greek prefix for "deep."

On June 3, 1930, Beebe, Barton, a crew, and the bathysphere sailed out to the deepest part of the sea around Bermuda. When the empty bathysphere was dropped 200 feet (61 m) into the ocean, its cables collapsed. Three days later the vessel was dropped into the sea again. This time it was raised intact.

Finally, Beebe and Barton climbed inside the bathysphere and curled up in its hard bottom as the lid was hammered in place. The bathysphere was lowered to a depth of 800 feet (244 m)—deeper than any human had gone before. Beebe decided they should return to the surface with news of their experience.

On June 11, after seven attempts at a deeper dive, the bathysphere dropped into the darkest sea depths ever seen by humans. Beebe spoke during the journey:

At 285 feet (87 m): "The *Lusitania* is resting at this level."

At 383 feet (117 m): "We are passing the deepest submarine record."

At 600 feet (183 m): "Only dead men have sunk below this."

The vessel continued to drop to 1,426 feet (435 m) below sea level before being raised.

On September 22, 1932, Beebe's voice was broadcast live from the bathysphere at a depth of 2,200 feet (671 m) during a North American and British television special celebrating the historic sea descent. Not yet done with their adventure, the men dropped down 3,048 feet (929 m) on August 15, 1934.

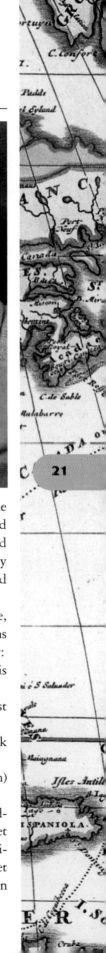

Gertrude Lowthian Bell

(1868–1926) TRAVELER·GOVERNMENT LIAISON

With her wealthy father's encouragement, Gertrude Bell made two voyages by boat around the world and climbed in the SWISS ALPS for several seasons by the time she was 35. The British adventurer's wanderlust also extended to the unmapped sands of the Middle East, where she traveled by camel frequently and was able to use Persian and Arabic language skills she learned at Oxford University. "Few moments of exhilaration can come as that which stands at the threshold of wild travel," she once wrote.

Besides filling 16 journals with her observations, Bell wrote books about her travels, most notably a description of SYRIA in *The Desert and the Sown* (1907), which is considered to be one of the finest works ever written on that region. Even when she wasn't traveling, Bell didn't want to return to England. "I like Baghdad and I like Iraq," she wrote. "It's the real East, and it's stirring; things are happening here, and the romance of it touches me and absorbs me."

When World War I broke out in 1914, Bell put her knowledge of the Middle East to work. The British hoped to encourage an Arab revolt against the Turks, who were then allied with GERMANY. Bell provided information on Arab culture and traditions to British intelligence officials, including T. E. Lawrence (AKA "Lawrence of Arabia"), who sought to better understand the Arabs in order to mobilize them into the war.

WORK IN IRAQ

Renowned for her relationships with Arab sheiks and tribal and religious leaders, Bell was assigned to the Arab Intelligence Bureau in 1915. Her vast knowledge of Middle Eastern geography, language, and leaders was considered a great asset. She helped the bureau map uncharted lands, noting the location of wells and railroads, and she was instrumental in figuring out which Arabs would be friends or enemies of the British. Two years later, Bell visited BAGHDAD's leaders as an advisor to the British civil administrator of the MESOPOTAMIAN region (modern IRAQ), a position she held through the end of the war.

At the end of the war, in 1921, Bell was the only woman in a committee of 40 scholars and politicians who were summoned by British Minister of War Winston Churchill to decide the fate of Mesopotamia. Guided by her belief that Arabs should have political independence, Bell encouraged the committee to approve the state of Iraq and install Prince Faisal I as its first ruler. For years after Iraq's creation, Bell worked as one of Faisal I's closest advisors.

Bell went on to found the Iraq Museum in the capital of Baghdad. This national archive holds some of the 7,000 photographs Bell captured on her travels through the Middle East, between 1900 and 1918. The pictures continue to hold great value because they show structures that have since been eroded or destroyed.

Persian Poems

IN HER SPARE TIME, Gertrude Lowthian Bell translated the poems of famous Persian poet Hafez to make them available to an English-speaking audience.

Hiram Bingham (1875–1956)

EXPLORER·LEGISLATOR

Hiram Bingham's father and grandfather were distinguished missionaries in the Gilbert Islands and HAWAII, who helped the native islanders learn to read and write and also to translate the Bible into the local languages. Born in Honolulu, Hawaii, Bingham completed his undergraduate degree at Yale University and received a Ph.D. from Harvard in 1905. After finishing school, Bingham was eager to explore undiscovered areas in South America by the following year.

In South America, Bingham first explored the route traveled by Venezuelan general **Simón Bolívar** across VENEZUELA and COLOMBIA in the early 1800s. Then, from 1908 to 1909, Bingham trekked along the old Spanish trade route from BUENOS AIRES, ARGENTINA, to LIMA, PERU.

Bingham's next adventure was to serve as director of the Yale Peruvian Expedition. In 1911, he set out from CUZCO, an ancient Incan city that is now one of Peru's major cities, in the hopes of finding Vilacabamba, the legendary Incan city rumored to be filled with treasures. Bingham followed a new trail that had just been blasted along the Urubamba River by the Peruvian government, who hoped to open the remote region up to commerce.

THE LOST CITY

Fifty miles northwest of Cuzco, Bingham met a farmer who said he knew of some nearby ruins. Bingham met the farmer the next day and was led 2,000 feet (610 m) up a slippery, jungle-filled canyon wall to see Native Indians, who were planting maize on top of ancient Inca stone terraces. While chatting with the men, Bingham was approached by a boy who wanted to show him where he played. Bingham followed the boy toward blocks of stone, and set his eyes on the lost Incan city of MACHU PICCHU. The first thing he saw, Bingham later recalled in his book, *Lost City of Incas* (1948), was "a great flight of beautifully-constructed stone-faced terraces, perhaps hundreds of them, each hundreds of feet long and ten feet high."

Undiscovered by those outside of Peru for more than 400 years, Machu Picchu was an amazing sight. Bingham discovered two temples while climbing a series of steps in what is now called the Sacred Plaza. "The walls contained blocks of Cyclopean size, higher than a man," Bingham later wrote. "The sight had me spellbound....Would anyone believe what I had found?"

While in Peru, Bingham also located the last Incan capital of Vitcos, and became the first person to climb the 21,763-foot (6,633-m) Mt. Coropuna. He further explored the Inca lands for Yale and the National Geographic Society between 1912 and 1915.

From 1907 to 1924, Bingham taught history on-and-off at Yale, Harvard, and Princeton, interrupted by a period during World War I when he became head of the Air Personnel Division in Washington, D.C., and later of the Aviation Instruction Center at Issoudun, France. As a Republican, Bingham served as Connecticut's lieutenant governor in 1924 and was elected governor a year later. He resigned to fill a vacancy for Connecticut in the U.S. Senate, and then was elected to a full-term there in 1926.

> In 1948 the road to Machu Picchu was named the Hiram Bingham Highway

23

Arlene Blum (1945–)

MOUNTAIN CLIMBER

Arlene Blum began mountain climbing while studying physical chemistry for a Ph.D. at Reed College in Oregon. Although she went on to become a college professor and complete research studies about environmentally hazardous chemicals, Blum also continued to climb mountains.

In 1967 Blum fell into a crevasse while ascending Mount Pisco in PERU. The scare didn't deter her, nor did being told she couldn't join a climbing team on an expedition to MOUNT MCKINLEY in ALASKA because, the team leader said, women weren't strong enough or emotionally stable enough to make the difficult trip. Instead, Blum's experiences made her more eager to succeed—and see other female climbers succeed.

ENDLESS WINTER

"I saw the movie *The Endless Summer* and loved it, and I decided to do an endless winter," Blum told the *Boston Globe* in 1999. "I would climb mountains in Europe, Africa, Asia, Australia, and New Zealand… looking for the world's best mountain. I planned and did it, 15 consecutive expeditions.… " The first of these climbs was an all-female trek up Mount McKinley in 1970.

Another mountain peaked Blum's interest in 1974. No American and no woman of any nationality had ever climbed the avalanche-prone peak of ANNAPURNA in the HIMALAYAS. At 26,500-feet (8,077-m) tall, Annapurna is the tenth highest peak in the world, and Blum worried she would not be able

to find enough sponsorship to make the climb. Not only would sponsors feel skeptical about the element of danger, but also the fact that Blum wanted to take an all-female team up with her—and an all-female team had never climbed any of the world's highest peaks. Plus, the Nepalese government was slow in getting Blum the permit she needed before making the climb. In the meantime, Blum joined a climbing expedition to demonstrate women's stamina at high altitudes at the 1976 American Bicentennial Expedition to MOUNT EVEREST.

With Annapurna still on her mind, Blum reapplied for a permit in 1977. In the fall of 1978 she received word that her team could finally go up. Blum carefully chose climbers for the American Women's Himalayan Expedition and raised $80,000 through sponsorship and fundraising. In August 1978, Blum and 12 others left SAN FRANCISCO for NEPAL.

The women battled avalanches, logistical problems, and ice climbing, but on October 15, two of Blum's climbers, Irene Miller and Vera Komarkova, reached the top of Annapurna with their Sherpa guides. Tragically, two days later, two other women on Blum's expedition fell to their deaths before making the summit.

The finale of Blum's climbing career came in 1982. Blum and climber Hugo Swift became the first westerners to complete the 2,000-mile (3,219-km), nine-month trek—up peaks and down riverbeds—along the Himalayan regions of BHUTAN, INDIA, and Nepal. Soon after, Blum had a daughter and decided to put climbing behind her and use her experiences from more than 20 climbs for motivational speaking engagements.

The Discoverer

ARLENE BLUM'S research at California's University College at Berkeley was instrumental in the discovery that a flame-retardant chemical used on children's sleepwear caused cancer. The chemical, tris, was later taken off the market.

Nellie Bly (1867–1922)

INVESTIGATIVE REPORTER·TRAVELER

Born in Pennsylvania with the given name Elizabeth Cochran, Nellie Bly was the third of five children. Her father died when she was six, leaving her family with financial troubles. In 1879, when she was only 12, Bly dropped out of school and found a job to help support her family.

A few years later, Bly grew angry reading Erasmus Wilson's "Quiet Observations" column in the *Pittsburgh Dispatch*, in which he stated that "girls were useless outside the sphere of marriage." She wrote an eloquent letter arguing the point to *Dispatch* editor George Madden, who—along with Wilson—was impressed with Bly's spirit and style. Bly was hired for $5 a week to write investigative articles for the paper, and given the pen name of Nellie Bly, which was taken from a then-popular song.

her that she could have a position at the newspaper if she came back with a great story. For her first article, Bly pretended she was insane so she could plant herself inside Blackwell's Island (now Roosevelt Island), one of New York's biggest mental institutions. After ten days, the *World* sent a lawyer to get her released. Bly then wrote about the horrific treatment of patients in a series of articles, which were again applauded by readers. Her articles were so effective that the city government quickly allocated money for reforms at the asylum. By the end of 1887, Bly was one of the *World*'s first female reporters, and she continued to write undercover stories about sweat shops, slum life, and minor crimes.

UNDERCOVER REPORTER

Bly's first assignment was to disguise herself as a poor woman and land a job at a copper cable factory in order to get an insider's view of working conditions. The resulting articles were filled with so many troubling details that factory owners threatened to pull their advertising if Bly was not fired. Still, factory workers and other readers cheered Bly's articles and the newspaper's circulation increased to ten times its normal rate.

> **Nellie Bly's obituary called her "the best reporter in America."**

By age 20, Bly was ready for bigger challenges, and she decided to move to NEW YORK CITY. In the summer of 1887, she left a note on Wilson's desk: "Dear Q[uiet].O[bserver].—I am off for New York. Look out for me. Bly."

In New York, Bly presented several story ideas to the *New York World*. Its publisher, Joseph Pulitzer, told

WORLD TRAVELER

Then, in November of 1889, Bly set out in her trademark checkered coat with a single bag to make an around the world trip by train, horse, and steamboat in the spirit of writer Jules Verne's fictional character, Phileas Fogg, in *Around the World in Eighty Days*. "I would rather go back to New York dead than not a winner," she said of her goal to make the trip in less time. Bly stopped in France to interview Verne and still managed to make the trip in just 72 days, 6 hours, and 11 minutes. She described her adventures in *Nellie Bly's Book: Around the World in Seventy-two Days* (1890).

In 1895, Bly married and retired from journalism. After her husband's death and the end of World War I, Bly again began writing, this time for the *New York Journal*.

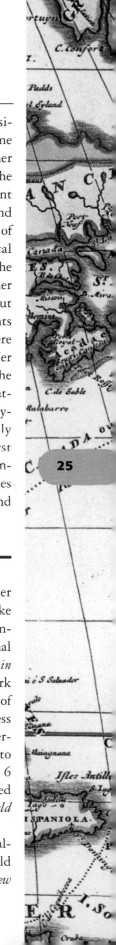

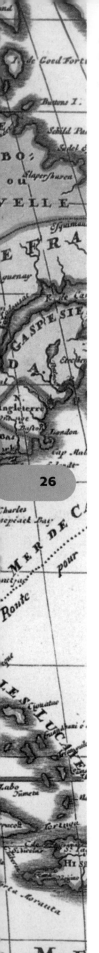

Simón Bolívar (1783–1830)

TRAVELER·SOLDIER·GOVERNMENT OFFICIAL

Simón Bolívar was born into a wealthy family in CARACAS, VENEZUELA, and educated by private tutors. In 1801, Bolívar visited PARIS, FRANCE, and saw Napoleon's rise to power after the French Revolution. He was upset by Napoleon's sudden popularity and saw it as a betrayal of the ideals on which France was built. On August 15, 1805, Bolívar climbed atop the Aventine Hill in ROME, ITALY, and declared that he would dedicate his life to South America's emancipation so that his homeland would not face the same fate as France.

STRUGGLE FOR INDEPENDENCE

In 1807, France invaded SPAIN, and Bolívar, among others, rose up to fight for Venezuelan independence. Caracas's city council removed the Spanish viceroy, and selected Bolívar to lead a mission to LONDON, ENGLAND, to ask the British for protection against France. To Bolívar's dismay, British leaders refused to help, citing a growing friendship with the French. Still in London, Bolívar met with compatriot Francisco de Miranda, who had led two past revolts against Spain. Together, the men returned to Caracas and encouraged the Venezuelan Congress to declare the country's independence on July 5, 1811.

The attempt at independence failed, and Bolívar fled for New Granada (modern COLOMBIA) to join its fight for liberation. On December 15, 1812, Bolívar wrote the first of many essays on the importance of independence, the "Cartegena Memorial," which explained Venezuela's failure and renewed a call for its freedom. With the help of New Granada's forces, Bolívar again attempted to take over Venezuela and declare independence on August 6, 1813. He succeeded, but in July 1814, he was forced out of the country by horsemen backed by the French. With his home country once again under the control of a foreign nation, Bolívar sailed to New Granada. However, when Spanish troops took control of that country in May of 1815, Bolívar moved on to JAMAICA.

Finding little help for his cause in Jamaica, Bolívar sailed on to HAITI, where President Alexandre Pétion offered to help him set up a liberation expedition. Bolívar and his crew made two failed attempts to travel inland at Venezuela. Realizing he needed a new strategy, Bolívar sailed up the ORINOCO RIVER and built a base at ANGOSTURA (modern CIUDAD BOLIVAR) in order to gain control of eastern Venezuela. Bolívar called a congress at Angostura on February 15, 1819, with the goal of laying the political foundation for northern South America's future.

Finally, on December 17, 1819, Bolívar's men had gained enough ground to witness the declaration of the new Republic of Gran Columbia, which would unite New Granada, Venezuela, and Quito (modern ECUADOR). Still, Venezuela was not completely liberated. Bolívar's forces resumed fighting in 1821.

By May 24, 1822, Gran Columbia became a reality, and Bolívar was made its President. He encouraged other counties to become states under the united Gran Columbia and to organize that country's government, but had little luck because the states were still divided in their loyalties. In 1830, Venezuela and Quito seceded from Gran Columbia. Defeated and tired, Bolívar resigned as president on April 27.

Daniel Boone (1734–1820)

EXPLORER · PIONEER

Growing up in Berkins County, Pennsylvania, as the sixth of eleven children, Daniel Boone received little education, but became a skilled hunter and trapper. He learned to hunt with a spear and a rifle with the guidance of Native Americans who lived near his home.

Just after his 20th birthday, Boone served in the French-Indian War of 1754 at Fort Duquesne (modern Pittsburgh). There, he met John Finley, a hunter who spoke often of hunting adventures in KENTUCKY. Boone was anxious to see the vast wilds Finley spoke of and, although he had just married at the war's end, he left home for two years to explore Kentucky with Finley and five other men.

KENTUCKY PIONEER

Boone's party reached Kentucky while clearing a hunting trail called the Wilderness Road. Immediately Boone was amazed by the land's beauty and by the many buffalo that roamed it. Yet he also realized that he was not safe because many of the Native American camps in the area felt threatened. "We were then in a dangerous, helpless situation," Boone later wrote of his travels, "exposed daily to perils and death...not a white man in the country but ourselves."

Before long, Boone and his fellow hunters were captured by Shawnee and held for seven days. They escaped, and after exploring more of Kentucky, Boone journeyed home to NORTH CAROLINA in 1771. After two years, Boone was ready to set out for Kentucky again. This time he built a log cabin near Harrodsburgh and took a job with the Transylvania Company, which was looking to build settlements in the area. After bringing his family to Kentucky, Boone began work on his new town, Boonesborough, near the Kentucky River. He also helped other settlers travel through uncharted territory and negotiate with angry Native Americans along the way.

> **Among the settlers Boone brought to Boonesborough were Abraham Lincoln's grandmother and grandfather.**

Boone himself had many problems with the Shawnee. At one point he had to rescue his daughter and other young girls from his settlement who were kidnapped by the tribe. Then, in 1778, Boone was captured by the Shawnee. He lived with them for four months, until June 16, 1778, when he heard them discussing an attack on his settlement. Boone found the strength to escape and raced 160 miles (258 km) in four days to return home and warn the settlers. Still, Boone was happy in Kentucky, and would have stayed there for good, had the British not made Kentucky part of VIRGINIA in an attempt to hinder the colonists. This act made all of the Transylvania Company's contracts worthless and, although Boonesborough later became a permanent village, Boone was not a part of it.

Boone moved to Bourbon, Kentucky, and became the town's sheriff and surveyor. From 1788 to 1789, Boone settled in Point Pleasant, VIRGINIA (modern West Virginia) and became a member of Virginia's new state assembly. However, politics were not for the earthy Boone, who brought his family to present-day Missouri in 1798. He later lost his land due to debts he owed in Kentucky, and had to spend his last days living in his son Nathan's home.

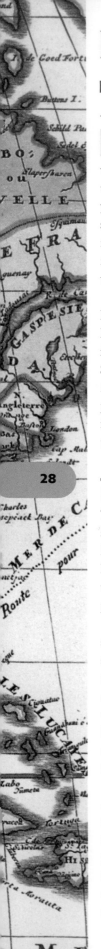

Louise Arner Boyd (1887–1972)

EXPLORER·AVIATOR·SCIENTIFIC RESEARCHER

Louise Boyd was born into a wealthy family in San Rafael, California. Her two brothers, sick with rheumatic fever and frail from birth, died in their teens, and later Boyd's parents died within a year of each other. At 32, Boyd was a wealthy socialite, having inherited her father's mining business and the rest of the family inheritance. Alone, rich, and without roots, Boyd chose to busy herself with travel.

She spent the next few years traveling through Europe, including stops in post-World War I FRANCE and Belgium. In 1924, she saw the ARCTIC for the first time aboard a tourist boat to SPITSBERGEN, an island off the coast of NORWAY and in the Arctic sea, and fell in love with its beauty and promise of adventure. "On that trip were laid the foundations of my subsequent seven expeditions to the Arctic," said Boyd later.

NORTHERN ADVENTURE

Two years later, Boyd chartered the *M.S. Hobby*, a ship once used by explorer **Roald Amundsen**, for herself and a group of friends. The ship sailed from Norway to FRANZ JOSEF LAND, a group of 70 of the world's northernmost islands, where Boyd hunted polar bears and seals.

In 1928, upon hearing that Amundsen had disappeared while flying to the Arctic, Boyd financed and set out on a roughly 10,000-mile (16,100-km), three-day expedition to find him. Although Boyd did not find the explorer, Norway presented her with the Chevalier Cross of the Order of St. Olav for her heroic attempt. She met so many scientists and explorers in the process that she decided studying the Arctic would become her life's work.

Boyd began making yearly expeditions to the Arctic in 1931. She sailed with an exploring party to GREENLAND'S northeastern coast, where they studied glaciers and photographed animal and plant life. Two years later, Boyd led a scientific team back to the area to study the fjords and glaciers. The crew also used a sonic device to measure ocean depths. During Boyd's 1937 and 1938 trips around the Arctic sea, her team located an underwater mountain range between BEAR ISLAND and JAN MAYEN ISLAND.

ARCTIC EXPERT

Due to World War II, Boyd stopped exploring until 1941. Then she led another expedition to the Arctic to study the effects of polar magnetic fields on radio communications. She later served as a military strategy advisor in the Arctic, appointed because of her knowledge of the area's geography.

At age 68, Boyd chartered a private plane to fly over the NORTH POLE. The flight made history as the first nonmilitary plane to fly over the Pole and the first plane to make the trip from mainland Norway, but for Boyd it was a longtime dream fulfilled. "In a moment of silent and reverent awe, the crew and I gave thanks for this priceless sight," she later wrote in *Parade* magazine. "We crossed the Pole, then circled it, flying 'around the world' in a matter of minutes.... My Arctic dream had come true."

James Bridger (1804–1881)

FUR TRADER · FRONTIERSMAN · SCOUT

James Bridger was born to an innkeeper and his wife in Richmond, VIRGINIA. Around 1812, the family moved to a farm near ST. LOUIS, MISSOURI. Yet, by the time Bridger was 13, both of his parents had died. Orphaned and in need of work, he began an apprenticeship with a blacksmith, but was attracted to a help wanted ad in the *Missouri Republican* seeking "enterprising young men." The ad, placed by William Ashley on March 12, 1822, offered employment to 100 men willing to take part in a fur-trapping venture near the mouth of the MISSOURI RIVER.

Life and Death

THROUGH ALL OF HIS WORK, Bridger managed to marry three times—always to Native American women. His first wife was a Flathead who died in 1846, leaving Bridger with three children. His second wife, a Ute, died in 1849, after giving Bridger another daughter. A third wife, a member of the Snake tribe, died in 1858.

FRONTIERSMAN

Over the next 20 years, Bridger took part in various beaver fur-trapping expeditions between CANADA and the southern tip of COLORADO and from the Missouri River west to IDAHO and UTAH. Though he could not read, he communicated well with Native Americans and, as a result, developed many good relationships as well as some enemies. The tall Virginian managed to become an expert in the ROCKY MOUNTAIN region and its people, and in the fall of 1824, it is believed he was the first white man to visit the GREAT SALT LAKE.

By 1843, the growing western migration encouraged Bridger and partner Louis Vásquez to establish the supply post of Fort Bridger on the Oregon Trail in southwestern WYOMING. The fort and Bridger himself became points of interest for westward-traveling explorers and colonizers. Among the many who noted Bridger's helpful expertise and hospitality were Brigham Young, the Mormon leader who established Utah, and explorer **John Frémont**. Still, business is business, and because the Mormons sought to monopolize the supply and fur needs of others traveling westward, Bridger's fort was forced to close in 1853.

Bridger retired to a farm in Kansas City for a short while to care for his three children. Before long, he was asked to serve as a government scout. Back in 1849, he had guided a government-funded expedition through Utah, on which he informed the government about a little traveled short-cut in central Wyoming that later became popular with those moving west. The route was named Bridger's Pass in honor of the explorer.

With his expert reputation, Bridger was given assignments that included participation in an expedition to present-day Yellowstone National Park in 1859–1860 and guiding an engineering team to find a direct route from Denver, Colorado, to the Great Salt Lake. He contributed to recollections about each area, though until his descriptions of geysers and other unique features in the Yellowstone area were verified, they were discussed as "Jim Bridger's lies." In 1866, Bridger traveled on the Bozeman trail from Fort Kearny, Nebraska, to Virginia City, MONTANA, in order to measure its distance (967 miles [1,556 km]).

Bridger retired from his travels for the last time in 1868. As his health was growing worse, he finally settled in Kansas City, where he gradually went blind.

Sir Richard Francis Burton

(1821–1890) EXPLORER · TRANSLATOR

As the son of a British navy colonel and wealthy mother with royal ancestors, Richard Burton traveled frequently around Europe with his parents throughout his youth. Thus, he received his education infrequently through tutors. Burton later attended Oxford University, where he had the nickname "Ruffian Dick" and preferred to study topics that interested him, such as Arabic and mysticism, rather than standard curriculum. He was expelled from the university in 1842.

At age 21, Burton joined the British East India Company's army and was appointed to Sind (modern southern PAKISTAN). There, he lived among Muslims and learned several Eastern languages and dialects, including Persian, Arabic, and Hindustani.

INCOGNITO

He took leave in 1853 to make a journey to CAIRO and the sacred Muslim cities of MECCA and MEDINA. At the time, Arab governments did not allow Europeans or Americans into holy cities. In fact, they were to be executed, if caught. Yet Burton disguised himself as a Muslim doctor and was able to use his perfect Arabic language skills to enter the holy cities. Later writings about his journey provided information on the rituals of pilgrimage and a sketch of Mecca's central shrine, the Kaaba. Because he was one of the first non-Muslims to enter Mecca, Burton's book—*Personal Narrative of a Pilgrimage to El-Medinah and Meccah* (1855)—made him famous across Europe.

On leave again the next year, Burton traveled to HARER (part of modern ETHIOPIA), a walled Islamic city-state forbidden to non-Muslims, and became the first European to enter it and survive to tell about it. Next, Burton sailed with British explorer John Speke and two officers of the East India Company to Somaliland (modern SOMALIA) in eastern Africa to find the source of the NILE RIVER. The trip was unsuccessful, and the men were attacked by Africans, who killed the officers. Burton escaped with spear slashes through both of his cheeks.

After a time as a soldier in the Crimean War, Burton sailed back to Africa with Speke in 1858. Sailing hundreds of miles, they finally discovered LAKE TANGANYIKA, which Burton believed was the source of the Nile. Too ill with malaria to travel any further, Burton allowed Speke to continue explorations without him. Speke later announced that he had traveled up LAKE VICTORIA, the biggest lake in Africa, and believed it was the Nile's source. Although Speke was correct, the men had a public feud and never spoke again. In 1861, Burton accepted the first of many consul posts, which allowed him to travel though West Africa, BRAZIL, PARAGUAY, ARGENTINA, PERU, and SYRIA.

SIR BURTON

Throughout his travels, Burton wrote 43 books that described the remote areas he was viewing. In 1872, as a consul in TRIESTE, Austria-Hungry (modern ITALY), Burton began to translate the works of other authors. One of the best-known translations was *Arabian Nights (The Thousand Nights and a Night)*, a collection of stories from western Asia which filled 17 volumes (1885–1888). Burton was knighted by Queen Victoria in February of 1886.

Richard E. Byrd (1888–1957)

EXPLORER·AVIATOR·NAVAL OFFICER

Richard Evelyn Byrd was born into one of Winchester, Virginia's, most prominent families. At age 14, he went alone to live in the PHILIPPINES for a year with a family friend. Byrd then traveled around the world by himself, taking a British steamer to INDIA, SUEZ, ENGLAND, and NEW YORK. Upon his return, he wrote in his diary that he wanted to be the first person to reach the NORTH POLE.

Byrd began to study law at the University of Virginia, but soon decided to transfer to the U.S. Naval Academy at Annapolis, Maryland. There, the athletic trainee broke his ankle twice. After serving as a gunnery officer, Byrd broke his ankle a third time in 1916 and was forced to take a two-month naval leave. Upon his return, Byrd was sent to the Naval flight school in Pensacola, Florida, to learn to pilot aircrafts.

THE NORTH POLE

In 1925 Byrd took part in an Arctic expedition sponsored by the National Geographic Society. He became the first person to fly over ELLESMERE ISLAND and the GREENLAND ice cap, and was inspired to become the first to fly over the North Pole. With financial support from John D. Rockefeller and Edsel Ford, Byrd flew to SPITSBERGEN on April 29, 1926. From there, he flew to the pole. Despite take-off troubles, Byrd and warrant officer Floyd Bennett reached the North Pole at 9:02 AM on May 9, 1926.

THE SOUTH POLE

The pair was welcomed back to the States as heroes. Byrd next set his sights on the SOUTH POLE. He sailed to the continent in 1928, and set up a base camp on the BAY OF WHALES. Named "Little America" by Byrd, it would become the main scientific camp for later expeditions by other explorers and scientists.

At 3:29 PM on November 28, 1929, Byrd and four others began to fly over the pole. Despite a harrowing moment when 250 pounds (13 kg) of emergency rations had to be thrown out of the plane so they could gain enough height to clear a large glacier, the men reached the South Pole at 1:14 AM on November 29, and circled it twice. In honor of this feat, Byrd was promoted to the rank of rear admiral, and retired.

He set out for the ANTARCTIC again in 1933 as part of a two-year research expedition. Byrd's main goal was to establish a weather post 125 miles (201 km) south of Little America. After Bolling Advanced Weather Station was built in a tiny hut buried deep in the snow, Byrd entered it alone to conduct meteorological research in March 1934. Blizzards kept him in the hut constantly. After two months, Byrd's radio transmissions back to Little America became irrational as, it was realized later, he was being poisoned by carbon monoxide from a defective stove. A rescue mission fortunately reached Byrd in time and sent him home in July.

In November 1939, Byrd made a third trip to Antarctica to map the continent so military bases could be set up. He made four flights and suggestions for two bases. His good work was rewarded with a bigger mission. At the end of World War II, Byrd was asked to command the then-largest Antarctic expedition. In Operation Highjump, he oversaw 4,100 men, 19 airplanes, 13 ships, 4 helicopters, and a submarine with the goal of exploring and mapping approximately 845,000 sq miles (2,188,500 sq km) of land.

The admiral's final expedition to the Antarctic came in 1955 when he was named commander of the exploration mission Operation Deep-Freeze. On January 8, 1956, as part of the research, 67-year-old Byrd made his last flight over the South Pole.

Álvar Núñez Cabeza de Vaca

(c.1490–1557) EXPLORER

Álvar Núñez Cabeza de Vaca was born into Spanish nobility, and began his career as part of the military. In early 1527 Cabeza de Vaca sailed from SPAIN to the Americas as second in command of a crew of 250 to 300 men on an expedition led by Pánfilo de Narváez. Hit by a hurricane off the coast of CUBA, the ship landed in modern TAMPA BAY in March 1528. Narváez immediately claimed the land for the Spanish empire.

Cabeza de Vaca and the rest of the expedition crew lived among the Apalachee tribe of Native Americans in northern FLORIDA for a time, but were kicked off the land after a dispute. In late 1528, the crew built several rafts from horsehides and trees and attempted to sail to Cuba. By the time a hurricane forced the crew toward the Gulf Coast near modern Galveston, TEXAS, starvation and storms had caused Narváez's death and reduced the crew to 80 men. They were at first welcomed by local Native Americans, but were again driven away by some tribes after many of the natives began to catch deadly diseases and blamed Cabeza de Vaca and his men.

across what is now Texas, through NEW MEXICO, ARIZONA, and northern MEXICO in an attempt to reach the Spanish Empire's outpost in Mexico. The men became the first non-Native Americans to travel through southwestern North America, as well as the first Europeans to see the American buffalo.

In July 1536, the men finally came across fellow Spaniards, who were on a slave-taking expedition, in modern Sinaloa, Mexico. Cabeza de Vaca later recalled that the men were "dumbfounded at the sight of me, strangely dressed and in the company of Indians. They just stood there staring for a long time."

SOUTHWEST TRAVELS

For the next four years, the dwindling crew lived in East Texas, and Cabeza de Vaca became a trader and healer. By 1532, only four members of the original crew survived, including Cabeza de Vaca and Estevan, an African slave. They are believed to have traveled

Cabeza de Vaca returned to Spain the next year and published an account of his experiences. In it, he noted that he was discouraged by Spain's treatment of the Native Americans. His writing inspired other Spanish explorers to venture to America, including **Hernando de Soto** and **Francisco Vasquez de Coronado**.

Cabeza de Vaca was appointed governor of the Spanish settlement on the Rio de la Plata (modern PARAGUAY), but was removed when he was accused of corruption—a charge some scholars suggest might have been made because of Cabeza de Vaca's friendly position on Native Americans. Although he was convicted, Cabeza de Vaca was pardoned in 1552, and later became a judge in Seville, Spain.

Name Game

CABEZA DE VACA TRANSLATES in Spanish to "cow's head." A distant relative of Cabeza de Vaca was famous for marking an unguarded pass in the Sierra Morena with the skull of a cow, an act that helped bring the Christians to victory in 1212 during the Crusades.

John Cabot (c. 1450–c. 1498)

EXPLORER

Originally a seaman and citizen of Venice (and born Giovanni Caboto), John Cabot settled in BRISTOL, ENGLAND, with his sons around 1495. He had read **Marco Polo**'s description of the Far East—the source of "all the spices n the world"—and hoped to find a more direct westward passage to Asia. Bristol appeared to be a good starting point to Cabot because he learned that for the past 15 years Bristol sailors had been making regular voyages to the west, seeking better fishing areas, and in their travels they had sighted land. Cabot believed the land they sited was part of Asia. He assured the British that he could sail a more northern route than that of the one followed by **Christopher Columbus** in his 1492–1493 voyage. Thus, Cabot's passage would be shorter and more direct than any other explorer's route to Asia.

On March 5, 1496, King Henry VII authorized a letter that allowed Cabot and his sons to discover and possess lands "unknown to all Christians." Cabot attempted his expedition that year, but rough sea conditions forced him to turn back.

ACROSS THE ATLANTIC

He finally set sail with a crew of 18 from Bristol in his ship *Matthew* (named for his wife, Mattea) on May 2, 1497. After 35 days battling rough seas, Cabot came ashore in present-day MAINE or southern NOVA SCOTIA, and claimed the land for Henry VII. While exploring the area, he sailed eastward toward Cape Race in NEWFOUNDLAND by the coast of New England, and named many islands and capes along the Canadian coastline. He then made a quick 15-day sail back to Bristol.

Arriving home in early August, Cabot told the court of England that he had found "a part of Asia...the country of the Great Khan." The British accepted his claim and Cabot became a hero, even receiving a financial bonus from the king. One fellow Venetian living in LONDON wrote home that Cabot was "called the Great Admiral...and these English run after him like mad."

SECOND VOYAGE

In December 1497, Cabot asked the king for permission to organize a second voyage. He planned to sail to the spot he began his last trip and then follow the coast to the southwest until he came to Cipangu (JAPAN) in East Asia. Two months later, Cabot received word that he could make the journey and recruited a crew of 300 and prepared five ships. Cabot set sail in early May 1498. While the fate of the expedition is uncertain, it is believed that Cabot sailed along the eastern coast of GREENLAND and sailed north along the coast until his crew, suffering from the cold, forced him to turn back toward England. While Cabot didn't find a route to Asia, he enabled England to make its first claims in CANADA. Scholars also suggest that Cabot made an "intellectual discovery of America" because from that point on, English explorers didn't confuse the land of America with Asia.

Sebastian Cabot (c. 1476–1557)

EXPLORER

Sebastian Cabot, born in Venice, Italy, learned about the excitement of exploration from his father, **John Cabot**. He moved to ENGLAND with his father and brother in 1495, and took part in the elder Cabot's first expedition to North America in 1497.

THE NORTHWEST PASSAGE

After his father died, King Henry VII sent Cabot to search for the fabled Northwest Passage. The explorer hoped to find a route around the New World that would make trade with Asia easier. Cabot led two ships with 300 men on board north to ICELAND, southern GREENLAND, and along the southern coast of LABRADOR. When his crew refused to go any further, Cabot sailed south along the eastern coast of North America toward CUBA. Maps he drew of his journeys show that he may have found the HUDSON BAY and believed it was the Northwest Passage.

By 1512 Cabot had settled in Spain where he was appointed SPAIN's Pilot Major. As Pilot Major, he kept records of Spanish voyages of discovery and helped plan two voyages to North America, but both expeditions fell through.

In 1524, the Spanish king joined with a group of Seville merchants to invest in a voyage to South America to find an easier passage to the Pacific Ocean than the one **Ferdinand Magellan** had found in 1520. Cabot was asked to lead the expedition.

SOUTH AMERICA

Cabot set sail from CÁDIZ in April of 1526 with four ships and more than 150 men to RECIFE on the northern coast of BRAZIL. There they met an abandoned sailor who told them about a previous Spanish expedition to South America that reaped a large supply of silver. They also picked up other sailors who told tales of "a mountain two hundred leagues inland containing many mines of gold and silver and other metals." The sailors were referring to the wealth of the Inca Empire.

After hearing the news of riches, Cabot decided to change the goal of his expedition: he would now focus on ARGENTINA—and its riches. Cabot docked in the great estuary there and named it the RÍO DE LA PLATA ("Silver River"). He climbed ashore, leaving behind at least three sailors who disagreed with his decision, and explored the URUGUAY and PARANÁ RIVERS that make up the estuary. He oversaw the building of a fort called Sancti Spiritus near present-day Rosario, Argentina. Cabot and his men explored the area, but found no silver. After local Native Americans destroyed the fort, Cabot decided to return to Spain. Only 24 of his men had survived to return home.

While in Spain in August 1530, Cabot was put on trial for his conduct towards his fellow commanders and his lack of success. He was sentenced to between two and four years of banishment, but King Charles V pardoned him. Cabot returned to Seville and remained Pilot Major, though he spent much of his time working on the growing debate surrounding how to determine longitude.

In 1547, Cabot returned to England, where he received the title of Great Pilot. Five years later, as governor of the Muscovy Company, Cabot guided trade with RUSSIA and prepared for more (unsuccessful) attempts to find the Northwest Passage.

Sole Survivor

ALL THAT REMAINS of Cabot's charts is a map of the world he drew in 1544. It is now preserved in the National Library at Paris.

Jacques Cartier (1491–1557)

EXPLORER • NAVIGATOR

Not much is known about Jacques Cartier's early life, except that he was born in the French port of SAINT-MALO in the province of Brittany. As a crew member, he later made several sea voyages to BRAZIL and NEWFOUNDLAND, among other foreign lands. Some believe he was part of **Giovanni da Verrazzano's** expeditions to America in 1524 and 1528.

In 1532, Cartier was selected by King François I of FRANCE to lead an expedition to the New World in an attempt to discover the Northwest Passage to Asia. Two years later, on April 20, Cartier sailed from Saint-Malo with two ships and 61 men. Not only were they to explore the New World, but they were also expected to return with great wealth. Their instructions were "to discover certain islands and lands where it is said that a great quantity of gold and other precious things are to be found."

NEW FRANCE

Within 20 days they reached the northern tip of Newfoundland and sailed through the STRAIT OF BELLE ISLE, the narrow body of water between Newfoundland and LABRADOR. Sailing southward along the north coast of present-day QUEBEC, Cartier named many of the rivers and harbors he saw. His ships explored the GULF OF ST. LAWRENCE, and Cartier became the first European to report on PRINCE EDWARD ISLAND and the NEW BRUNSWICK mainland.

After sailing into Chaleur Bay, or as he named it *Baie des Chaleurs*, the ships landed on the GASPÉ PENINSULA. Cartier claimed the land for France. He also met the Iroquois chief Donnacona, and brought two of the chief's sons aboard so they could visit France. Cartier later sailed into the present-day ST. LAWRENCE RIVER estuary. The ships returned to Saint-Malo on September 5, 1534, and were heartily welcomed even though they brought back no gold.

The following year the king asked Cartier to return to CANADA. His three ships left Saint-Malo on May 15, 1535, with a crew that included the chief's sons, who had learned French and served as translators. Guided by the Iroquois, Cartier crossed Belle Isle again. By August, he sailed up the St. Lawrence River, which he named, to the village of Stadacona (modern Quebec). From there, he traveled to the village of Hochelaga (modern MONTRÉAL) where he climbed a hill behind the village to observe the Ottawa River. Cartier named the hill *Mont Réal* (Mount Royal); the city of Montréal's name is derived from this hill.

Cartier's crew became the first Europeans to spend the winter in Canada—in Stadacona—though many suffered from scurvy and the freezing temperatures. Fortunately, the Iroquois taught them how to make tea out of white cedar, which was a source of vitamin C, curing the scurvy. They returned home to France with Chief Donnacona on July 16, 1536. Again, the king was pleased with Cartier's work—not only had he found the St. Lawrence, which they believed led to Asia, but he also brought back gold he had found.

Cartier's third expedition to Canada reached Stadacona on August 23, 1541. With five ships and a crew of a thousand, he again sailed up the St. Lawrence, this time traveling as far as Lachine Rapids. He established a camp at the present-day town of Charlesbourg, north of Quebec. There he found what he believed to be diamonds and gold. Yet the camp was not a permanent one, as the winter was harsh and the Iroquois, now under a new chief, grew hostile.

Cartier's ships sailed to the port of St. John's, Newfoundland, where Cartier had orders to help French nobleman Sieur de Roberval found a new colony. One night, Cartier—unhappy with his role as helper—returned to France. Once home, he was embarrassed to learn that the gold he found was actually iron pyrite and the diamonds were quartz crystals. Cartier settled in Saint-Malo and wrote an account of his expeditions that was published in 1545.

Samuel de Champlain (c. 1567–1635)

EXPLORER·COLONIST

Born in Brouage, France, Samuel de Champlain followed in his father's footsteps and pursued a career as a naval captain. After various sailing expeditions to the West Indies and Central America, Champlain was appointed royal geographer by his former captain, King Henry IV. In 1604, he sailed to Acadia, where he spent three years mapping the Atlantic coast, from NOVA SCOTIA to CAPE COD and Martha's Vineyard. He set up a small settlement at Port Royal (modern Annapolis Royal, Nova Scotia).

TROUBLE WITH THE IROQUOIS

By 1608, the French were more interested in the land around the ST. LAWRENCE RIVER valley than Acadia. Champlain led an expedition to the valley, and set up QUEBEC with 32 colonists. Few settlers survived the first winter there, but more settled there in the spring. Champlain made friends with the Algonkin and Huron tribes in the area in order to promote the fur trade that would help the colony flourish.

In 1609, Champlain accompanied a band of these Native Americans searching for an enemy tribe of Iroquois up the Richelieu River to, what would later be called Lake Champlain, becoming the first European to explore that lake. Champlain helped his allies defeat the Iroquois, but in the process made a longtime enemy. The Iroquois threatened to destroy all French settlements along the St. Lawrence River.

By winter, Champlain was back in France, looking for support from merchants and the French court for his new colony. He was appointed commandant in New France, the French's land in CANADA, in 1912. A year later, Champlain sailed up the Ottawa River to Allumette Island to encourage the Algonkin to enter into more trade with the French.

FRENCH FUR TRADE

In 1615, Champlain again sailed up the Ottawa River. This time, he was in search of the best route—and what would become the main route—for the French fur trade. Soon after, Champlain was asked to join another war against the Iroquois. This time he was so severely wounded that he had to spend a winter under the care of the Huron before returning to Quebec.

Although Champlain's explorations were finished, he now had knowledge of the Native Americans' main trade routes from Acadia to the GREAT LAKES. He sent out younger men to learn the Native American languages and introduce trade with the French. In 1627 he became governor of New France, but his title didn't hold for long, as English privateers began stealing provisions sent from FRANCE to Québec. They soon took over Quebec and brought Champlain to ENGLAND as a prisoner.

The French negotiated to regain control of Quebec in 1632. Champlain was sent back to Quebec, and worked to rebuild the settlement and reestablish trade with the Native Americans until his death.

Lasting Title

IN 1607 SAMUEL DE CHAMPLAIN was named New France's lieutenant-governer. Although he traveled back to France, he continued to hold this position until his death in 1635.

Chang Ch'ien (c. 160 BC– c.107 BC)

EXPLORER·GOVERNMENT ENVOY

In 138 BC, Chinese Emperor Wu-ti of the Han dynasty decided to seek a military alliance with the Indo-European tribe of the Yueh-chih in order to deal with Hsiung-nu nomads (the Huns) who were causing disorder in northwest CHINA. He chose the young court official, Chang Ch'ien, to send on the diplomatic mission to deliver his request. Ch'ien, and a group of 100 men, eagerly took on the task.

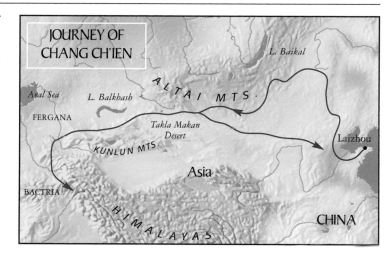

JOURNEY OF CHANG CH'IEN

IN SEARCH OF ALLIES

While journeying through the Kansu corridor to Central Asia, the group was captured by the Huns and brought to their headquarters in the ALTAI MOUNTAINS. After ten years as a prisoner, Ch'ien escaped and continued his journey southwest through Fergana (modern UZBEKISTAN) to Bactria (modern AFGHANISTAN), which was then ruled by the Yueh-chih. When Ch'ien finally met the Yueh-chih leaders, he learned that they had no interest in joining the fight with Han China. He did however set up a trade arrangement wherein the Chinese gave gold and silver for the Yueh-chih's strong horses.

Ch'ien returned home by taking a southern route along the KUNLUN MOUNTAINS, toward a lake at LOP NUR and then to the Tsaidam Depression. Again, Ch'ien was captured by the Huns. He escaped a year later, and finally arrived home in 126 BC. Upon his return, Wu-ti named him supreme counselor of the palace. Although he was not able to find an alliance to fight the enemy, Ch'ien was able to report on the lands he had passed through and many countries he had heard about, including INDIA, Persia (modern IRAN), MESOPOTAMIA, and Roman provinces in Asia.

ESTABLISHING A TRADE ROUTE

Ch'ien also told Wu-ti that he had seen Szechwan products in Bactria that he knew had come through India. Ch'ien proposed that his people create a new route to the West from SICHUAN through India, so that they could trade with India. Wu-ti agreed, and

sent out four missions to explore the TIBET to YUNNAN borders. All of the missions met with tribes at war and none survived.

In 122 BC Ch'ien fought with the Huns and was fined because he did not come to the aid of his commander during an attack. However, when the Chinese won a major battle against the Huns the next year, Ch'ien fell back into good favor with the Emperor.

Seven years later, Ch'ien led another mission to seek an alliance against the Huns. This time he sought another Indo-European tribe, the Wusun, who lived in northwest China (modern TURKESTAN and KAZAKHSTAN). Although the mission failed, Ch'ien sent assistant envoys to other countries, including Fergana and Bactria, with gifts of silk made in China. The act was the start of the Chinese silk trade. Later the Silk Road became the main channel for east-west communication, and played an especially important role in linking China to the Roman Empire.

Trade Route Span

THE SILK ROUTE, for which Ch'ien was largely responsible, stretched from Merv (in Turkmenistan) through northern Iran to Ecobatana. It then went to the city of Seleucia-Ctesiphon (near Baghdad) through northern Mesopotamia and Syria to the port of Antioch, which was 6,000 miles (9,656 km) from China.

Cheng Ho (1371–c. 1434)

EXPLORER · ADMIRAL

Cheng Ho (Zheng He) was named Ma Ho at birth by his Muslim parents of Mongol-Arab descent, who lived in southwestern China's YUNNAN province. When the rulers of CHINA's Ming dynasty stopped a rebellion by the Muslims in 1381, 10-year-old Ma Ho was one of the many boys captured and then castrated to become eunuchs in the service of the Chinese emperor. Ma Ho served the prince Chu Ti (renamed Yung-lo when he became emperor in 1402) and accompanied him on many battles against the Mongols on China's northern border.

In his new role as emperor, Yung-lo gave his former servant the new surname of Cheng, as well as the titles of Grand Imperial Eunuch and admiral before commanding him to lead a series of voyages to promote the Chinese as rulers of the world. With a massive fleet for each trip, Cheng Ho's intentions were to make a strong impression, bring each country's rulers gifts of silk and porcelain, and take representatives back to China to meet the new emperor.

THE MAIDEN VOYAGE

Cheng Ho's first trip began in 1405 at the YANG-TSE RIVER with a fleet of 65 large (444 feet long [135 m]) and 255 small (180 feet [55 m] long) ships holding a total crew of 27,800. They sailed to Champa (modern southern VIETNAM) to successfully battle Sumatra's ruler, Chen Tsu-I, who had been causing trouble for the Chinese. With the mission accomplished, Cheng Ho sent the ruler to China to be executed. He sailed to CEYLON next (modern SRI LANKA) and INDIA's spice-trading port of CALICUT (modern KOZHIKODE), before returning home in 1407.

Later in the year, Cheng Ho and a large crew sailed on a two-year voyage that made stops in THAILAND and JAVA. A third trip (1409–1411) returned to ports visited in the past. Cheng Ho's fourth fleet in 1413, sailed along the southern coast of ARABIA and stopped in the MALDIVE ISLANDS as well as PERSIA's (modern IRAN's) port of ORMUZ. He also sent some of the crew to EGYPT and the holy Muslim city of MECCA by land. In 1415 the fleet returned to China with envoys from 30 countries.

On his fifth voyage (1417–1419), Cheng Ho discovered the island of TAIWAN and sailed on to the nearby RYUKYU ISLANDS. He sent out smaller fleets to the East African shores of MOGADISHU (in modern-day SOMALIA), ZANZIBAR, and port cities in TANZANIA and MOZAMBIQUE.

FINAL VOYAGE

In the middle of Cheng Ho's sixth expedition (1421–1422, which built on his previous journey to Africa, Emperor Yung-lo died. Cheng Ho returned to China to learn that the remaining members of the court thought his voyages were wasteful because they believed China could gain nothing from dealing with other countries. The new emperor, Chu Chan-chi, commanded that Cheng Ho travel on a final voyage in 1431 to announce his installment. Cheng Ho died on an early stop in Calicut.

Many of Cheng Ho's maps were destroyed by the new court, but monuments he built to commemorate his travels still remain in India and Southeast Asia. On one Taoist temple, Cheng Ho wrote: "We have traversed…immense water spaces and have beheld in the ocean huge waves like mountains rising sky-high, and we have set eyes on barbarian regions far away hidden in a blue transparency of light vapors…."

Jacqueline Cochran (1906–1980)

AVIATOR

Jacqueline Cochran was orphaned as a child and brought up by a poor foster family in a lumber mill town in northern FLORIDA. By the time she was 13, she was cutting hair professionally in a beauty salon. Urged to find a more serious career by one of her customers, Cochran, who had little formal education, enrolled in nursing school. Even with three years of medical training, Cochran said in her autobiography that she was never comfortable with the sight of blood.

Cochran went back to hairstyling, this time at Antoine's in New York's Saks Fifth Avenue. Still, Cochran had bigger dreams of setting up her own cosmetics company. In 1932, when future husband, millionaire financier/pilot Floyd Bostwick Odlum told Cochran that to succeed with her dream, she'd need to learn how to fly so she could travel and make contacts that her competitors could not, she took his advice. "At [the] moment when I paid for my first lesson," Cochran said later, "a beauty operator ceased to exist and an aviator was born."

A CAREER IN AVIATION

By July of 1941, two years into World War II, England was in such desperate need of pilots for homeland transport missions that the Royal Air Force began using already-trained female pilots. Cochran flew to LONDON to learn more about the operation. When she returned home, President Theodore Roosevelt asked her to lead a team of more than 1,000 American female pilots who would help England during the war. Cochran's female pilots helped train B-17 turret gunners, worked as test pilots, and trained other pilots. Cochran herself became the first woman to fly a bomber across the North Atlantic.

Not Forgotten

COCHRAN RETIRED from the U.S. Air Force Reserve at the rank of colonel in 1970. Seven years later, she successfully helped lobby Congress for veterans' benefits for the female pilots she supervised during World War II.

In 1938, Cochran also became the first woman to win the Bendix Transcontinental Air Race by flying 2,042 miles (3,286 km) from LOS ANGELES to Cleveland in a then-record of 8 hours, 10 minutes, and 31 seconds. Her silver B-35 had a new fuel system that enabled her to become the first pilot to finish the course non-stop. A year later she created a new women's altitude record by climbing to 33,000 feet (10,058 m).

Cochran also broke several speed records, including one in 1950 for propeller-driven aircraft. Three years later, she became the first woman to break the sound barrier by dropping her plane vertically. "I was hanging face downward diving at Mach 1 [the speed of sound] with my blood surging into my brain, not looking forward to what pilots call a 'red-out' [bursting blood vessels]," explained Cochran, in her autobiography. "You don't hear the sound of your plane. That sound passes behind you because you are going faster than sound can travel."

Once, when asked what fueled her to fly, Cochran replied: "I might have been born in a hovel, but I was determined to travel with the wind and the stars."

Bessie Coleman (1893–1926)

STUNT AVIATOR

Bessie Coleman was born and raised in TEXAS. As one of 13 children, she contributed financially to her family by picking cotton and washing clothes.

DREAMS OF FLYING

When Coleman was ten, she heard about Wilbur and Orville Wright's historic first airplane flight. Coleman dreamed of a way to make her life better— she wanted to become a pilot. "I read everything I could get my hands on about aviating," she said later. "Some of the libraries wouldn't let black girls who picked cotton borrow books, but the books I wanted were about piloting, and folks were so surprised they let me have them anyway."

After attending one semester of college, lack of money forced Coleman to move to CHICAGO to live with her brother. She attended beauty school while working as a manicurist. Coleman saved enough money for flying lessons, but soon found that few U.S. flight schools taught women, and no schools were open to black women.

Coleman's dreams of flying were brought to the attention of Robert Abbott, publisher of the *Chicago Weekly Defender*. After hearing that French flight schools were more liberal, Abbott helped Coleman gain acceptance to a school there. She entered flight school with a new dream—to open her own flight school for African American men and women. After ten months of training, she graduated on June 15, 1921. Coleman returned to the UNITED STATES as the only black woman with a pilot's license.

Because Coleman's savings were drained from the trip, she decided the best way to make money was to become an air show performer. At her first show in 1922, Coleman shocked the crowd with flying maneuvers such as loops and figure eights. During another show, Coleman thrilled spectators when she parachuted out of her plane. Soon Coleman was being introduced at shows as "Brave Bessie."

Coleman experienced her first crash while flying in California in the early 1920s. She suffered fractured ribs and a broken leg, among other injuries, but told reporters she would soon return to flying. Coleman began flying again within a year.

BLACK HERITAGE

USA 00

BESSIE COLEMAN

TRAGEDY STRIKES

In 1926, Coleman was asked to perform at the annual Negro Welfare League in Orlando, FLORIDA. She flew there in her plane, along with her mechanic and public relations manager, William Wills. Mechanical troubles forced her to make two emergency landings before she finally touched down in Florida. There, Wills made repairs to the plane, while Coleman greeted Abbott, who had come to see her perform.

When Wills finished his work, he indicated to Bessie that a flight check would be needed before the show. Abbott told Coleman he was concerned with the plane's safety, but Coleman assured him that it was fine. While in the sky, Coleman allowed Wills to take over the controls to perform the stunt maneuvers. At 3,000 feet (914 m) up, Wills put the plane into a dive. The plane slipped into an upside-down position, and Coleman, who had not put on a seatbelt, fell to the ground. She died that night, and it was later found that a wrench had been left in the machine, thereby jamming the controls.

Eileen Marie Collins (1956–)

ASTRONAUT·SHUTTLE COMMANDER

Eileen Collins was born in Elmira, New York, and grew up in a public housing complex. In her teens, she decided she wanted to fly. "I began reading voraciously about famous pilots, from **Amelia Earhart** to Women Airforce Service Pilots (led by **Jacqueline Cochran**) who played an important role in WWII," said Collins. "Their stories inspired me. I admired the courage of these women to go and fly into dangerous situations."

THE AIR FORCE

Collins's family didn't have enough money to pay for flying lessons, so at 16 she got a job and began saving. By 19, she had saved up $1,000, enough for her first flying lessons. After she earned a degree in math and economics from Syracuse University in 1978, Collins's good grades, flying experience, and a letter of recommendation from her college ROTC supervisor enabled her to become one of the first women to go straight from college into the Air Force. There, she flew as a T-38 instructor pilot and a C-141 aircraft commander and instructor pilot. She considered a career as an astronaut and knew that she'd need at least 1,000 hours of flying high-performance aircraft for the job, so she stayed in the military to earn more flying hours.

From 1986 to 1989, Collins was assigned to the U.S. Air Force Academy in Colorado, where she was an assistant professor in mathematics and a *T-41* instructor pilot. The next year, she was finally selected for NASA's astronaut program. Collins became an astronaut in July 1991, and was first assigned numerous ground jobs, including spacecraft communicator at Mission Control.

Between February 3 to 11, 1995, Collins served as the first female shuttle pilot, the cockpit's second-in-command. "This is really a dream come true for me, something that as a child I didn't think I could do," she told reporters, explaining that she thought being a woman would hold her back. Collins's mission was the first to take part in the joint Russian-American Space Program. Besides making a tricky connection with the Russian Space Station *Mir*, Collins had to maneuver the shuttle to retrieve an astronomy satellite. She served as pilot again on a May 15 to 24, 1997 mission, in which she also had to dock with *Mir*.

COMMANDER COLLINS

On July 23, 1999, Collins lifted off as commander of *Columbia*, and became the first female to command a shuttle mission. One of her biggest successes on that four-day mission was guiding the launch of the $1.5 billion *Chandra X-Ray Observatory*, which allowed scientists to study exploding stars, quasars, and black holes. From its start, the launch was full of surprises. During lift-off, an electrical short blew out computers that were set to run *Columbia*'s main engines and the shuttle's engines ran out of fuel several seconds early, which made the shuttle orbit lower than planned. Collins handled all of the problems with ease, and released *Chandra* on schedule with all satellite systems in working order.

Collins is now an Air Force colonel with more than 5,000 hours of flying time in 30 types of aircraft. She is scheduled to fly as commander on another mission in early 2003.

Christopher Columbus (1451–1506)

EXPLORER

Born in Genoa, Italy, Christopher Columbus began his career at sea at age 14. In 1476, he sailed on a ship bound for ENGLAND that was attacked by privateers. Columbus jumped overboard and swam to nearby PORTUGAL.

He settled in LISBON and married there. Columbus enjoyed studying his father-in-law's maps and ocean current charts. At the same time, he read **Marco Polo**'s accounts of his expedition to CHINA. Columbus decided he could reach the East Indies by sailing west on what he thought was a more direct sea route. (To Europeans of this time, all land east of the INDUS RIVER in Asia were "the Indies.") Unfortunately, Columbus underestimated the Earth's circumference and the distance between Europe and Asia.

After being turned down for sponsorship by Portugal, Columbus moved to SPAIN in 1485 so he could present his ideas to rulers King Ferdinand V and Queen Isabella I. At a monastery in the town of Palos de la Frontera, he made friends with Friar Juan Pérez, who introduced him to the monarchs. Although they were unhappy with his requested payment (one-tenth of all riches found), they realized that the rewards could be great.

On August 3, 1492, three Spanish ships—the *Niña*, the *Pinta*, and the *Santa Maria* (commanded by Columbus)—set sail with a crew of approximately 100 men. At 2:00 AM on October 12, land was spotted. As the men went ashore, Columbus named the island San Salvador and claimed it for Spain. It is not known where they actually landed, but historians believe it may be Samana Cay in the BAHAMAS or Watling Island (modern EL SALVADOR). The native inhabitants of the island were eager to trade, but didn't understand Spanish. Columbus was sure he had landed in the Indies—Asia—and began calling the natives "Indians."

THE CARIBBEAN AND SOUTH

The "Indians" brought Columbus to the coast of CUBA. He also found islands that he named HISPANIOLA (modern HAITI and the DOMINICAN REPUBLIC), before returning home with plenty of gold on March 15, 1493.

With his new title, "Admiral of the Sea Oceans," Christopher Columbus was ready for a second expedition (September 25, 1493–June 11, 1496). He sailed to Hispaniola with 17 ships holding at least 1,200 men, and discovered PUERTO RICO on the way. At Hispaniola, the men began to establish a settlement, but soon complained that they wanted to search for more gold. Columbus enslaved Native Americans to work on the settlement.

On Columbus's next voyage (May 1498–October 1500), he sailed further south, discovering TRINIDAD and VENEZUELA. When he returned to Hispaniola, where his brother Bartholomew had established Santo Domingo, Columbus found angry settlers who wanted a share of the riches. They complained to the king, who responded by taking Columbus's titles from him.

On his final expedition, Columbus set sail on May 9, 1502, and found MEXICO, HONDURAS, PANAMA, and Santiago (modern JAMAICA) before arriving home on November 7. Though Columbus was very rich, he was heartbroken about losing his titles and petitioned the court to get them back, to no avail. While Columbus never actually found a route to Asia, he did manage to open the west to trade with the Europeans.

James Cook (1728–1779)

EXPLORER·CARTOGRAPHER

James Cook was born in the rural English village of Marton, Yorkshire. At age 17, he moved to the coastal town of Whitby and worked as an apprentice to a merchant and ship owner. By 1755, 27-year-old Cook yearned for travel. He joined the British Royal Navy and within two years he sailed to CANADA, where he assisted an army surveyor in mapping ENGLAND's new territories along QUEBEC and the ST. LAWRENCE RIVER. Cook was then assigned to map the coast of NEWFOUNDLAND.

TERRA AUSTRALIS

In the late 1760s, Cook was asked to map a unique astronomical phenomenon only visible in the southern hemisphere—the transit of Venus as it passed between Earth and the Sun—and to search for "Terra Australis," a large land mass believed to exist in the southern part of the world. In 1768, the *Endeavour* set sail from Plymouth, England, captained by Cook. After crossing the Atlantic Ocean, the ship rounded CAPE HORN, and sailed to TAHITI, where Cook wrote notes on Venus.

While other explorers had noted the presence of AUSTRALIA and NEW ZEALAND, their maps were incomplete. Cook set out to fix that. The *Endeavour* circumnavigated the north and south islands of New Zealand and sailed along Australia's eastern coast, the latter of which had never been seen by a European. Cook claimed the area for Britain and called it New South Wales before returning home in July 1771.

Among the observations Cook made on this trip was sailors' need for vitamin C. Scurvy, a disease caused by lack of the vitamin, had been a primary killer of sailors on long journeys. Cook was the first to realize the sailors' need for fresh fruit and vegetables, and made port stops to have the men eat fresh sauerkraut.

In 1772, Cook embarked on another expedition with two ships, the *Resolution* (which he commanded) and the *Adventure*. They sailed around the CAPE OF GOOD HOPE and then headed toward the Atlantic Ocean. In the process, they made the first recorded crossing of the Antarctic Circle. The ships then crossed the southern Indian Ocean to New Zealand and Tahiti, where Cook spent a winter mapping nearby islands.

SOUTH PACIFIC ISLANDS

From there, Cook sailed west, and he and his crew became the first Europeans to sight a group of islands (modern Cook Islands). By early 1774, the ships returned to the tropics and found Easter Island and a group of islands far west of Tahiti that Cook named the New Hebrides (modern VANUATU) before returning home in 1775.

The following year, Cook set out to look for the much talked about Northwest Passage. His two ships sailed to Tahiti, then traveled north. In 1778 they became the first Europeans to find the HAWAIIAN ISLANDS, which Cook named the Sandwich Islands.

With the weather growing colder, Cook decided to spend the winter at the Sandwich Islands and then return north in the summer. After a few weeks at a camp in Kealakekua Bay, the native inhabitants stole a small boat. Cook was angry and attempted to take the tribe's chief hostage. Violence broke out, and Cook was beaten and killed by a mob.

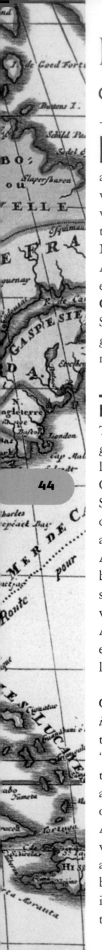

Francisco Coronado (1510–1554)

CONQUEROR·EXPLORER

Born in Salamanca, SPAIN, Francisco Vásquez de Coronado came to America at age 25 to serve as an assistant to New Spain's (modern MEXICO's) first viceroy. Over the next four years, Coronado became wealthy by marrying the colonial treasurer's daughter, and was named governor of the province of Nueva Galicia (modern Jalisco, Zacatecas, and Aguascalientes, Mexico). Coronado was very interested in the travels of Spanish explorer **Álvar Núñez Cabeza de Vaca** and had heard about the legendary Seven Cities of Cíbola, which were believed to be gold-walled cities filled with treasures and located northeast of his province.

IN SEARCH OF GOLD

Thinking another PERU or Mexico or something even greater lay in the distance, New Spain's leaders sent Coronado to investigate. On February 23, 1540, he led 300 Spanish soldiers on horseback wearing colorful silk and velvet suits and armor, as well as 1,000 Tlaxcalan Native Americans herding cattle and pigs (to be used for food) along the western slope of the SIERRA MADRE and northward toward the modern-day border of ARIZONA. They then traveled northeastward to Cíbola, which was populated by a tribe of Zuni.

Upon approaching the Zuni, Coronado began reciting the *requirimientor*, a standard Spanish speech read to Native Americans. It began with an order to "acknowledge the Church as the ruler and superior of the whole world, and the high priest called the Pope, and in his name the King and Queen." The speech went on to explain what would happen if the Native Americans didn't obey, "…we shall forcefully…make war against you…take you and your wives and children and shall make slaves of them." The Zuni were angered by Coronado's words and began firing arrows. In retaliation, Coronado and his men killed many Zuni and tore apart their pueblo. They found no gold.

Coronado was frustrated, but decided to continue the search for gold. He sent parties to explore along the COLORADO RIVER and much of present-day NEW MEXICO. Another small group, led by Garcia López de Cárdenas, traveled westward. The group became the first Europeans to see the GRAND CANYON. The whole party spent the winter in SANTA FE, New Mexico.

Coronado soon turned his attention to a wealthy city, called Quivira, which he had heard about from a Zuni nicknamed "the Turk." By the spring of 1541, Coronado led his followers eastward, where they crossed the upper RÍO GRANDE and present-day Texas's GREAT PLAINS. Coronado's party traveled into modern-day Kansas, but found only a village filled with thatched huts and Wichita Native Americans. When questioned by Coronado, the Turk admitted

that he used the Spaniards interest in gold to fool them, hoping the long journey would kill them. Coronado had his men kill the Turk.

The group returned to New Spain in 1542. Two years later, Coronado was relieved of his governorship when officials found him guilty of committing crimes against Native Americans. He moved to MEXICO CITY, where he worked in the local government and finished an account of his journey. The account provided a vivid description of the southwestern UNITED STATES before other European conquests.

Hernán Cortés (1485–1547)

EXPLORER·CONQUEROR

Hernán Cortés, born in Medellín, SPAIN, was studying law at the University of Salamanca when he decided to sail to the Americas to claim land for his country—and great wealth for himself. In 1511, Cortés joined Spanish soldier Diego Velázquez in the

fight for CUBA. After their conquest proved successful, Cortés became mayor of Santiago de Cuba while Velázquez became Cuba's governor. In 1518, Cortés asked Velázquez to allow him to make an expedition to the newly discovered MEXICO. Although Velázquez feared that an independent Cortés would ignore his authority and try to cancel the expedition, Cortés left for Mexico on February 19, 1519, with approximately 11 ships, 600 men, and 16 horses.

THE AZTEC EMPIRE

Cortés reached Mexico on April 22 and entered the town of Tabasco with his horses. The townspeople had never seen the animals before and were frightened, enabling Cortés to quickly take over the town. There, he learned about Mexico's rule by the Aztec Empire and its emperor, Montezuma II. He also took some locals captive, including a woman named Malinche, who became his mistress and interpreter. Cortés established the town of La Villa Rica de la Vera Cruz (modern VERACRUZ) with a government independent from Aztec rule. He renounced Velázquez's authority and claimed to recognize only the Spanish crown.

Cortés spoke with Montezuma, who asked him not to enter the Aztec capital of TENOCHTITLÁN. Regardless, Cortés decided to overcome the city of Tlaxcala, and then join with the Tlaxcalans to overcome their enemies, the Aztecs. On November 8, 1519, Cortés and a group of 600 men entered Tenochtitlán.

Most Aztecs thought Cortés was Quetzalcoatl, a light-skinned, bearded god who they believed would return from the east to take over their country. As a result, Cortés and his men were allowed to roam freely and take gold and other treasures. Still, Cortés was insecure about his enemies and took Montezuma hostage.

In April 1520, Cortés left the capital city, Tenochtitlán, in the command of explorer Pedro de Alvarado while he traveled to the coast to capture a group of Spaniards sent by Velázquez. He forced the men to join his army, and returned to Tenochtitlán to find the Aztecs in a revolt. Cortés and his army were attacked, and he asked Montezuma to speak up to end the fighting. Montezuma was stoned to death and many Spaniards were killed while the rest were pushed out of the city by the Aztecs.

On July 7, 1520, Cortés reached Tlaxcala, where he spent months reorganizing his forces to take over the capital. He finally captured the new Aztec ruler, Cuauhtémoc, on August 13, 1521, and took control of Tenochtitlán. Cortés built MEXICO CITY on its ruins, and then informed the Spanish king and asked for colonists. He was named governor and captain general of New Spain, the areas in Mexico claimed for Spain, in 1523.

Meanwhile, some members of the Spanish court questioned Cortés's actions. In 1528, he was ordered to relinquish control and return to Spain. The king later dismissed many of the charges.

In 1536, Cortés explored Mexico's Pacific coast and discovered the peninsula now called BAJA, CALIFORNIA. Unsuccessful in appealing to the Spanish court to get permission for another expedition, Cortés settled at a small estate near Seville.

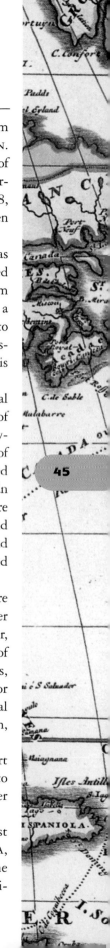

Jacques Cousteau (1910–1997)

EXPLORER·INVENTOR

Jacques Cousteau, born in Saint-André-de-Cubzac, FRANCE, spent much of his youth suffering the effects of chronic enteritis, a painful inflammation of the intestines, and anemia, a blood disease that made him weak. Frequently confined to his bed, Cousteau became an avid reader and his favorite book was Jules Verne's *Twenty Thousand Leagues Under the Sea*.

LEARNING TO DIVE

Cousteau loved the sea and made his first dive at age ten at a summer camp near Vermont's Lake Harvey. As

a teen, he developed two other loves: building and photography. When he wasn't filming with his first movie camera, he amused himself by taking it apart and putting it back together.

Upon graduation from boarding school, Cousteau enrolled in the French naval academy. He trained to be a pilot and was second in his class, but at age 26 a car accident left his right arm paralyzed and his left arm shattered. Cousteau, instead, was stationed at the Toulon Naval Base and began swimming and exploring underwater to strengthen his arms. He soon grew frustrated that he couldn't dive deep enough or stay underwater long enough to take good photographs.

In 1943, Cousteau and French engineer Émile Gagnan completed work on the aqualung, later renamed the "self contained underwater breathing apparatus" (SCUBA). It enabled divers to receive measured amounts of air from tanks, allowing them to swim at great depths for long periods of time. The device consisted of three cylinders of compressed air connected through a pressure-regulator (with two tubes for intake and exhaust) to a facemask.

A few years later, Cousteau turned a 360-ton (327-metric ton), 141-foot (43-m) minesweeper into a floating laboratory with underwater television cameras. *Calypso*, as he named it, allowed Cousteau to explore and make films and television documentaries about his findings. In them, Cousteau could be seen in his trademark back and yellow wetsuit talking to the audience about exotic undersea creatures, undersea wreckages, or pollution, as Cousteau was a fierce conservationist. Cousteau's *The Silent World* (1956) won an Academy Award for Best Documentary.

On July 29, 1956, Cousteau brought *Calypso* to the Romanche Trench near Africa's IVORY COAST. He sent a thin anchor cable over the side and set a record—it was the deepest anchorage ever achieved. While there, Cousteau used a submersible camera to take pictures 24,600 feet (74,981 m) below sea level, more than a half-mile (.8 km) deeper than the trench had ever been photographed before.

Cousteau spent the rest of the 1950s designing and building *Denise*, a saucer-shaped underwater vehicle that could carry two people more than 1,000 feet (305 m) below sea level. Unlike the bathysphere, *Denise* could be steered and was free of outside connections. It ran on a jet pump, motor, and batteries, and featured a claw that enabled divers to grab items off the sea floor and bring them close to a viewing window.

Cousteau also found success with his ocean conservation activism. In the 1970s, he convinced the Italian government to remove 500 drums of toxic chemicals they had buried in the MEDITERRANEAN. During the last two decades of his life, Cousteau took *Calypso* all over the world to film and study the pollution in oceans and rivers.

Davy Crockett (1786–1836)

FRONTIERSMAN · POLITICIAN

The fifth of nine children, David Crockett spent his early years in Jefferson County, TENNESSEE. He left home at age 12 when he found work driving cattle. Crockett then spent the next two years in VIRGINIA, earning a living as a farm laborer and wagon driver. At age 15, the 6-foot-tall (1.8-m) Crockett returned home to TENNESSEE, and began working for one of his heavily in-debt father's creditors. In addition to attending school for six months (his only formal education), Crockett bought a rifle and won many local shooting contests.

Crockett made a name for himself as a hunter, once killing 105 bears in a single season. In 1813 he fought alongside General Andrew Jackson as a commander during an uprising by the Creek tribe of Native Americans in ALABAMA and FLORIDA. He then moved his family to Shoal Creek, Tennessee, where he worked as a justice of the peace, town commissioner, and colonel of the local militia.

CROCKETT THE POLITICIAN

In 1821, Crockett was elected to Tennessee's state legislature, but continued to dress and act as he always had. "He wore that same veritable coon-skin cap and hunting shirt, bearing upon his shoulder his ever faithful rifle," said Tennessean James Davis. Crockett was popular with constituents and six years later was elected to the U.S. House of Representatives, though he had many critics in the press. "He attracted the

Tall Tale

CROCKETT BECAME an American legend when at least 50 "Crockett Almanacs"—which included fabled stories of how the frontiersman rode an alligator up Niagara Falls and tore the tail off Halley's comet—were published between 1836 and 1856.

general gaze by his grotesque appearance, his rough manners, and jovial habits," wrote the *Norristown Free Press*, "at the same time…he exhibited uncommon indications of a strong though undisciplined mind."

A year after Crockett's election to Congress, his old friend Andrew Jackson became president. Crockett made an enemy of Jackson, however, when he opposed the president's policies regarding pioneers' rights and the forced movement of western Native American tribes. His political opponents succeeded in ruining Crockett's reelection hopes in 1831, but he was reelected to Congress in 1833.

Two years later, Crockett unsuccessfully ran for Congress again, but his constituents believed he was more interested in becoming a national celebrity. At age 49, Crockett's political career was over. He decided moving to TEXAS would bring new opportunities. Texas was MEXICO's territory, but the Mexican government encouraged Americans to settle there. The settlers, unhappy with Mexican rule under General Antonio Lopez de Santa Anna, declared Texas to be independent of Mexico and built an army to defend themselves. Crockett joined the army and led a unit named the Tennessee Mounted Volunteers.

Crockett was asked to help defend an old Spanish mission, the Alamo, in San Antonio. The Mexican army approached the Alamo on February 23, 1836, and heavy fighting continued through the next month. By March 6, Crockett and fewer than 20 others were left defending the fort. Although some historians say Crockett fought to the death, most believe he and the others surrendered and were killed when Santa Anna ordered his men to slash them with their sabers.

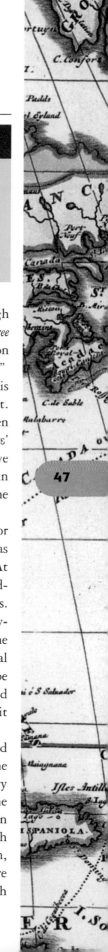

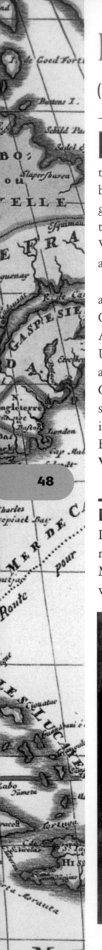

Frank Hamilton Cushing

(1857–1900) ETHNOLOGIST

Frank Hamilton Cushing was born in Northeast, Pennsylvania. When he was 13 his family moved to Media, New York, an upstate town with plenty of backwoods that once served as Native American burial grounds. Inspired by his surroundings, Cushing practiced the arts of stone chipping and basket weaving. When he was 15, his skill for making arrowheads attracted the attention of local ethnologists.

Two years later, the teen wrote his first scientific article, on his archaeological findings in New York's Orleans County, for the Smithsonian Institution's Annual Report. He began attending Cornell University in 1875, but spent most of his time assembling a collection of aboriginal material for the Centennial Exposition in Philadelphia. By 19 he left school to become a curator at the National Museum in Washington, D.C., where he worked with the Bureau of American Ethnology's director **John Wesley Powell**.

LIFE WITH THE ZUNI

In 1879 he was asked to be an assistant on a three-month-long expedition to observe the Zuni in NEW MEXICO. He and his colleagues made observations while living in tents outside the Zuni pueblo.

Fascinated by the experience and frustrated that he couldn't see more, Cushing asked for permission to stay behind for further study. He then settled himself in a room belonging to the Zuni head chief, who didn't invite him, but allowed him to stay. As a result, Cushing became one of the first professional anthropologists to live with the people he was studying.

Cushing learned the Zuni's language and participated in ritual ceremonies. After a few months, some Zuni became angry at Cushing's constant note taking, especially during ceremonies. According to Cushing, one confrontation escalated to the point where he had to take out a knife to defend himself. The act, he said, helped earn him the respect of the tribe. He became so close-knit with the Zuni that in 1881, Cushing was initiated into the tribe's secret "Priesthood of the Bow."

Not only did Cushing try to learn Zuni culture, he also introduced them to his culture. For example, before asking about their myths, Cushing told them European and American folktales. Then, in 1882 he led a group of Zuni leaders on a tour of the UNITED STATES. Two Zuni stayed in Washington to help Cushing write his required reports for the Bureau of Ethnology, which sponsored most of his studies.

Cushing returned to the Zuni pueblo in late 1882 and stayed until 1884, when he was asked to return to Washington. Officials at the bureau were concerned with the amount of money Cushing was spending on research while providing fewer reports than expected as well as his involvement in a Zuni–Navajo clash.

In 1886, Cushing led archaeological expeditions in ARIZONA, finding "lost cities" of Native Americans, including the legendary Cíbola. By 1889 he was removed from the project and suffered from poor health that he said made him unable to complete all of the bureau's reports.

Yet, in 1895, Cushing persuaded a wealthy benefactor—Phoebe Hearst, wife of publisher William Randolph Heart—to fund a three-month archaeological expedition to the FLORIDA KEYS. There, he found remains of lake dwellings as well as many objects. Some scientists suggested Cushing forged one of these artifacts, but Cushing denied the charges.

Alexandra David-Neel (1868–1969)

TRAVELER·ADVENTURER

Alexandra David, born in the Paris suburb of Saint-Mandé, had an unhappy childhood and ran away many times—once getting as far as the Italian ALPS. As a young loner, she spent much of her free time reading about Eastern religions and philosophy.

In 1889, David received an inheritance and used it to travel around INDIA and CEYLON (modern SRI LANKA) to learn first-hand about the religions she had read about. Within three years she ran out of money and returned to FRANCE, where she found work with a traveling opera company as a singer by the stage name of Mademoiselle Myrial. At a stop in TUNIS, she met and married a distant cousin, Philippe Neel. Though they ended up spending much of their lives apart, he adored her and financed many of her travels.

Soon after the marriage, Mrs. David-Neel returned to PARIS to study Asian religions. In 1910 the French Ministry of Education sponsored her trip to India to further her research. The next year, she interviewed the Dalai Lama, TIBET's chief spiritual leader, in Bhutan after she learned he had moved there when CHINA invaded his country. (At that point, the British forbade Europeans from entering Tibet).

David-Neel traveled to the kingdom of Sikkim in 1913, where she lived in a monastery and studied the Tibetan language. A 15-year-old Sikkimese student lama, Yongden, became her guide. David-Neel spent the following winter of 1914 to 1915 living as a Buddhist nun in a cave in Sikkim. She and Yongden (now her constant companion) then traveled to the monastery of Tashilhumpo, on the edge of Tibet, in hopes of meeting Pachen Lama, the second-ranking lama. Before she could do so, she was caught by British soldiers and forced to leave.

LHASA: FORBIDDEN LAND

In 1916 David-Neel began a tour of BURMA, JAPAN, and China, where she lived in a Buddhist monastery for more than 20 years while translating Tibetan texts. She made an attempt to enter Tibet's capital of LHASA from the north in the winter of 1922–1923 by disguising herself as a Tibetan woman and traveling across the GOBI DESERT in southern MONGOLIA. Unfortunately, before she reached her destination she was recognized as a European and led out of the country.

In the summer of 1923, David-Neel attempted to enter Lhasa again by trying to blend in with Buddhist pilgrims traveling through southeastern Tibet. She posed as Yongden's mother by dying her hair with Chinese ink and darkening her face. (Yongden traveled freely because he was a lama.) They traveled throughout the countryside, until Yongden sprained his ankle. David-Neel tried to carry her 24-year-old guide, but they got lost and were approached by robbers, though David-Neel scared them away by firing her gun. By early 1924, David-Neel reached Lhasa and toured the Potala, the Dalai Lama's palace.

In May 1925 David-Neel and Yongden went to France, where David-Neel wrote a series of articles (turned into a book in 1927) about her travels as the first European woman to visit Lhasa. She convinced her husband to adopt Yongden, and in 1936, David-Neel and Yongden lived in a Chinese monastery until the end of World War II. When they returned to France, David-Neel worked as a journalist. Yongden died from alcoholism in 1955.

Bartholomeu Dias (c. 1450–1500)

EXPLORER·NAVIGATOR

Little is known about Bartholomeu Dias's early life. He was asked by King John II of Portugal to command a ship on an expedition to Africa's Gold Coast in 1481. Five years later, the king asked Dias to command another expedition that would further explore the western coast of Africa, a challenge first attempted in 1482 by explorer Diego Cam, who had sailed as far south as WALVIS BAY. Dias was invited

to find the kingdom of the Christian African king Prester John, with whom the Portuguese wished to develop a trade relationship.

After ten months of preparation, Dias's expedition set sail with two ships from LISBON in August 1487. On board were two African men and four African women who were to climb ashore first and explain the purpose of the expedition to natives. A smaller supply ship, commanded by Dias's brother, Pero, accompanied the expedition.

MOSSEL BAY

The ships reached Cape Cross, which was then the southernmost point of Portuguese exploration, and left the coastline. Sailing further south, then turning east and north, Dias finally sighted land, which he named *Bahia dos Vaqueiros* (MOSSEL BAY). The location is about 200 miles (370 km) east of the present-day CAPE OF GOOD HOPE, but Dias did not sight the cape.

THE CAPE OF GOOD HOPE

By February 1488, Dias's ships became the first to round the southern end of Africa as far as the estuary of the present-day Great Fish River, which he named after the commander of one of his ships. In rounding Africa, Dias had found a good sea route from Europe to East Asia (INDIA), which Europeans felt was necessary for their future wealth. Yet supplies were running low and the crew was demanding Dias to allow them to return to PORTUGAL.

After exploring approximately 1,260 miles (2,028 km) of African coastline previously unknown to Europeans, Dias was ready to end his expedition. On the return voyage, he stopped at the southeastern tip of Africa. He named the land *Cabo Tormentoso* (Cape of Storms), though King John II later renamed it *Cabo da Bõa Esperança* (Cape of Good Hope) to commemorate Dias's successful expedition. Dias reached Lisbon in December 1488.

In 1500 Dias commanded one ship in an expedition to discover BRAZIL, led by fellow Portuguese explorer Pedro Álvares Cabral. On the return trip, Dias's ship sunk during a storm in the South Atlantic Ocean, off the Cape of Good Hope.

Mossel Bay Museum

SOUTH AFRICA'S COASTAL town of Mossel Bay is home to the Bartolomeu Dias Museum. The most popular attraction there is the Old Post Office Tree, a more than 500-year-old milkwood tree under which early explorers used to leave important letters and records of their findings in an old shoe. The museum also houses a replica of Dias's ship, built for a commemorative voyage from Portugal to the bay in 1988.

Charles Montagu Doughty

(1843–1926) TRAVELER

The son of a wealthy clergyman from Suffolk, England, Charles Montagu Doughty attended at least three different universities, including Cambridge and Oxford, while studying a variety of topics that interested him. In 1874, he decided he wanted to study the ancient ruins of the Middle East.

Doughty made many expeditions to the SINAI PENINSULA, financed by the Royal Geographic Society in London, before moving to DAMASCUS, where he spent a year learning Arabic, adopted the Arabic name of Khalil, and began wearing Arab robes. Doughty refused, however, to disguise his nationality or Christian faith to fit into Arab culture—a fact that would make his future travels challenging.

On November 12, 1876, Doughty left Damascus with a caravan of Arabs. By December 4, the caravan reached Med'in Salih, a pre-Islamic town carved out of rock in northwestern ARABIA. Doughty was initially not allowed to enter the ruins, but he befriended a local sheikh, Zeyd Sbeychan, who helped him gain entry. Doughty spent the next two months writing notes about and sketching the city, which was once a prosperous trade center for gold, frankincense, and cinnamon for people between the MEDITERRANEAN and southern Arabia.

LIFE WITH THE BEDOUIN

Instead of returning with the caravan, Doughty decided to travel with his new friend's band of nomadic Arabs called Bedouin. The band was just one Bedouin tribe that Doughty lived with, studied, and wrote about. In the summer of 1877, he left Sbeychan's band and literally entered the tent of another. While the men weren't pleased to have a Christian with very little money traveling with them, they felt obliged to take care of him. Still, he was often threatened by band members and given smaller amounts of food.

Doughty met new bands of Bedouin in TAYMA and HA'IL, northern Arabia's capital city. He was greeted by the local emir in Ha'il and given a place to stay. However, after several weeks, Doughty was beaten by the emir's guard and asked to leave the city. In

November 1877, he entered the town of Khaybar in the western Arabian province of Hejaz. The governor believed Doughty to be a spy, and as a result took his travel documents and most of his cash and forced him to stay in town for four months.

In mid-March 1878, Doughty was free to leave, so he traveled to the town of BURAYDAH, where he was again beaten and robbed. He walked to the nearby town of UNAYZAH and found a local merchant who cashed a check for him. The merchant then suggested Doughty join a caravan traveling to the city of JIDDA near the RED SEA.

On the caravan, Doughty—who had torn clothes and was behaving like a beggar—was threatened with a gun by a camel driver, but a servant from MECCA came to his aid. When he reached Jidda, Doughty was turned over to the British consulate, which arranged to have him sent back to ENGLAND.

Doughty spent ten years writing about his experiences in *Travels in Arabia Deserta* (1888). T. E. Lawrence (AKA Lawrence of Arabia) said the book was an enormous influence on his later work and writings on Arabia.

51

Sir Francis Drake (c. 1540–1596)

EXPLORER

Francis Drake was born near the small town of Tavistock, England. He apprenticed as a mariner, and began commanding his own ships on trading missions by 1567. In 1572 he led two ships in a fight against Spanish ports in the CARIBBEAN SEA. During this voyage, Drake—working for the first time as a privateer—sailed to the Pacific Ocean, captured the Panamanian port town of Nombre de Dios, and pillaged the Panamanian town of Portobelo. He returned with a load of Spanish silver.

AROUND THE WORLD

Drake was next assigned to Ireland from 1573 to 1576 to help end a rebellion there. Upon his return, Queen Elizabeth I asked him to take on a secret mission against the Spanish colonies on the Pacific coast of America. On December 13, 1577, Drake set out from Plymouth, ENGLAND, with five ships and 166 men. Two ships were abandoned early on, though the others sailed through the STRAIT OF MAGELLAN at South America's southern tip and reached the Pacific Ocean in 16 days. A series of storms destroyed one ship and Drake sent another home. Drake, on the *Golden Hind*, sailed where the wind took him—far south.

As the ship sailed along South America's Pacific coast, Drake and his crew robbed and destroyed many Spanish ports as well as a treasure ship off the coast of PERU. Drake also took control of some Spanish ships and used their more accurate charts for further explorations. In search of an eastward passage back to the Atlantic, Drake sailed north, reaching as far as the present U.S.-Canadian border. Finding no passage, Drake headed south and docked his ship for repairs

on June 17, 1579, at an inlet now called Drake's Bay. He claimed the land around it for England and named it Nova Albion ("New England;" modern SAN FRANCISCO area).

Drake set out again on July 23, 1579. He sailed west across the Pacific, until he finally reached the MOLUCCAS, a group of islands located in the South Pacific, in November. Drake also stopped at the Indonesian islands of Sulawesi (modern CELEBES) and JAVA, before rounding the CAPE OF GOOD HOPE at the southern tip of Africa and returning to England with a shipload of spices and treasures in September 1580. He was celebrated as the first Englishman to circumnavigate the world.

In April 1581, Queen Elizabeth knighted Drake and assigned him as mayor of Plymouth. He also served as a member of Parliament in 1584 and 1585. At the end of 1585, Drake set sail again, this time with a large fleet. He attacked and robbed many settlements, including ST. AUGUSTINE in present-day FLORIDA, before setting up the first British colony in America on Roanoke Island (the coast of modern NORTH CAROLINA). He returned to England with treasures as well as tobacco, which was new to his homeland.

In 1587 England and SPAIN were on the brink of war when Drake led an attack on Spanish ships in the harbor of CÁDIZ, at the queen's request. Afterwards, Drake was made vice admiral of the English fleet. He returned to Parliament until 1595, when the queen assigned Drake and Sir John Hawkins to lead another attack on the Spanish. The mission was a failure, as the two men contracted dysentery on the journey and died.

Amelia Earhart (1897–1937)

AVIATOR

Born in Atchison, Kansas, Amelia Earhart was a tomboy who loved to climb trees and hunt rats with a .22 rifle. She also kept a scrapbook with newspaper clippings featuring women who were successful in then male-dominated fields, such as law and film direction.

Earhart saw a plane for the first time at a state fair when she was ten years old. "It was a thing of rusty wire and wood and looked not at all interesting," she

said. Almost a decade later, Earhart watched a stunt plane show and suddenly felt her interest in planes grow. Then, on December 28, 1920, she took her first flight with pilot Frank Hawks. "By the time I got two or three hundred feet off the ground," she later said. "I knew I had to fly."

After caring for injured soldiers as a nurse's aide in Toronto during World War I, Earhart obtained a medical degree from Columbia University. Upon graduation, she took flying lessons from female pilot Neta Snook, and then made her first solo flight in 1920, buying a used plane soon after.

TRANSATLANTIC FLIGHT

In 1928, Earhart was asked to be a log-keeper on a transatlantic flight by Wilmer Stultz and Louis Gordon. The trip, lasting 20 hours and 40 minutes, put Earhart into the record books as the first woman to fly over the Atlantic.

Four years later, on May 20, 1932, Earhart made the trip across the Atlantic Ocean alone. She battled bad weather and a gas leak and landed in an Irish meadow, but managed to set a new record for transatlantic airplane crossing: 13 hours and 30 minutes.

"FIRST" FLIGHTS

Earhart tackled the Pacific Ocean, from HAWAII to CALIFORNIA, in 1935, becoming the first woman ever to make the journey. Later that year, she set another speed record by flying nonstop from MEXICO CITY to Newark, NEW JERSEY, in 14 hours and 19 minutes. Between her flights, Earhart worked as aviation editor at *Cosmopolitan* and helped establish an organization of female pilots, the Ninety-Nines.

Determined to make another amazing "first" flight, Earhart took off from MIAMI, FLORIDA, in June 1937 on a quest to become the first woman to complete an around-the-world journey. Because planes were not then made with navigation equipment, Earhart brought along navigator Fred Noonan.

After a routine stop, Earhart took off on July 2 for the most challenging part of the trip, from Lae, PAPUA NEW GUINEA, to Howland Island in the Pacific Ocean. The plane never made it to its island destination, and the U.S. Navy and Coast Guard were sent to search for it. Although Earhart's fate remains a mystery, tests on a piece of a plane found years later near Howland Island showed it was from Earhart's plane.

Last Flight

AFTER EARHART DIED, her husband, George Palmer Putnam, edited and published a book, *Last Flight* (1937) about her journey. The book includes Earhart's flight notes, letters she cabled to him from her brief stops, and log records. "When I go," Earhart had told her husband, "I'd like best to go in my plane. Quickly."

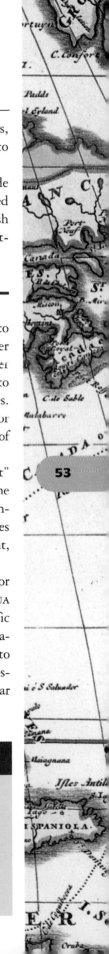

Sylvia Earle (1935–)

OCEANOGRAPHER·MARINE BIOLOGIST

Raised on a farm near Camden, NEW JERSEY, Sylvia Earle found an interest in the sea at an early age. "When I was three, the ocean along the New Jersey shore sent up a wave that knocked me off my feet," said Earle. "I fell in love."

Her family moved to Clearwater, FLORIDA, on the GULF OF MEXICO, when Earle was 13. Three years later, she made her first underwater dive in Florida's Weekiwachee River. From then on, she spent much of her free time making dives near her home.

Earle won a scholarship to Florida State and supported herself by working on research in the college's laboratories while earning a B.A. Though she was interested in underwater exploration, Earle decided to major in botany because she felt that the first step to understanding an ecosystem is understanding its vegetation. During this time she began a continuing study of underwater plant life in the Gulf of Mexico. To date, she has catalogued more than 20,000 marine plant specimens.

UNDERSEA EXPLORER

In 1964, after earning a Master's Degree from Duke University, Earle joined the National Science Foundation's studies in the Indian Ocean. Two years later, Earle received a Ph.D. from Duke. She continued on various undersea expeditions, including a 1968 exploration 100 feet (31 m) below the waters of the Bahamas in a submersible while she was four months pregnant with her third child.

A year later, Earle applied for the first Tektite Project, sponsored by the U.S. Navy, the Department of the Interior, and NASA, in which researchers live in an underwater shelter and study marine life. Though she had spent more than 1,000 research hours underwater—more than any other scientist who applied to the program—Earle was rejected because the organizers didn't want men and women living together in the underwater habitat. Undaunted, in July 1970, Earle led *Tektite II*, in which five women spent two weeks 50 feet (15 m) below sea level in an underwater shelter off the U.S. Virgin Islands.

Throughout the 1970s, Earle took part in expeditions with undersea photographer Al Giddings, including a journey from HAWAII to NEW ZEALAND, AUSTRALIA, SOUTH AFRICA, Bermuda, and ALASKA to follow sperm whales. In 1979, Earle set a record for the deepest untethered dive. Wearing a pressurized suit that enabled her to walk 1,250 feet (381 m) below sea level near Oahu, Hawaii, Earle spent two and a half hours making observations and gathering specimens. Six years later, she made a record 3,000-foot (914-m) dive into the Pacific Ocean in a submersible. Such dives have enabled Earle to discover many new species of fish, including the hatchetfish.

In 1990, Earle became the first woman to serve as lead scientist at the National Oceanic and Atmospheric Administration, which oversees the weather service and marine sanctuaries. Earle found that working at a federally funded organization with lawmakers didn't suit her conservationist tendencies and stayed only a year and a half. She then founded Deep Ocean Exploration and Research (now called DOER Marine Operations), an ocean engineering company that designs and manages human-operated and robotic underwater vessels.

Earle is currently the leader of Sustainable Seas Expeditions, a five-year project to explore the 18,000 square miles (28,968 sq km) of federally protected marine sanctuaries along U.S. coastlines.

Erik the Red (c. 950–1001)

EXPLORER

Erik the Red's actual last name was Thorvaldsson, but he got his nickname because of his red hair and beard. He was born in Jaeren, NORWAY, but when his father, Thorvald Asvaldsson, was exiled after committing several murders in the late 960s to early 970s, his family settled in ICELAND.

There Erik met and married a woman named Thjódhild. The couple was forced to move several times due to fights Erik had with neighbors. He fought one battle with another family in which several men died. From then on, Erik kept a team of fighters on his farm.

GREENLAND

In about 981, Erik was charged with manslaughter and banished for three years. He decided to explore some islands to the west of Iceland, first sighted by Gunnbjörn Úlfsson many years earlier. Accompanied by a crew, he sailed from the SNAEFELLSNES PENINSULA in 982 and reached the islands Gunnbjörn had spoken of off the eastern coast of GREENLAND. He then landed on the eastern coast of what would later be known as the largest island in the world. He named the icy spot Midjokull ("middle glacier") and then sailed south, rounded the southern tip of the island (modern CAPE FAREWELL) and landed on the southwestern coast.

In the west, Erik found a choice parcel of land, where he built a settlement, Brattahlid. He spent the next two winters exploring the southern tip of the island. Members of his crew explored the northwest and discovered DISKO ISLAND (modern QEQERTARSUAQ). Though much of Erik's newfound island was ice, legend has it that before returning home, he named it Greenland so new settlers would flock to it, thinking it held rich farmland.

With his banishment over, Erik returned to Breidafjord, Iceland, in 985, and persuaded others to join him in the new land. It wasn't hard because Iceland was suffering from a famine due to excessive farming and grazing. The following summer, 25 ships, carrying 750 men, women, and children, sailed with Erik to Greenland. Only 14 made it to their destination. The 11 other ships sank or sailed back to Iceland when their commanders were threatened by a huge storm.

Erik found that the eastern coast was covered in ice, so he brought the ships around Cape Farewell and settled in the town of Brattahlid (modern Julianehåb) with his wife and children. Erik's farm lay 60 miles (97 km) inland, was made of stone, and included a 12-foot (4-m) by 45-foot (14-m) main room with a stream flowing through it. At least 190 other homes dotted the landscape nearby. Other members of Erik's party established a settlement at GODTHAAB (modern NUUK).

By the year 1000 there were approximately 1,000 settlers in Greenland, but an epidemic two years later vastly reduced the population. Erik was supposed to sail to Vinland (North America) with his son, **Leif Eriksson**, in 1001, but an injury forced him to cancel those plans. Erik died the winter after his son returned home with word of the new land.

Viking Ship

LIKE OTHER VIKINGS, Erik had long wooden ships, called *knorrs*, which featured a large, square sail as a central mast. They were sturdy enough to handle the ocean, yet didn't need a harbor. They could land on beaches or river banks.

Leif Eriksson (c. late 970's– c. 1020)

EXPLORER

Leif Eriksson, born Leiv Erikkson Den Hepne in Iceland, was the middle son of Norwegian explorer **Erik the Red** and his wife, Thjódhild. Eriksson's family moved to GREENLAND soon after his father discovered the island. Just before the year 1000, Eriksson

sailed to Norway, as was customary among sons of prominent Icelandic families. From there, he made a trip to the shores of North America, though historians disagree on how Eriksson ended up there.

NORTH AMERICA

Scholars consider an ancient record called *Groenlendinga* ("Tale of the Greenlanders") to be the most reliable resource for Eriksson's travels. It notes that Icelandic trader Bjarni Herjólfsson saw North America 14 years before Eriksson when he got lost in the fog on his way to Greenland. Eriksson later bought Herjólfsson's ship and followed the trader's notes in order to retrace his voyage.

On the way, Eriksson stopped in parts of North America that he named Helluland ("Flatstone land" in Icelandic old Norse; believed to be modern BAFFIN ISLAND), Markland ("Woodland;" believed to be LABRADOR), and Vinland ("Pastureland" or "Wineland.") While some scholars believe Vinland is NOVA SCOTIA or New England, most agree Vinland is

NEWFOUNDLAND because ruins of a Viking settlement found there in 1963 correspond to Eriksson's description of Vinland as a place with fertile land, wheat, and wild grapes.

Another account of Eriksson's journey, the ancient Icelandic document called *Eiríks saga* ("Saga of Eric"), suggests that Norwegian King Olaf I encouraged the explorer to convert to Christianity and sent him to Greenland to spread the religion to the Viking settlers there. Sailing westward, strong winds knocked Eriksson off course and his ship landed in Vinland.

Whichever account is true, both note Eriksson stayed in Vineland for a year, built settlements, and found grapes and timber, which he brought back with him. On his return trip, he rescued the crew of a wrecked Nordic trading ship. The appreciative crew nicknamed him Leif the Lucky and gave him their cargo, making Eriksson quite rich. Upon leaving North America and docking in Greenland, Eriksson spread the message of Christianity to Greenland's settlers. His father was a devout believer in the Norse god of thunder, Thor, and refused to be converted. However, Eriksson's mother became a Christian. After Erik the Red argued with his wife about her new religious beliefs, he gave in and allowed her to supervise the building of a small Christian church near—but out of sight from—the family farm at Brattahlid. It was Greenland's first church.

Eriksson took over Brattahlid when his father died. He gave his ship to his brother, Thorvald, so he could explore Vinland. In the winter of 1005, Thorvald and his crew attacked some Native Americans, who in return killed Thorvald. Eriksson's other brother, Thorstein, died on a voyage to bring his dead brother's body home from North America.

Ancient Remains

ARCHAEOLOGIST'S FOUND the ruins of Thjódhild's church in 1961. Made of wood and dirt, the church could only hold a few people. In its cemetery is an unmarked grave with remains believed to be those of Eriksson.

Sir Ranulph Fiennes (1944–)

EXPLORER·TRAVELER

Ranulph Twistleton-Wykeham Fiennes was born into a wealthy British family. His father died at war before Fiennes was born, and he grew up hoping to follow in his footsteps by becoming a commanding officer of a Scottish regiment. Yet, Fiennes received such poor grades at Eton College that he was barred from being a regular officer. He was able to join the army on a series of short missions, and even spent some time working with Britain's elite regiment, the Special Air Service (SAS), during which time he learned how to climb mountains, ski, and canoe.

GENEROUS ADVENTURER

He was kicked out of the SAS for blowing up a Twentieth Century Fox movie-set in Castle Coombe, Wiltshire, according to BBC reports, and began making expeditions to raise money for charity. After seven years of planning, Fiennes and actor Charles Burton began a three-year journey in 1979 to become the first to reach both poles in one circumnavigation of Earth.

Earlier than that, Fiennes had grown fascinated with the legend of the Lost City of Ubar which was the frankincense trading center of the ancient world. After 26 years and eight expeditions to the ARABIAN DESERT, Fiennes realized the city was probably in OMAN, which was forbidden to international archaeologists. Since Fiennes was once posted in service to the Sultan of Oman, he was granted permission to film parts of the country for a documentary in 1991. After six weeks of secret digging, his team unearthed a 2,500-year-old chess set, and later, a city wall.

In 1993 Fiennes and Mike Stroud made the first unsupported crossing of ANTARCTICA. Traveling approximately 14 miles a day for 97 days the men walked across the continent through snowstorms while dragging 500-pound (227-kg) sledges. This feat, coupled with a 1980 trip to the SOUTH POLE, made Fiennes the first man to reach the South Pole and the Antarctic twice. The expedition also raised £1 million (approximately $1.5 million) for charity.

That same year, Fiennes was knighted for his exploration and charitable work. His expeditions have raised more than £5 million ($7.8 million) for

charities, while Fiennes has managed to live off money he earned writing books. Fiennes' charity money has built Europe's first multiple sclerosis research center in Cambridge, England, as well as the first breast cancer clinic in Europe.

In February of 2000, Fiennes set out to become the first person to reach the true NORTH POLE without any assistance. Reaching the real North Pole takes

approximately four times as long as reaching the magnetic North Pole, which is presently much further south. Fiennes trained for months by running up and down hills near his farm in Exmoor, ENGLAND, with truck wheels attached to his waist. The weights were to prepare him to journey the 700-plus miles (over 1,126 km) in about 100 days in subzero temperatures while pulling the weight of all of the necessary food and equipment over icy ridges and around gaps.

One week into the journey, Fiennes suffered frostbite after attempting to rescue a pair of sledges that had fallen through the ice. The expedition was cancelled, as Fiennes lost the lower portions of all fingers on his left hand. In 2000, Fiennes said that he would focus on finding lost cities in the future.

Steve Fossett (1944–)

BALLOONIST·SAILOR·PILOT

Steve Fossett earned an M.B.A from Washington University in St. Louis, Missouri, in 1968, and later earned millions as a business leader. Yet he has gained fame from his participation in endurance sports. He has swum the English Channel, driven in the 24 Hours of Le Mans sports car race, participated in Alaska's Iditarod Dogsled Race, and completed the Ironman Triathlon in Hawaii.

RECORD-BREAKER

Still, world's records are what really excite Fossett. He earned ten sailing world's records, including one for a

Steve Fossett
PILOT

solo crossing of the Pacific Ocean. In 2000, Fossett also broke a number of flying records, the most celebrated being U.S. transcontinental records for nonmilitary planes flying from San Francisco to New York (3 hours, 42 minutes) and Jacksonville, Florida, to San Diego (3 hours, 29 minutes).

In the 1990s, Fossett's attention turned to ballooning. In February 1995 he made the first solo Pacific crossing, and by January the next year he was ready to attempt the first solo around-the-world balloon flight. Thirty-six hours after launching from St. Louis, storms brought the craft down. A year later,

Fossett tried again and set a distance record, traveling 10,361 miles (16, 673 km) before running out of fuel.

SOLO SPIRIT

He tried again in 1998, but this time decided to travel around the southern hemisphere. After launching in Mendoza, Argentina, on August 7, Fossett's balloon, *Solo Spirit*, ruptured during a violent thunderstorm. Fossett fell 29,000 feet (8,800 m) into the shark-infested Coral Sea, but he still managed to set a new distance record for ballooning—14,235 miles (22,909 km). "This is the closest I have come in my entire life to being killed," he told reporters after being rescued.

In December 1998, Fossett, fellow millionaire businessman Richard Branson of Britain, and balloonist Per Linstrand of Sweden, sailed more than halfway around the world—from Morocco to Hawaii. Though the flight made a crash landing, it marked the first crossing of Asia by a balloon.

Fossett attempted the solo around-the-world balloon flight for a fifth time in 2001. His balloon was made larger (140 feet {43 m} tall and 60 feet {18 m} wide) and he had enough fuel for a 22-day flight. The 57-year-old launched from Northam, Australia, on August 4, 2001.

His balloon was mostly set on autopilot, controlling the burner, as wind currents moved it forward. He breathed liquid oxygen from cylinders and lived in a cramped 7-foot-long (2.1-m), 5-foot-wide (1.5-m), and 5-foot-tall (1.5-m) capsule. After crossing the South Pacific, he landed in southern Brazil after severe thunderstorms hit.

On June 19, 2002, Fossett launched from Northam, Australia, once again, this time on his sixth attempt. Fourteen days, 19 hours, and 51 minutes later Steve Fossett became the first person to complete a solo around-the-world hot air balloonflight. Despite bad weather, Fossett landed smoothly in Australia's eastern outback. His balloon, *Spirit of Freedom*, will be displayed next to **Charles Lindbergh**'s plane, *Spirit of St. Louis*, in the National Air and Space Museum at the Smithsonian Institution in Washington, D.C.

Dian Fossey (1932–1985)

PRIMATOLOGIST

Dian Fossey's parents divorced when she was six. Her mother quickly remarried, and she never saw her father again. By age 14, Fossey was extremely shy and embarrassed about her 6-foot, 1-inch (1.85-m) height. The lonely girl spent most of her time around animals, particularly horses.

In 1954 Fossey graduated from San Jose State College with a degree in occupational therapy, and began work at Kosair Crippled Children's Hospital in Louisville, Kentucky. She would quietly work around the children, never forcing them to interact with her. While some co-workers thought her aloofness was odd, Fossey knew that gradually the children would trust her and open up—and she was right. She used the same approach with gorillas later.

AFRICAN SAFARI

In 1963, Fossey decided she wanted to take a seven-week safari and took a bank loan to finance it. On September 26, she flew to Africa and traveled with a guide for 1,000 miles (1,609 km) through East Africa. At the Olduvai Gorge in TANZANIA, Fossey met anthropologists Dr. **Louis** and Mary **Leakey**. She also traveled to Mount Mikeno in the Congo (modern DEMOCRATIC REPUBLIC OF THE CONGO [DRC]) to observe mountain gorillas. Fossey fell in love with the animals and returned to Kentucky with a heavy heart.

Three years later, Fossey visited Dr. Leakey during his U.S. book tour. He encouraged her to set up a camp and expand a 1959 gorilla research study by zoologist George B. Schaller. Fossey didn't have a science background or research skills, and she had acrophobia, which would make mountain climbs difficult. Still, Dr. Leakey insisted the work called for someone to be instinctive, not science-oriented. He persuaded Fossey to return to Tanzania in 1966 and meet with primatologist **Jane Goodall** to gain expertise.

On December 15, 1966, Fossey traveled to Africa and set up a study site in the Virunga Mountains on the borders of DRC, RWANDA, and UGANDA. Her site, the Karisoke Research Center, became the base for an 18-year study to, in her words, "form more intimate contacts with gorilla groups and individuals, to observe up close their behavior, their interactions, and to do this in such a way that my presence did not affect their behavior."

NEW DISCOVERIES

She discovered that gorillas make 25 distinct sounds and learn to communicate using those sounds. Fossey also learned to imitate their eating and grooming habits to gain their trust. After six years of close contact with the gorillas, Fossey began to fight with anyone she saw as a threat to them, including hunters, herdsmen who allowed their cattle to graze on their land, tourists, and the Rwandan government. Fossey was also very reclusive. The Africans called her *nyiram acibili* ("the woman who lives alone in the forest"). She left the site only to visit family and take classes at Cambridge University in ENGLAND, where she spent three to six months at a time to complete a Ph.D. in zoology by 1974.

In 1985, Fossey was found murdered by a machete at her campsite. Her death remains a mystery, though some authorities suspect that it was in retaliation for her efforts to stop the poaching of gorillas in Africa. Fossey's best selling book, *Gorillas in the Mist* (1983) was made into a movie in 1988.

John Franklin (1786–1847)

EXPLORER · BRITISH NAVY OFFICER

The youngest of 12 sons, John Franklin was born in Spilsby, Lincolnshire, England. He entered the British Navy as a midshipman at age 14, fighting in the Battle of Copenhagen on April 2, 1801. That same year he joined an expedition to explore the coast of AUSTRALIA. In 1803, he returned to ENGLAND to fight in other battles.

Fifteen years later, Franklin was commander of the ship *Trent* on an unsuccessful ARCTIC expedition. He was promoted to lieutenant in 1819 and began the first of three sailing explorations of the Arctic coast.

CANADIAN WILDERNESS

On his first trip, Franklin docked in HUDSON BAY in northwest CANADA and traveled overland eastward for more than 500 miles (800 km) from the mouth of

the Coppermine River. Franklin and his crew almost died of starvation when a promised supply ship never arrived. Crew members resorted to murder and cannibalism of their own men, until Native Americans took care of the remaining survivors.

Franklin arrived back in England in 1822. He was promoted to captain and settled down to write an account of his travels. Three years later, Franklin made a second Arctic expedition. This time, he and his crew explored 1,200 miles (1,900 km) of Arctic coastline, including Alaska's coast.

After returning home, Franklin was knighted in 1829. Seven years later he was appointed lieutenant governor of the new penal colony at Van Diemen's Land (modern TASMANIA). In the seven years he served there, Franklin tried to dignify the settlement by establishing a college and scientific society.

When Franklin returned to England he learned that the Navy was preparing for a search of the Northwest Passage, the fabled icy link between the Atlantic and Pacific Oceans. He was insistent that he lead the expedition, though Navy officers felt his age, 59, was a concern. Finally, Franklin was granted his wish and given command of two ships, *Erebus* and *Terror*, and a crew of 130. The ships set sail in May 1845, and entered LANCASTER SOUND, northwest of BAFFIN ISLAND on July 26. They were last seen by another crew on that day.

IN SEARCH OF FRANKLIN

Three years later, many expeditions set sail to find Franklin. In 1854, John Rae of the Hudson Bay Company met Inuit who told him they saw white men dragging a boat near KING WILLIAM ISLAND, east of VICTORIA ISLAND. The Inuit also gave Rae spoons that were later found to have belonged to Franklin and his crew.

In 1857, Lady Jane Franklin, his wife, organized a search expedition that found the ship's log, which noted that Franklin's ships had gotten stuck in the ice near Victoria Island and that Franklin died on June 11, 1847. More crew members died walking inland, but not before they reached Simpson Strait, from which a passage to the BERING STRAIT was already established. Thus, Franklin's expedition is generally credited with being the first to find the passage.

In 1984, Canadian anthropologist Owen Beattie studied skeletons, some well preserved in ice, found during a U.S. expedition to the area. His research indicated that the crew most likely died of lead poisoning from cans of tainted meat.

John Frémont (1813–1890)

EXPLORER · MILITARY OFFICER · POLITICIAN

John Charles Frémont, son of a Virginia woman and a French immigrant, was born in Savannah, Georgia. His father died when he was five, and he moved with his mother to Charleston, SOUTH CAROLINA, where he attended school and entered the College of Charleston, South Carolina. Before graduation, he was expelled for "incorrigible negligence."

SURVEYOR

Frémont found work as a math instructor on the warship *Natchez* in 1833 and later spent summers surveying for railroad projects and a winter studying the Cherokees. In 1838 he was commissioned as second lieutenant in the U.S. Army Corps of Engineers. The following year, Frémont joined French explorer Jean-Nicolas Nicollet on an expedition to survey and map the land between the upper MISSISSIPPI and MISSOURI RIVERS. He used the geology, topography, and astronomy skills Nicollet taught him to head an expedition to survey the Des Moines River in 1841.

Frémont led the first of three expeditions into OREGON territory the following year. Under the guidance of the War Department, he mapped most of the Oregon Trail and climbed a 13,730-foot (4,185-m) peak (now called Fremont Peak in modern WYOMING). A year later, Frémont finished his work on the Oregon Trail all the way to the mouth of the COLUMBIA RIVER on the Pacific coast. He was led by scout Kit Carson, who suggested they make a midwinter crossing of the SIERRA NEVADA to CALIFORNIA.

THE BEAR FLAG REPUBLIC

In 1845, Frémont made his third expedition, further exploring the Pacific coast into Sonoma, California. There, Frémont supported a group of Americans, who created the Bear Flag Republic, in an uprising against Mexican rule. He accepted the rights to California from Mexican officials at Cahuenga Pass, near LOS ANGELES, and was later appointed military governor of the 31st state by U.S. Navy commodore Robert Field Stockton. However, because Frémont refused to follow Army brigadier general Stephen Watts Kearny's orders, he was arrested for mutiny and insubordination and let go from the army. Even though President James Polk formally dismissed Frémont's penalty, he resigned from his army post.

In winter 1848–1849, Frémont led an expedition to find a route for a proposed railway line from the upper RÍO GRANDE to California. The area was too rugged, however, and 11 of his 33 men died on the trip. Frémont gained great wealth during the California gold rush, and was elected in 1850 as one of the first two senators from California. He served only one year, but ran as a presidential candidate of the new Republican Party in 1856. Democrat James Buchanan defeated him.

In 1964 Frémont became a nominee for president. He withdrew to give his party's nomination to Abraham Lincoln, but his political career was not over. Frémont served as ARIZONA's governor from 1878 to 1883. Shortly before his death, Congress voted to return Frémont to the rank of army major general and restore his pension.

> **Alameda county, California, and Sandusky county, Ohio, are just two places with cities named for Frémont.**

Yuri Alekseyevich Gagarin

(1934–1968) COSMONAUT

Yuri Gagarin was born in Klushino, Union of Soviet Socialist Republics (USSR; modern RUSSIA), and attended primary school until 1941. At that time the Germans invaded and forced Gagarin's family and others out of their homes.

Gagarin's family settled in the town of Gzhatsk, where the schools reopened in 1945. Four years later, Gagarin attended a manufacturing trade school before training as a metalworker. During this time, he learned to fly planes. His instructor recommended him to the Soviet Air Force cadet training school at Chkalov (modern Orenburg, Russia) in 1955. The 5-foot, 6-inch (1.7-m) pilot needed a seat cushion to see downward far enough to land his training plane.

In 1960, Gagarin applied to be one of the first cosmonauts. After six weeks of training, Sergei Korolev, the USSR's "Chief Designer" of the space program, picked Gagarin as one of six cosmonauts to possibly become the first human to orbit Earth. Korolev had the cosmonauts learn to parachute, run for miles, and practice gymnastics. He also challenged their mental capabilities by placing each of them in a dark, sound-proof chamber with extreme heat, cold, and vibrations for hours, and later days. Finally, on April 8, 1961,

Korolev interviewed each man for hours, carefully watching for any sign of frustration.

Just four days before *Vostok 1* was to launch, Gagarin got word that he would be in it. On April 12, 1961, Gagarin told a crowd of engineers and Soviet military and government officials gathered to watch lift-off: "To be the first to enter the cosmos, to engage single-handed in an unprecedented duel with nature—could one dream of anything more!"

At 9:07 AM, *Vostok I* took off on its 108-minute flight. Gagarin, exposed to approximately six times Earth's normal force of gravity as the craft rose, shouted: "Poyekali!" ("Off we go!")

While orbiting Earth, Gagarin ate, recorded his observations on tape, monitored the craft's systems, and evaluated the ability to view objects in space. All of the capsule's controls were automated or controlled from the ground—though Gagarin had a sealed envelope with a code to enable him to work the controls, if there was an emergency.

RETURN TO EARTH

Approximately 78 minutes later, the capsule's retro-rockets fired, bringing the craft down. The rockets accidentally didn't separate and Gagarin was thrown around the capsule as it shook and fell. *Vostok 1* landed in a field near Saratov, USSR. In the late 1980s, Soviet space files were released to show that Gagarin actually parachuted separately from the capsule at 23,000 feet (7010 m). The Soviets had hidden this fact because they worried the flight wouldn't count if the world learned that Gagarin landed separately.

Gagarin went back into cosmonaut training, and was on the backup crew for *Soyuz 1*. He was killed when a jet he was piloting crashed.

In Memory of...

GAGARIN'S ASHES are stored in a Kremlin wall. Also, the town of Gzhatsk was renamed Gagarin, and the center for cosmonaut training in Star City, Russia, is called the Gagarin Cosmonaut Training Center.

Vasco da Gama (c. 1469– 1524)

EXPLORER·NAVIGATOR

Vasco da Gama was born in the Portuguese seaport of Sines, Alemtejo (modern Baixo Alentejo). After receiving an education and serving in the military, in 1492 da Gama assisted King John II during a dispute with the King of France. He was later commissioned by the new Portuguese ruler, King Manuel, to sail to the new Portuguese territories in Africa and the East (a treaty with the Spanish divided the world into equal shares; Spain took the western half—the New World.) The trip would make da Gama the first European to reach INDIA by sea.

INDIA

On July 7, 1497, da Gama spent the night praying for a successful journey at a chapel built by **Henry the Navigator**. The next day, he sailed from LISBON with approximately 170 men on four ships. Several of the sailors were convicts who were deemed expendable and, thus, perfect to perform dangerous tasks.

The ships sailed to the CANARY ISLANDS, the Cape Verde Islands, and then turned south. On November 22 they rounded the CAPE OF GOOD HOPE and set anchor at MOSSEL BAY. There, da Gama traded with the African tribe, the Hottentots, to get cattle, and built a stone monument, called a *padrao*, to mark the progress of his expedition. The Hottentots destroyed the *padrao* as soon as da Gama sailed onward.

On January 25, 1498, the ships docked at the Kilimane River on the coast of MOZAMBIQUE. Da Gama erected another *padrao* and stored more supplies though many of his men were dying from scurvy. At the next stop in MALINDI, da Gama picked up a local pilot, Ahmad Ibn Majid, to guide the ships eastward to India.

The ships sailed into CALICUT (modern KOZHIKODE, India) on May 20, 1498, but the Muslim merchants refused to trade with

the Christians. Da Gama left another *padrao* behind and sent a letter to his king that stated the merchants would trade spices and gems if the Portuguese brought back gold, silver, coral, and scarlet cloth on a future visit.

Da Gama and his crew—minus those who died of various diseases—returned to PORTUGAL by early September 1499. Da Gama was welcomed as a hero who opened the Portuguese to enormous financial possibilities, rewarded with an annual income, and named Admiral of the Indian Seas. The king followed up da Gama's work by asking Pedro Álvares Cabral to lead an expedition to India to establish a Portuguese trading post in Calicut the following year.

RETURN TO CALICUT

When news of a massacre at Calicut reached Portugal, da Gama was sent with more than 15 ships on February 10, 1502, to avenge the dead. On the way, da Gama established Portuguese colonies at Mozambique and Sofala (part of modern Mozambique) in east Africa. In Calicut, da Gama forced the local ruler to make peace and swear loyalty to the king of Portugal. The ships returned to Portugal with a cargo of many spices on October 11, 1503.

Da Gama stopped sailing for the next 20 years as he fought with the king over the value of his accomplishments. In February 1524, the new king, John III, appointed da Gama as Viceroy of Portuguese India. The explorer sailed to India with 14 ships carrying 3,000 men including his own two sons. Da Gama had instructions to stop the corruption among the Portuguese authorities in India, but he died in COCHIN three months after he arrived. His body was taken back to Portugal and buried in the very chapel where he prayed the night before he left on his first voyage.

John Glenn (1921–)

ASTRONAUT • POLITICIAN • WAR PILOT

John Herschell Glenn, Jr., was born in Cambridge, Ohio, but grew up in nearby New Concord, where his father had a Chevrolet dealership. In 1942, during World War II, Glenn cut short his studies at Muskingum College, where he later received a degree in engineering, to begin taking pre-flight training in the Naval Aviation Cadet Program. As a Marine pilot, he made 59 combat missions during World War II and 63 during the Korean War.

> **John Glenn's high school, New Concord High, was later renamed John Glenn High School.**

THE FIRST ASTRONAUTS

Glenn later served as project officer at the Bureau of Naval Weapons, where, in 1957, he became the first person to make a nonstop supersonic flight from LOS ANGELES to NEW YORK CITY. Two years later, NASA chose Glenn to be among the first astronauts. He flew on the third piloted mission, *Mercury*, which lifted off on February 20, 1962, with a crew of seven. It was Glenn who flew aboard *Mercury's* capsule *Friendship 7* to become the first American to orbit Earth.

During the 4-hour, 55-minute flight, Glenn was supposed to take pictures, perform exercises to test his body's reaction to weightlessness, and make observations. Glenn would only control the capsule during test periods while the capsule's automatic control system would guide the vessel the rest of the time. Yet, at the end of the first orbit, the system began to malfunction and Glenn had to take over as pilot.

During the second orbit, NASA engineers at ground control realized that the capsule's heat shield, needed for reentry, had come loose. Glenn was instructed to steer the capsule so that outside pressure would hold the heat shield in place during the descent. *Friendship 7*—with Glenn aboard—landed safely by parachute in the Atlantic Ocean.

Glenn returned home a hero and was so popular that NASA refused to send Glenn back into space, for fear that the public would turn against the space program if something happened to their hero. Frustrated, Glenn retired from NASA and the Marine

Corps in 1965 and became an executive for beverage-maker Royal Crown International.

In 1974, he was elected as a Democrat from Ohio to the U.S. Senate, where he served four terms. Glenn also made an unsuccessful run for the Democratic presidential nomination in 1984. During this time, Glenn began to speak to NASA officials about returning to space.

On October 29, 1998, the 77-year-old lifted off into space aboard the shuttle *Discovery* with the goal of studying the effects of space travel on aging humans. He wore a heart monitor to measure his heart rhythms and blood pressure as well as a sleep monitor to keep track of his brain waves and eye movements as he slept.

After 134 Earth orbits, the shuttle landed. Tests showed Glenn had no muscle atrophy and recovered his sense of balance within a day. "Maybe prior to this flight we were looked at as old geezers who ought to get out of the way," he told *People* after the flight. "Just because you're up in years some doesn't mean you don't have hopes and dreams."

Jane Goodall (1934–)

PRIMATOLOGIST·ETHNOLOGIST

When London-born Jane Goodall was a little girl she was fascinated with tales of animals and Africa. She loved to read about Dr. Doolittle and Tarzan. "All through my childhood people said, 'You can't go to Africa. It's the Dark Continent,'" said Goodall. "But my mother used to say, 'If you really want to, there's nothing you can't do.'"

Goodall's parents divorced when she was 12, and she saw little of her father after that. With almost no money for college, Goodall attended secretarial school and found a job in LONDON. Her dream of seeing Africa became reality when a former classmate invited Goodall to visit her farm in KENYA.

LOUIS LEAKEY

At 23, Goodall sailed to Kenya, where she learned about anthropologist Dr. Louis Leakey's work and made an appointment to meet him. Leakey was quite impressed by Goodall's passion for animals and Africa and hired her as an assistant on a fossil-hunting expedition in Olduvai Gorge.

After three months, they returned to Kenya, and Goodall found a job in a NAIROBI museum. She and Leakey spoke often about Goodall leading a study on chimpanzees at LAKE TANGANYIKA in Tanganyika (modern TANZANIA). Leakey felt that although Goodall had little training, her research would benefit from her non-biased mind, patience, and keen observation skills. Authorities at the study's sponsor, the National Geographic Society, were against the idea of the young woman living in Africa, but they reconsidered after Goodall's mother, Vanne, volunteered to stay with her daughter for the first three months.

In July 1960, Goodall and her mother set up camp at Gombe National Park in Tanganyika. At first Goodall could not get close to the chimps; when she came near, they'd run away. Worried that her funding only allowed for a five-month stay unless she found something major, Goodall began to watch the chimps through binoculars from a peak above the forest. She became familiar with the personalities of each chimp and gave them names.

BREAKTHROUGH

Finally, in October, Goodall saw the revelation for which she had hoped. The chimp she'd named David Greybeard stuck a blade of grass into a termite mound, pulled out the blade, and ate the bugs. It was the first time a researcher had ever seen a chimpanzee using tools. She later saw another chimp take leaves off a twig, which showed that the animal could modify an object to create a tool—another major find. Because Goodall had little training, scientists were wary of her research. To be taken seriously, she returned to ENGLAND to receive a Ph.D. at Cambridge University in a program that accepted professional experience in lieu of undergraduate degrees.

Back at the site, the chimps grew used to Goodall's presence and allowed her to interact with them, furthering her research. She continued studying the chimps on and off for 25 years and established chimpanzee sanctuaries for the care of orphaned chimps in four African countries. In 1977, she founded The Jane Goodall Institute for Wildlife Research, Education, and Conservation in Silver Spring, Maryland. She spends most of her time lecturing around the world to raise money for her institute and promote conservation.

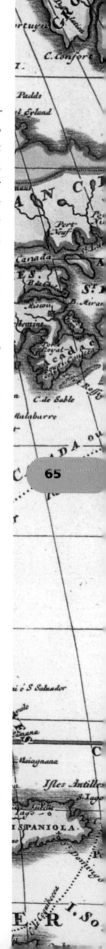

Virgil "Gus" Grissom

(1926–1967) ASTRONAUT

Virgil Ivan Grissom, born in Mitchell, Indiana, received a degree in Mechanical Engineering from Purdue University and entered the Air Force. By 1951, he piloted fighter planes, and flew at least 100 combat missions in Korea. Upon returning to the UNITED STATES, Grissom became a jet instructor at a base in Bryan, Texas, and attended Air Force Test Pilot School at Edwards Air Force Base in California, before becoming a fighter test pilot at Wright-Patterson AFB in Ohio in 1957.

Grissom was one of the first astronauts selected by NASA in 1959. On July 21, 1961, he boarded the bell-shaped capsule *Liberty Bell 7*. It was launched from a rocket to make a 15-minute sub-orbital flight above Earth. His mission was to verify results Alan Shepard, the second U.S. astronaut in space, made on the first U.S. sub-orbital capsule flight on May 5, 1961, and test enhancements which had been made to the capsule since then.

CLOSE CALL

As Grissom recorded the positions of dozens of switches inside the capsule, it made a planned splashdown in the Atlantic Ocean. As Grissom lay waiting for a helicopter to pluck the capsule out of the water, the emergency exit hatch blew open and the capsule was flooded with water. Grissom was able to grab onto a line dropped from a rescue helicopter as the capsule sank 3 miles (5 km) to the bottom of the sea.

On March 23, 1965, Grissom and astronaut John Young blasted into space aboard *Gemini 3*, which Grissom jokingly dubbed the "Unsinkable Molly Brown." The astronauts became the first to maneuver their own spacecraft, making three orbits in five hours. Their capsule splashed down in the sea 50 miles short of a recovery ship, so the astronauts had to wait inside for half an hour.

Next up for Grissom was *Apollo I*. On January 27, 1967, three weeks before *Apollo's* launch, Grissom and astronauts Roger Chaffee (then the youngest astronaut at age 31) and **Edward White** (the first American to walk in space) boarded the craft as it sat on the launch pad. They spent the day practicing countdown and simulating launch. There were so many problems that after lunch, Grissom hung a lemon on the side of the craft.

At 6:31 PM, Chaffee calmly said, "Fire. I smell fire." An explosion rocked the craft and loud screams were heard. Then silence. The capsule burst into flames, killing all three astronauts. Investigators later concluded that a bunch of wires near Grissom's chair may have sparked the fire, as the cabin was highly pressurized with pure oxygen. For 20 months, NASA halted their program and refined their capsules.

Recovered Capsule

Liberty Bell 7 rested for 38 years on the ocean floor until members of a Discovery Channel expedition making a documentary recovered it, along with Grissom's word map, checklist, diver's knife, and survival kit that included shark repellant, soap, and a vial of morphine. The capsule was refurbished at the Kansas Cosmosphere and Space Center so it could be displayed at future museum exhibitions.

Hanno (c. 530–c.470 BC)

EXPLORER·ADMIRAL

Hanno served as an admiral in the North African city of Carthage (modern TUNISIA), which was founded by Phoenicians from LEBANON. In approximately 500 BC, Hanno was commissioned to take a major expedition to explore and colonize the northwest coast of Africa. The expedition is now considered to be the first voyage with a main goal of exploration.

FIRST KNOWN EXPLORER

Although Hanno wrote about his voyage in the Phoenician language, only a Greek translation from the 10th century AD survives. According to it, Hanno set sail past the Pillars of Hercules (the STRAITS OF GIBRALTAR) with 60 ships holding 50 oarsmen each and a total of 30,000 men and women (scholars argue that the number of people was likely smaller). After two days, Hanno colonized his first city, Thymiaterium (modern MEHDIA in TUNISIA). Leaving some settlers behind, the fleet sailed west and stopped again at modern Cape Cantin. They built an altar to Poseidon before sailing further east.

A day later, they dropped off settlers, who built five new cities by the sea, including Carian Fort (modern MOGADOR) and Acra (modern AGADIR). Sailing on, Hanno's fleet cited a large river flowing from LIBYA, the Oued Draa, and noted that there were friendly nomads with animals on the banks of the river. The Lixites, as he called them, told him about the land and its people. "Beyond these dwelt inhospitable Ethiopians who inhabit a country full of wild animals," the translation quotes Hanno as saying. "...People of a different appearance, the Troglodytes, are said to live in the (Anti-Atlas Mountains) gorges...they are said by the Lixites to run faster than horses."

With Lixite interpreters, Hanno and his fleet set sail again, traveling south past deserts for two days and then east for a day. On a small island they founded the colony of Cerne (most likely modern Herne Island in the WESTERN SAHARA) and then sailed on through the SENEGAL RIVER.

They returned to Cerne and sailed south along the coastline for 12 days. The ever-dwindling fleet passed

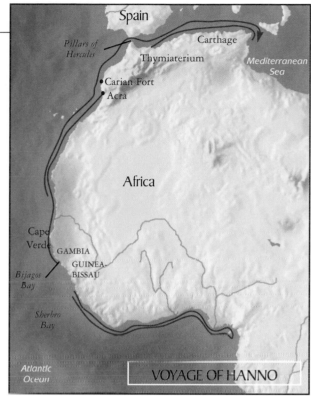

VOYAGE OF HANNO

the wooded mountains of CAPE VERDE, sailed into the GAMBIA estuary, and then onward another five days until they reached Bijagos Bay in modern GUINEA-BISSAU. They stopped near an island and heard the sound of pipes, drums, and human cries, though all they saw were trees and fires. Hanno and his men were scared, and their interpreters suggested they continue sailing.

"On the four following nights we saw land covered in flames," the translation quotes Hanno as saying. "In the center a leaping flame towered above all others and appeared to reach the stars. This was the highest mountain we saw: it was called the Chariot of the Gods." Historians believe Hanno is referring to a volcano erupting—most likely Mt. Cameroun.

The fleet sailed for another three days before docking in Sherbro Bay in SIERRA LEONE. On the shores of Macauley Island, Hanno noted seeing "wild people...with hairy bodies"—chimpanzees, which no Carthaginian had ever seen before. They skinned three chimps to bring home.

With their supplies running low, the fleet returned to Carthage. On the way, Hanno wrote his account on stone tablets.

Father Jean Louis Hennepin

(1640–1705) MISSIONARY·EXPLORER

Jean Louis Hennepin was born in the town of Ath in present-day Belgium. He studied there and became a student priest of the Franciscan order. As a novice, he journeyed to ROME and then preached in Belgium and northern FRANCE.

In May 1675, Hennepin's superiors sent him to serve as a missionary in New France (modern CANADA). He sailed there on a ship with explorer **René-Robert Cavalier Sieur de La Salle**, but upon arrival he made a preaching tour of the colony. In 1678, La Salle asked Hennepin to accompany him on his voyage of exploration to the MISSISSIPPI RIVER.

Hennepin traveled to meet La Salle at Fort Frontenac (modern Kingston, ONTARIO). On November 18, 1678, Hennepin left the fort with an

advance party to reach the Niagara River. When they reached NIAGARA FALLS, Hennepin became the first person to write a description of them. He stated that they were "the most beautiful and altogether the most terrifying waterfall in the universe." While there, the party built a fort and a boat, the *Griffon*, which enabled them to explore the GREAT LAKES.

MISSISSIPPI EXPLORER

Hennepin's journey with La Salle began on August 7, 1679, when they sailed to Fort Crévecoeur on the ILLINOIS RIVER. On February 29, 1689, La Salle sent

Hennepin and two other men ahead to explore the upper Mississippi. In a book he later wrote about his travels, Hennepin claimed that he sailed the length of the Mississippi between February 29 and March 25—beating La Salle's claim to have done so by two years. However, most historians believe Hennepin's claim was false.

Either way, by April 11, Hennepin and the two others reached the point where the upper Mississippi joins the Illinois River. There they were attacked and taken prisoner by 33 canoes filled with members of the Sioux tribe, who took the men up the Mississippi. The Sioux brought Hennepin and the others as far as St. Anthony Falls (near modern St. Paul, MINNESOTA), making them the first Europeans to see it.

By April 21, they had arrived at a Sioux village in the Thousand Lakes region. Hennepin joined one of their expeditions to the Wisconsin River, where he met Frenchman Daniel Greysolon Duluth (the namesake for Duluth, Minnesota), who had been sent to visit the Sioux. When he returned to the Sioux village in September they were all allowed to depart. They left for QUEBEC in April 1681, and by the end of the year, Hennepin had returned to Paris.

While in Europe, Hennepin wrote of his exploration adventures in *Déscription de la Louisiane* (1683). It was a best-seller that was printed in several languages. (It has since been found that parts of the work were plagiarized from La Salle's letters about the region.) Hennepin became quite popular and was given many important jobs, until four years later when he was expelled from his monastery. The reason for his expulsion is not clear, but Hennepin believed it was part of a plot masterminded by La Salle to ruin his good name and get even with him for making his claim of early exploration along the Mississippi.

Hennepin traveled to Holland, France, and Rome, where his words became the focus of many disputes. He continued to write about his explorations in North America, but his later books were never as popular as the first. In the last few years of his life, he settled into obscurity in Holland.

Henry the Navigator (1394–1460)

ROYALTY·PATRON OF EXPLORATION

Born in Oporto, Portugal, as the third son of King John I and Philippa of Lancaster (ENGLAND), Prince Henry grew up at a time when the monarchy's wealth was drained, mainly due to civil war. His mother, who was a devout Christian, instilled high moral standards in her children. In addition to their religious upbringing, Henry and his brothers received not only an education but also "bodily training"—fitness development, particularly in the arms.

Under their father, Henry and his brothers increased Portuguese influence by conquering Moorish North Africa, converting Muslims to Christians, exploring and conquering Atlantic island groups in the west and south, and opening the West African coast to slave and commerce trading. Henry fought in the battle that captured the commercial center of CEUTA in North Africa from the Moors (Muslims) in 1415. As a governor of the Order of Christ, Henry was obliged to wage a holy war against non-Christian "infidels," and his mother's death in the summer of 1415 made the battle against the spread of Islam and for the expansion of Portuguese influence even more important. His success earned him knighthood and the title of Duke of Viseu at age 21.

HENRY THE PATRON

Henry made no voyages of exploration, but found funding, defined missions, and worked with map-makers to document their findings. His first major sponsored expeditions were to the islands of Madeira and Porto Santo in the Atlantic. He had his navigators return to colonize the islands and encourage fishing and sugar-making, among other commercial activities.

Henry sent explorer Gil Eannes toward Cape Bojador numerous times, until Eannes successfully rounded the North African cape in 1434. The trip was the southernmost made by any European at the time. Other voyages under Henry's guidance included a rounding of Cape Blanco in 1442, the settlement of Arguin Island the following year, and the discovery of the mouths of the SENEGAL and GAMBIA RIVERS by Nuno Tristão in 1444 and 1446.

Prince Henry sponsored a total of 1,500 miles (2,414 km) of African coastal exploration. The travels aided PORTUGAL economically and politically as the expeditions brought an increase of gold to Portugal and made it possible for the royal council to begin minting gold coins in 1457. Another major African export the Portuguese picked up was a coarse red pepper, *malagueta*, which assisted in their spice trade with ITALY. Portugal's economy was further aided by the start of the slave trade in 1442, wherein explorers found free laborers by raiding coastal African villages.

Henry later became reclusive and made a home alone at Vila de Infante in Sagres, Portugal. During this time he is believed to have established an observatory and the first school for navigators in Europe.

Family Ties

DURING AN ATTEMPT to conquer Tangier in 1437, Henry's younger brother, Fernando, was taken hostage. The Moors swore to return him only when Ceuta was returned to Moorish rule. Under objections from Henry and older brother, Duarte (then king and called King Edward I), the royal council refused the trade. Fernando was kept in a Fez dungeon until his death. When Duarte died in 1438, his 5-year-old son became King Afonso V. Henry dutifully helped govern the country until the boy reached his teens.

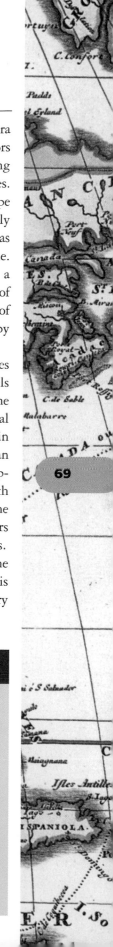

Matthew Henson (1866–1955)

EXPLORER

Two years after Matthew Henson was born to sharecroppers in Nanjemoy, Maryland, his mother died. His father remarried and died a few years later, leaving Henson with his stepmother. In 1877, 11-year-old Henson ran away to Washington, D.C., where he was taken in by a local café owner. At the café, Henson met Baltimore Jack, a sailor who thrilled him with stories about the sea.

At age 12, Henson found work as a cabin boy on the *Katie Hinds*, led by Captain Child. The captain taught Henson literature, math, history, navigation techniques, and survival skills as they traveled around the world. When the captain died in December 1883, a teenaged Henson found work in a D.C.-based furrier. There he met U.S. Navy officer Robert Peary, who was so impressed with Henson that he offered him a job as his assistant on a two-year expedition to NICARAGUA.

THE ARCTIC

In 1891, Peary decided to explore GREENLAND and asked Henson to come along as a volunteer. Henson, Peary, and four others sailed to the shores of Wolstenholm Sound, where Henson led in the building of a house. In spring, they attempted to cross Greenland in order to find its northernmost point, which would help Peary plan for his real goal: to be the first to reach the NORTH POLE.

On the way, Henson learned the Inuit language and became friendly with local Inuit, learning their survival techniques. Henson and Peary spent the next 18 years visiting the ARCTIC and attempting the polar expedition. By 1895, they had mapped the entire Greenland ice cap.

On July 6, 1908, Henson, Peary, and five others returned to the Arctic on the *Roosevelt*. They knew it would be their last attempt to reach the pole, as Henson was nearing age 40 and Peary was nearing fifty.

The *Roosevelt* sailed to CAPE SHERIDAN on the northernmost part of Canada's ELLESMERE ISLAND. Henson built all the necessary sledges and trained some members of the group on handling the dogs that would lead them. Henson and some Inuit then traveled by sledge to Camp Columbia, where they built a base camp with several igloos before the others joined them.

On March 1, 1909, Henson started breaking a trail northward toward the pole. At one point, he fell into an icy crevasse, but his Inuit assistant Ootah rescued him. By April 6, only Henson, Peary and four Inuit—who continued on when the others died or went back to base camp—noted on their chronometer and charts that they reached the pole.

LATE HONORS

While historians dispute which man actually reached the Pole first, Peary returned to the U.S. as a media hero, while Henson received little credit, most likely because of his race. Finally, at age 70, Henson was made an honorary member of New York's Explorer's Club for his work on the expedition. Other honors soon followed as reports of the expedition became public.

In 1987–1988, Henson biographer Dr. Allen Counter led a successful movement to have Henson's remains moved from Woodlawn Cemetery in the Bronx, New York, to the more venerable Arlington National Cemetery in Virginia, where he was reentombed near Peary.

Sir Edmund Hillary (1919–)

MOUNTAIN CLIMBER·EXPLORER

Edmund Percival Hillary was born and raised in Aukland, NEW ZEALAND. At age 16, he skied at a national park and found himself in awe of the

snowy peaks around him. During World War II, he served in the Royal New Zealand Air Force and gained experience climbing the SOUTHERN ALPS of New Zealand.

While he earned a living as a beekeeper in the family business, Hillary climbed 11 Himalayan peaks of more than 20,000 feet (6,096 m) in height between 1951 and 1952. With each climb he grew more eager to become the first to reach the summit of the world's highest peak, MOUNT EVEREST (29,028 feet [8,848 m]) on the TIBET/NEPAL border.

MOUNT EVEREST

Between 1920 and 1952, seven major expeditions failed to reach Everest's summit. In the early 1950s Hillary joined in rescue missions on Everest. His work caught the attention of Colonel John Hunt, leader of an Everest expedition sponsored by the Joint Himalayan Committee of the Alpine Club of Great Britain and the Royal Geographic Society.

Hillary served as one of the 1953 expedition's chief climbers, assisted by a Nepalese Sherpa named **Tenzing Norgay**. "We didn't know if it was humanly possible to reach the top of Mt. Everest," Hillary said later. "And even using oxygen as we were, if we did get to the top, we weren't at all sure whether we wouldn't drop dead, or something of that nature."

Hillary and Norgay made the climb while constantly monitoring their oxygen tanks as well as the dangerous terrain of soft snow, icy slopes, and crevasses. At one point, Hillary fell into a crevasse, stopped only by his spiked shoes. To climb out, he chopped steps with his ice pick.

The men finally reached the summit at 11:30 AM on May 29, but celebrated little. When Hillary reached the bottom of the mountain, his first words to fellow climber George Lowe were, "Well, George, we've knocked the bastard off!" Hillary was knighted by Queen Elizabeth soon after.

Two years later, Hillary led the New Zealand party on a three-year transantarctic expedition. Traveling by tractor, Hillary's crew reached the SOUTH POLE on January 4, 1958, and became the first to make a successful trip to the pole since Robert F. Scott in 1912.

Hillary went on to lead several more Himalayan expeditions. However, in the 1960s, he began to devote much of his time to environmental as well as humanitarian causes on behalf of the Nepalese people. Hillary developed clinics, hospitals, schools, and two airplane strips. He also persuaded the Nepalese government to make the area around Everest a national park, and helped get funding for the project from New Zealand.

Who Was First?

IN 1924, GEORGE MALLORY attempted to reach Everest's summit, and his body was later found near the top. While no one is sure if Mallory—who did not use oxygen—died on the way up or after reaching the summit, some climbers have suggested Hillary and Norgay should share credit with Mallory. Hillary has agreed to share credit, calling Mallory a pioneer in climbing Everest. Still, he has said, "It is one thing to reach the top, but to complete the job, you've got to get to the bottom."

Henry Hudson (c. 1565–c. 1611)

EXPLORER

Little is known about Henry Hudson's early life, besides the fact that he grew up in ENGLAND. In 1607, Hudson captained the *Hopewell* on an expedition for the English Muscovy Company. In an attempt to find a northeast passage from the Arctic Ocean to CHINA to promote trade, Hudson sailed as far north as 80° 23'—the farthest north anyone would sail for the next 100 years. Along the way, Hudson discovered JAN MAYEN ISLAND, off eastern GREENLAND.

The next year, Hudson used the same ship and sponsor to again try to find a northeast passage. This time, he sailed to the island of NOVAYA ZEMLYA in the BARENTS SEA. The ship was stuck in ice for some time, and once freed, the crew insisted on returning home. Hudson angrily gave in to the crew. The Muscovy Company was unhappy with news of another failed expedition and refused further business with Hudson.

He approached the Dutch East India Company, who granted him a new ship and more funding. In 1609, Hudson set sail from the Dutch island of Texel in the *Half Moon* with a crew of approximately 18 men. After sailing through icy waters to Novaya Zemlya, the crew threatened mutiny unless Hudson—described as obsessive—allowed them to sail away from the area. Believing that the Atlantic Ocean was separated from the Pacific by a narrow isthmus, Hudson commanded the ship to head southwest down the North American coast.

HUDSON RIVER VALLEY

On September 3, the *Half Moon* entered New York Bay. Hudson spent the next month exploring what is now called the HUDSON RIVER, traveling toward its mouth as far as present-day Albany. He noted the richness of the surrounding land, met Native American tribes of Delaware and Mohicans, and claimed the Hudson River Valley for the Dutch.

At the end of the year, Hudson sailed home to England. When word of his success reached the British government, they seized Hudson's ship, jailed him and his crew, and commanded him to serve only the country of his birth from that time onward.

Hudson set sail on his final voyage, sponsored by wealthy Englishmen, on April 17, 1610. This time, Hudson planned to search for the Northwest Passage. By the middle of the year, Hudson's ship, *Discovery*, docked on the shores of present-day HUDSON BAY. There, he and his 22-man crew, which included his son, John, spent three months exploring the land.

By November 10, they realized their ship was frozen in the water, forcing them to spend the winter there. The crew was angry since they were not prepared for this. Hudson grew frustrated with the men's complaints and threatened to hang a carpenter when he refused to build a house onshore because the ground was frozen.

Though the house was built, the cold, hunger, and onset of scurvy was too much for the crew. In late June 1611, when Hudson insisted he was still not ready to go home, they mutinied. They forced Hudson, his son, and seven others into a small boat in the bay and sailed home without them. Hudson and the others were never seen again.

Ibn Battuta (1304–1369)

TRAVELER·SCHOLAR

Born in Tangier, Morocco, to a family that had produced many Islamic judges, Ibn Battuta was well educated in Islamic law and literature. After turning 21, Battuta left home to make a pilgrimage to the Islamic holy city of MECCA, home of the prophet Muhammad. The journey was the duty of every strict Muslim, but the many side trips Battuta made, unusual for a person of his time, were based on his desire for adventure.

En route to Mecca, Battuta traveled along the NILE RIVER in EGYPT, the shores of the RED SEA, and through the city of DAMASCUS in SYRIA. In Damascus, Battuta studied religion with many noted Islamic scholars and religious leaders. After reaching Mecca, Battuta crossed ARABIA and traveled through PERSIA and Russian TURKESTAN, near the BLACK and CASPIAN SEAS. After sailing down the Red Sea and along the east coast of Africa, he returned through Persia to Mecca in 1332.

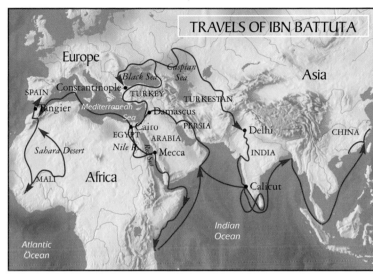

TRAVELS OF IBN BATTUTA

In the 1340s, Battuta was named Delhi's envoy to CHINA. On his way to China, Battuta faced pirates, survived shipwrecks, and ventured through ongoing wars. Though some scholars debate if Battuta ever made it to China, Battuta claimed in his notes that he traveled by river as far north as BEIJING.

JOURNEY TO DELHI

From Mecca, Battuta set out again, this time to DELHI, INDIA, which he heard had a Muslim sultan who was generous to visiting scholars. To get there, Battuta crossed through Egypt, Syria, and TURKEY, made a side trip through CONSTANTINOPLE and then traveled east and, finally, south across central Asia. He lead a caravan of slaves, wives, concubines, and other followers for most of the trip. Along the way, he made notes about how the areas had changed since the Mongols had conquered the lands several generations earlier.

Battuta arrived in Delhi in the mid-1330s. He found a position in service to the sultan, Muhammad ibn Tughluq. Tughluq was a cruel leader who was feared by many, including Battuta, who recalled later "there was no day that the gate of his palace failed to witness…the elevation of some object to affluence and the torture and murder of some living soul."

MUSLIM LANDS

From China, Battuta sailed to Baghdad and then went north into Syria, where in 1348 he saw people in the throes of the bubonic plague, which later hit Europe. Battuta made another trip to Mecca and then returned home to North Africa for the first time in 25 years. Vowing to finish seeing the rest of the world's principal Muslim countries, Battuta sailed to the kingdom of GRANADA, SPAIN, in 1350.

Battuta's last trip was across the SAHARA DESERT to the African kingdom of MALI, which was popular because its capital of TIMBUKTU was a trading center. Battuta's caravan was led by a blind guide, who—according to Battuta—planned his course by smelling the sand at the end of each day of traveling. Upon Battuta's return home in 1353, Morocco's sultan asked him to write about his travels, in which he journeyed 75,000 miles (120,701 km) and met at least 60 kings, sultans, and khans.

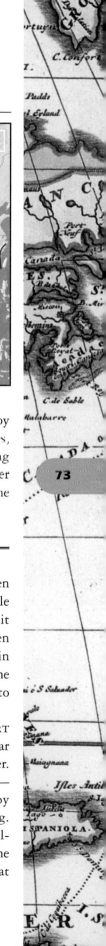

Naomi James (1949–)

SOLO SAILOR

Naomi Christine Power was born in Gisborne, New Zealand, and raised with a brother and two sisters on a dairy farm in Hawkes Bay. Power was shy and a self-described "loner," but loved to read and ride horses. At age 15, she dropped out of school and found work as an apprentice to a hairdresser. Two years later she began taking night classes to complete studies in art and design.

A SAILOR IS BORN

Power and her sister, Juliet, left home on New Year's Eve 1970 to move to England. Over the next five years, Power made trips to AUSTRIA, SWITZERLAND, GREECE, and FRANCE, before meeting Robert Alan James, a racing yachtsman. He offered to make Power a deck-hand/cook on his next trip, and she accepted. Though her seasickness was often a problem, Power learned everything about sailing and she loved it.

After marrying in May 1976, the new Mrs. James told her husband of her dream to be the first woman to sail around the world alone. He helped her find funding and resources, including a donated boat from Chay Blyth, who had previously sailed around the world. James named the boat *Express Crusader* to acknowledge the financial support of London's *Daily Express* newspaper. She set sail from Dartmouth, ENGLAND, on September 9 on a 30,000 mile (48,280 km) around-the-world journey with food, water, 100 books, and a kitten named Boris.

A few days later, James was in the BAY OF BISCAY when heavy winds caused a self-steering rudder to break. After she replaced it, she climbed the boat's mast to fix a loose sail. James found solace in her books and felt encouraged when she read in mountain climber Chris Bonington's autobiography that he had similar motives for adventure: "The satisfaction of exploring new ground…(and) of exploring one's own reactions to new, at times exacting, experience."

James had a radio to keep in touch with her father-in-law, as Rob was concurrently sailing around the world in the Whitbread Race, but it stopped working on October 7. She felt even lonelier when Boris fell overboard on October 30. By early November, a series of gale storms broke the rudder again. James stopped for radio and rudder repairs in CAPE TOWN, SOUTH AFRICA.

Within 60 hours, she was sailing again. Twice more the rudder broke in heavy storms—once causing the boat to lean on its side. Yet, on December 20, James managed to fashion another rudder from broken pieces. She was having a bad bout of seasickness on Christmas Eve, and it took her an hour to climb up the mast again to fix the sail. "No matter how I try to think of…what I shall do when I get home," she wrote in her log, "these thoughts are overshadowed by the fear that I might find death instead."

After a stop in TASMANIA for a new rudder, on February 27, 1977, James's boat did capsize. She pumped water out of the boat for nine hours, before continuing her sail. James rounded CAPE HORN on March 19 and docked in the FALKLAND ISLANDS for repairs. A brief stop in the Azores to meet her husband and the media was followed by 1,200 more miles (1,931 km) of sailing. On June 8 at 9:15 AM, after a record around-the-world sail of 272 days at sea, James sailed back into Dartmouth.

She wrote two books about her journey, sailed in the Observer Single-Handed Trans-Atlantic Race alone in June 1980 (first woman to finish), and the 1982 Double-Handed Round Britain race with her husband (first place), and then announced her retirement from racing. Her husband drowned a year later while sailing. James now lives in Curraghbinny, Ireland, with her daughter, and works as a travel writer.

Louis Jolliet and Father Jacques Marquette

(1645–1700) (1637–1675)

EXPLORER AND TRADER – EXPLORER·MISSIONARY

Louis Jolliet was born in New France (modern CANADA). At age 11, Jolliet decided he wanted to become a priest. He entered the Jesuit college in QUEBEC and learned philosophy and music.

By 1667, Jolliet realized the priesthood was not for him. He decided instead to work in New France's big business: the fur-trade. He made at least one trip west, in 1670, and was a cosigner of a document in which the French claimed the GREAT LAKES region.

In 1672, New France's leaders chose Jolliet to lead an expedition to discover the MISSISSIPPI RIVER. On October 4, 1672, Jolliet and a small party left Quebec. They reached the mission and trading post at St. Ignace (between LAKES HURON and MICHIGAN in modern Michigan) on December 6. There, Jolliet met Father Jacques Marquette who was in charge of the mission. Marquette was to accompany Jolliet on the expedition and preach to native tribes they met.

MARQUETTE'S LIFE

Marquette was the sixth child born to a family in Laon, FRANCE. Growing up he dreamed of becoming a priest and wished to die as a missionary in the wilderness. In 1666, he was sent to Quebec.

As he traveled to various missions, he met many Native Americans, including the Illinois, who told him about a great river they had seen—the Mississippi. Marquette told his superiors. In the summer of 1671 he founded the mission of St. Ignace on the north shore of the STRAITS OF MACKINAC.

DOWN THE MISSISSIPPI

The exploring party of Jolliet, Marquette, and five other men left the mission with two canoes in May of 1673. "…[We] resolved to do and suffer everything for so glorious an undertaking," Marquette later wrote. It is believed they traveled west along the north shore of Lake Michigan to Green Bay and then up the Fox River. They climbed overland to the Wisconsin River and sailed down until they reached the Mississippi on June 15, 1673.

The men stopped about 450 miles (724 km) south of the mouth of the OHIO RIVER. After climbing on land, they met the Quapaw tribe, who told them Spanish were approaching from the west. Realizing that the river must run into the GULF OF MEXICO, the men decided to turn back toward CANADA in mid-July.

Jolliet and Marquette split up at Saint Francis Xavier mission in Green Bay, Wisconsin. Marquette returned to Lake Michigan, where he helped establish a mission among the Illinois. Afterward, he realized he was very sick. He died at the mouth of the river now called the Pére Marquette. Two years later, Marquette's followers carried his remains to St. Ignace mission, where they were buried in a chapel. Two hundred years later, the remains were given to Marquette University in Milwaukee, Wisconsin.

Jolliet spent the winter after the expedition writing and making maps—which were ruined on the return trip. In 1679, he was asked to report on the British fur-trading posts in the HUDSON BAY. He later drew the first maps of Zoar, LABRADOR, and wrote about its Inuit inhabitants in July 1694.

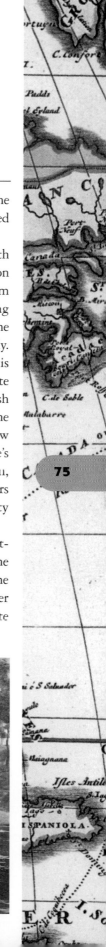

Mary Kingsley (1862–1900)

TRAVELER·WAR NURSE

Mary Kingsley grew up in ENGLAND caring for her bedridden mother, while her father Dr. George Kingsley traveled around the world to study religions of primitive societies. She was self-educated, but took classes in German to help her father with his research. When her parents died, Kingsley decided to take up where her father left off and travel to parts of Africa that no white person had ever reached.

TRAVELS IN AFRICA

In late 1893, she sailed by cargo ship along the West African coast. Kingsley made friends with missionaries, traders, and sailors who taught her key African trade phrases. Though she received a small stipend from the British Museum to collect beetle and fish specimens, Kingsley survived by trading with locals. She would offer them rum, gin, knives, cloth, and fish hooks while they gave her ivory and rubber, which she would trade at European trading posts for supplies she needed to continue traveling.

Led by Africans, Kingsley traveled through jungles, swamps, and canoed along rivers infested with crocodiles. In five months, she traveled as far south as LUANDA in ANGOLA, even exploring the CONGO RIVER area. All the while Kingsley was dressed as a Victorian spinster—high-neck black blouse, long black wool skirt, umbrella, buttoned leather boots, and sealskin hat. "Because one would never want to go about in Africa in a way that would embarrass one to be seen in Piccadilly," she explained. The clothing seemed more reasonable when she was saved one day from falling into a 15-foot-deep (4.6-m) animal pit because her skirt got caught on spikes around the hole.

On her second trip to Africa in December 1894, Kingsley spent several months studying wildlife along the Oil, Ogowe, and Rembwe Rivers. The Fan tribe of cannibals lived near the latter two rivers, but Kingsley felt fairly safe as she traded with them. "The trading method enables you to sit as an honored guest," she said. "…It enables you to become an associate of the confraternity of Witch Doctors, things that being surrounded with an expedition of armed men must prevent your doing."

Kingsley decided to explore the Rembwe with three Fan tribesmen. "We knew we would each have killed each other if sufficient inducement were offered," she wrote, "and so we took a certain amount of care that the inducement should not arise." She also became the first European to see Lake Ncovi, but refused credit, saying the Africans were the real discoverers.

Kingsley returned to England in 1895 and lectured on her travels and the more than 65 fish, reptile, and insect species she collected. She wrote a book about her father and two about West Africa before she volunteered as a nurse in SOUTH AFRICA during the Boer War between Great Britain and Dutch colonists.

She arrived in CAPE TOWN by ship in late March 1900 and was sent to care for Boer prisoners-of-war in Simonstown. There she saw Dr. Gerard Carré and two nurses caring for more than 200 patients who had been wounded or were suffering from delirium and fever caused by typhoid. The hospital was dirty and full of lice. Kingsley wrote to a friend, "Whether I shall come out of this, I don't know…."

By May, Kingsley caught typhoid. She begged Dr. Carré to give her a sea burial and then asked to die alone. The doctor reluctantly left Kingsley, who died the next morning.

Cultural Champion

MARY KINGSLEY DISAPPROVED of white missionaries's attempts to convert the Africans and became an outspoken advocate of African tribal culture in her writing and lectures.

René-Robert Cavelier Sieur de La Salle
(1643–1687) Explorer·Fur Trader

René-Robert Cavelier Sieur de La Salle was born in Rouen, France, and educated by Jesuit priests. He took initial vows to become a novice in the Society of Jesus in October 1660, but was considered unstable and paranoid, and had problems relating to his associates. Thus, he was released from his vows in March 1667. By that time, La Salle had immigrated to CANADA, and was granted land in 1666 on the ST. LAWRENCE RIVER. While he earned a living as a fur trader, La Salle explored the land south of LAKES ONTARIO and ERIE between 1669 and 1670. He claimed to discover the OHIO RIVER the following year.

On his travels, La Salle learned the languages and traditions of the Native Americans with whom he came in contact. French colonial governor Louis de Buade sensed these connections and skills would make La Salle an asset in trading, and appointed him commander of Fort Frontenac, a newly built Canadian trading station.

La Salle developed a plan to explore and trade farther west. In 1677 he sailed to France to get King Louis XIV's approval. La Salle returned to Canada with royal sponsorship and Italian explorer Henri de Tonti. Two years later, the men made a preliminary expedition to set up forts at the mouth of the St. Joseph River and along the ILLINOIS RIVER. Then, after the MISSISSIPPI RIVER was discovered by **Louis Jolliet** and **Father Marquette**, La Salle and his partner organized a group to explore and finding trading opportunities along the banks of the upper Mississippi in February 1680.

MOUTH OF THE MISSISSIPPI

After returning for a few months to pick up supplies at Fort Frontenac, La Salle led a party of French men and Native Americans to the Mississippi. They traveled down the Mississippi to the GULF OF MEXICO, a journey that made La Salle the leader of the first expedition to trace the Mississippi River to its mouth. On April 9, 1682, La Salle claimed the land around the Mississippi for France and named it La Louisianne (modern LOUISIANA), after French King Louis XIV. La Salle commanded the building of forts in this new

territory, but was called back to France by the king in 1682. While La Salle was gone, his rivals turned Louisiana's new governor against him.

In appreciation of La Salle's discoveries, the king named him viceroy of North America. On July 24, 1684, La Salle sailed from France with four ships and 100 soldiers and colonists on an expedition to establish a colony at the mouth of the Mississippi. He reached the Gulf of Mexico, but failed to find the Mississippi.

In early 1685, he finally landed on the shore of present-day Matagorda Bay in TEXAS, and led everyone overland to find the river. The search proved fruitless, and many people died along the way. La Salle decided to try to reach Canada overland with 17 survivors in order to find help and supplies for the people they left behind. In frustration over what they saw as La Salle's poor leadership, his men mutinied and killed him near the Trinity River in Texas.

Lost Now Found

ONE OF LA SALLE'S supply ships, *Belle*, which sank during a 1686 storm, was discovered at the bottom of Matagorda Bay in 1995.

Louis Leakey (1903–1972)

ARCHAEOLOGIST · ANTHROPOLOGIST

Louis Seymour Bazett Leakey was born to British missionaries living in Kabete, KENYA. He spent his youth among the Kikuyu people of Kenya, learned their language, and was even initiated into manhood according to their tribal rites. When he found his first fossil at the age of 12, he decided to be an archaeologist. He entered Cambridge University in ENGLAND in 1922, but a rugby injury caused him to postpone his studies. In his time off, Leakey helped manage a paleontological expedition to Africa. In 1926 he returned to Cambridge to receive degrees in anthropology and archaeology.

Leakey began archaeological research in East Africa—often aided by his second wife, fellow archaeologist Mary Douglas Leakey (formerly Nicol)—in 1924. He chose Africa because he wanted to prove Darwin's theory that Africa was where humans originated, though in the early 20th century many other scientists believed that early man began in Asia.

HUMAN FOSSIL

By 1931, Leakey moved to Olduvai Gorge in TANZANIA, where he and Mary made their most famous discoveries. Initially, they found small fossils and crude stone tools, but in 1959 Mary located the first significant hominid fossil of a skull with huge teeth. Leakey studied it and named the fossil, *Zinjanthropus boisei* (now believed to be a form of *Australopithecus*), which was determined to be 1.7 million years old.

Leakey had led four East African expeditions by 1935. He and Mary moved to Kenya in 1937 to complete a study of the Kikuyu people. From 1940 to 1961, Leakey served as curator of the Coryndon Memorial Museum (modern National Museums of Kenya) in NAIROBI, and continued his expeditions.

Political Ties

IN THE LATE 1940s through early 1950s, Leakey served as a spy in Africa for the British government. He was also court translator in 1952–53 during the trial of Jomo Kenyatta, the leader of the Kenya African Union.

In 1948 Leakey's excavation team was working on Rusinga, an island in LAKE VICTORIA, when they discovered the skull of *Proconsul africanus*, a 25-million-year-old ancestor to both humans and apes. Fourteen years later on another expedition east of Lake Victoria at Fort Ternan, Leakey's team dug up the remains of *Kenyapithecus*, a 14-million-year-old link between apes and humans.

Leakey theorized that another fossil—named *Homo habilis*—was in fact an ancestor to Homo sapiens (modern humans), lived with *Australopithecus* in East Africa, and was the first true toolmaker. Many scientists argued with Leakey's interpretations and whether *H. habilis* was even different enough from *Australopithecus* to warrant being classified separately. Yet, later finds by the Leakeys proved Leakey was correct.

Leakey's fossil discoveries in East Africa helped him prove conclusively that humans had been on Earth much longer than previously believed and were closely related to apes. His work also proved that human evolution did indeed center in Africa. Leakey is remembered as a great conservationist, who was active in promoting game preserves in East Africa.

Meriwether Lewis (1774–1809)

EXPLORER

Born in Albemarle County, outside Charlotte, VIRGINIA, Meriwether Lewis grew up in Virginia and Georgia as part of a wealthy planter family. He excelled in school, especially natural history, taking a keen interest in plants and animals.

Lewis joined the Virginia army during the Whiskey Rebellion, a series of uprisings in 1794 against the new federal tax on whiskey. He transferred to the U.S. Army and fought in the Indian wars of the Ohio Valley, where he spent time in the same rifle company as William Clark.

In 1801 President Thomas Jefferson chose Lewis as his personal secretary. Jefferson soon asked him to make preparations for the first expedition to cross the continent to the Pacific Ocean. By late December 1802, Lewis was estimating travel expenses, purchasing supplies, and finally consulting with scientists in the spring of 1803.

CORPS OF DISCOVERY

In June 1803, the president drafted expedition instructions for Lewis. Concerned that the trip had become bigger than he expected, Lewis requested that the party have a co-leader. He suggested his old friend, William Clark, who agreed to take the job as a lieutenant to Lewis's captain, though in theory they'd be partners. The party, known as the Corps of Discovery, came together at Wood River camp outside ST. LOUIS, MISSOURI, in December 1903 and trained through the next year. Lewis studied astronomy, plant taxonomy, and medicine, and gathered equipment.

On May 14, 1804, 45 men and Lewis's dog, Scannon, left St. Louis for Fort Mandan (modern NORTH DAKOTA) where they spent the winter. Only half the men made the full trip, and others, including Native American guide **Sacagawea**, would join them as the journey progressed. The men took turns walking, rowing through navigable rivers, and later riding the horses they were given by Native Americans. Along the way, they stopped in Native American villages to offer gifts and learn about the land ahead.

Lewis served as the expedition's naturalist, taking notes about plants and animals—including the grizzly bear and prairie dog—that were new to Americans and Europeans. He also kept in mind the president's hopes of expanding the reach of U.S. resources in the west, which led to the expedition's only fight with Native Americans. In late July 1806, on the return trip, Lewis led a small party into present-day central MONTANA to find the northern end of the Marias River in hopes of laying claim to the fur-rich area. When a group from the Piegan Blackfoot tribe tried to take the party's horses and guns, a fight ensued and two Blackfoot were killed.

After two years, four months, and ten days, Lewis and Clark's party completed the 8,000-mile (12,875-km) trip. Upon returning to St. Louis in September 1806, Lewis and Clark were presented as national heroes. In reward for his work, Lewis was appointed governor of the LOUISIANA Territory by President Jefferson. Yet Lewis had many problems in the position, and politicians and locals questioned his effectiveness. At the same time, Lewis was having personal financial problems and trouble writing the necessary formal report to the government on the expedition. On the night of October 10, 1809, he apparently committed suicide (some people claimed he was murdered, though there was no evidence of that) near Hohenwald, Tennessee.

Budget Woes

LEWIS AND CLARK'S Corps of Discovery expedition's had travel expenses budgeted at $2,500, but it actually cost the government $38,000.

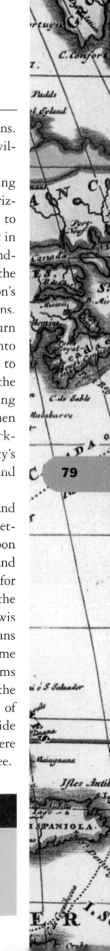

Charles Lindbergh (1902–1974)

AVIATOR

The only child born to a lawyer and a high school chemistry teacher, Charles Augustus Lindbergh grew up on a farm near Little Falls, Minnesota. He disliked school and eagerly accepted the principal's offer during World War I to give boys their diplomas early if they wished to do farm work instead.

Lindbergh went on to study engineering at the University of Wisconsin in 1920, but dropped out in his sophomore year to avoid expulsion. His attention turned to airplanes, and he enrolled in a Nebraska flying school. On April 9, 1922, Lindbergh made his first flight.

SOLO FLIER

Lindbergh graduated from an Army pilot training program in 1925, and became a mail plane pilot between ST. LOUIS, MISSOURI, and CHICAGO, ILLINOIS. While making his rounds in the fall of 1926, Lindbergh decided to make the first nonstop solo flight from NEW YORK to PARIS—a 3,600-mile (5,633-km) trip across the Atlantic. He collected $15,000 in sponsorship money from St. Louis businessmen, and named the plane he designed the *Spirit of St. Louis*, in their honor. The plane's cockpit was so small that the pilot could touch both sidewalls with his elbows and there was a wall of piloting instruments where the windshield would normally be. To see ahead, Lindbergh had to slip a periscope out of a side window.

After two weeks of test flights, Lindbergh flew first to his take-off point at Roosevelt Field, Long Island. On May 20, 1927 at 7:52 AM, Lindbergh climbed into his cockpit. He took off two minutes later to the delight of a small crowd.

Lindbergh hadn't slept the night before. After 24 hours, his grogginess made him temporarily lose control of the plane and dip down to 100 feet (31 m) above the ocean. He became energized when he realized he was near Europe. He recalled thinking. "In an emergency…I would have turned back toward America and home. Now, my anchor is Europe: on a continent I've never seen…Now I'll never think of turning back."

After 33 hours, 29 minutes, and 30 seconds, Lindbergh landed at Le Bourget Aerodrome near Paris at 10:22 PM. To the 25-year-old pilot's surprise, 100,000 people were waiting for him. On an international goodwill tour, Lindbergh met a U.S. ambassador's daughter, Anne Morrow. After they married, they flew all over the world, mapping more than 30,000 miles (48,000 km) of air routes for the newly created airline industry. Lindbergh also flew over the YUCATÁN in 1929 and the Far East in 1931.

In 1932, the Lindberghs's 19-month-old son was kidnapped from their home in NEW JERSEY. Though they complied with the kidnapper's demands for $50,000, the baby's body was found in the nearby woods six weeks later. A major criminal trial ensued.

To avoid the media frenzy, the Lindberghs moved to Europe. In 1938, Lindbergh went to GERMANY to review the country's air force at the request of the U.S. military, and accepted a medal from Adolf Hitler. Soon after, Lindbergh returned to America and urged the country to stay out of the coming war. Lindbergh was criticized as being a pro-German traitor, and forced to resign his membership in the National Advisory Committee for Aeronautics. Yet when the UNITED STATES entered World War II, Lindbergh released a statement urging Americans to unite and served as a consultant to U.S. Army fighter pilots.

By 1945, the Lindberghs moved to Connecticut, to raise their five children. Lindbergh lectured on conservation issues in the last decade of his life.

David Livingstone (1813–1873)

MISSIONARY·EXPLORER

Born in Blantyre, Scotland, to religious, poor parents, David Livingstone was working 14-hour days in a cotton mill by age 10. Each night he attended two hours of school, which enabled him to enter Anderson's College (modern University of Strathclyde) in Glasgow to study medicine in 1836. Two years later, he was accepted into the London Missionary Society, which sent him to South Africa.

TRAVELING MISSIONARY

As a 27-year-old missionary, Livingstone was stationed at Kuruman, on the southern fringes of the KALAHARI DESERT. He was unhappy that the area had few people to convert, and traveled northward to find more Africans to whom he could preach.

Livingstone began his own station at Mabotsa, near the mouth of the LIMPOPO RIVER. Yet he felt that he should be on the move, reaching new converts. As he did this, his goal became broader—he wanted to open central Africa to Western civilization in ways that could benefit the people as they lived within their own culture. Livingstone was disturbed by the slave trade and hoped that commerce and Christianity would end slavery. "I will open a way to the interior (of Africa) or perish," he said.

In 1849 Livingstone and three others crossed the Kalahari Desert and discovered Lake Ngami. After failing to reach the Makololo people farther north, Livingstone attempted to reach them again two years later by crossing the desert—this time with his wife and children. He later found the upper ZAMBEZI RIVER, which he noted was a navigable waterway to reach Africa's interior.

Beginning in 1852, Livingstone worked on a four-year venture to build a mission and trading center near the Makololo. For it to be successful, he knew he had to find a route from the upper Zambezi River to the coast. Livingstone traveled from CAPE TOWN to the Zambezi, then west to the Atlantic Ocean's coast at LUANDA (modern ANGOLA) to find a waterway. Unsuccessful, he returned to the Zambezi and sailed down river in a canoe. Despite malaria and dysentery, Livingstone made geographical notes, which helped further Europe's knowledge of Africa. In 1855 he became the first European to see the Zambezi's waterfall, which he named VICTORIA FALLS in honor of Britain's Queen Victoria. When Livingstone reached the mouth of the Zambezi at the Indian Ocean, he became the first European to cross the width of southern Africa.

Livingstone returned to ENGLAND in 1856 as a hero, and his book *Missionary Travels and Researches in South Africa* (1857) sold well. The following year Livingstone resigned his missionary post when his directors argued that he wasn't doing enough to spread religion.

In 1858 Livingstone began a five-year African expedition to explore the Zambezi, the SHIRE RIVER, LAKE NYASA, and the RUVUMA RIVER. A final African expedition began in 1866. Aided by two freed African slaves, Chuma and Susi, Livingstone explored LAKES Nyasa, MWERU, and BANGWEULU, as well as the rivers flowing through them. He followed a group of Arab slave traders westward to become the first European to reach the LUALABA RIVER, the headwaters of the CONGO RIVER. It was during this journey that he met journalist **Henry Morton Stanley**, who was sent to find the increasingly frail Livingstone. Together they explored LAKE TANGANYIKA.

Finally, Livingstone became so weak from dysentery that he had to stop traveling. He died in Chitambo (modern ZAMBIA), where Chuma and Susi buried his heart at the foot of a tree and wrapped his body for burial back in London's Westminster Abbey.

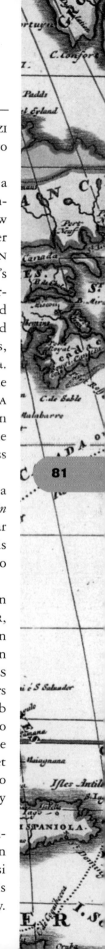

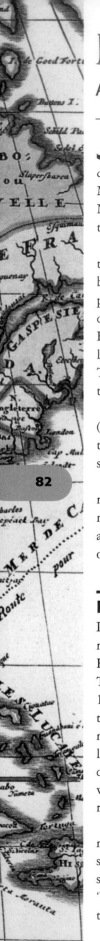

James Lovell (1928–)

ASTRONAUT

James Lovell was born in Cleveland, Ohio. As a child he loved to build model rockets. After receiving a degree from the U.S. Naval Academy at Annapolis, Maryland, in 1952, he attended Test Pilot School at the Naval Test Center in Patuxent River, Maryland, and then served as a fighter jet test pilot for four years.

In September 1962, Lovell was selected by NASA to enter their astronaut-training program. He was a backup pilot on *Gemini 4*, but first entered space as pilot of *Gemini 7* (December 4–18, 1965), which was commanded by Frank Borman. The two men orbited Earth 206 times on the then-record 14-day mission and linked with *Gemini 6A*, which had Wally Schirra and Tom Stafford on board. It was the first rendezvous of two manned spacecrafts.

Next, Lovell served as commander on *Gemini 12* (November 11–15, 1966) with pilot Buzz Aldrin. On this mission, Lovell directed a linking with an *Agena* satellite and Aldrin's space walk.

On his third flight, Lovell served as command module pilot on the first manned mission to orbit the moon. *Apollo 8* (December 21–27, 1968), with Borman and William A. Anders also on board, made 10 lunar orbits in 20 hours.

FINAL FLIGHT: *APOLLO 13*

Lovell's final space flight, *Apollo 13*, was launched as a mission in which he, John L. Swigert, Jr., and Fred W. Haise, Jr., were to attempt NASA's third moon landing. Though it launched without incident on April 11, 1970, the mission was cut short when the main oxygen tank in the service module exploded on the way to the moon. The astronauts were forced to seek safety in their lunar module, where, working closely with mission control, they spent more than an hour finding the best ways to conserve enough electrical power and water to return to Earth.

At one point, the crew disconnected their medical monitors so mission control couldn't monitor their vital signs. Lovell recalled that they had more than just conserving energy in mind. "It was my way of saying, 'We're in control,'" he said. "'You don't have to monitor our body readings to see how scared we are.'"

They returned to Earth in their lunar module on April 17 by splashing down in the Pacific Ocean. NASA classified the mission as a "successful failure" because of their positive efforts to rescue the crew.

Lovell, however, had had enough of flying. "It changed me in a major way," he said. "I live my life one day at a time. Nothing rattles me. I could be dead." He retired from NASA as the first astronaut to make four space flights, and completed Harvard Business School's Advanced Management Program in 1971. In May of that year, Lovell was named deputy director for science and applications at the Johnson Space Center. Two years later, he was deep in the private sector, serving in top positions at three businesses.

Lovell is now president of Lovells, Inc., which opened a restaurant—Lovells of Lake Forest—in 1999 in Lake Forest, Illinois. A NASA flight suit and Lovell's awards and space memorabilia decorate the restaurant. Lovell flies a Baron jet regularly between his homes in Lake Forest and Horseshoe Bay, Texas.

Earth Trekker

IN ADDITION TO HIS SPACE travel, Lovell traveled to the North Pole (April 13, 1987) and the South Pole (January 2000).

Sir Alexander Mackenzie

(1764–1829) FUR TRADER·EXPLORER

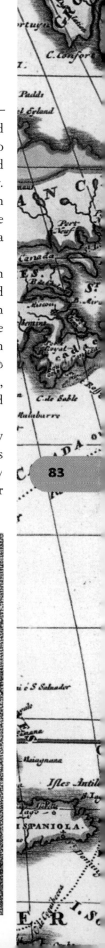

Alexander Mackenzie was born in Scotland and immigrated to New York with his family in 1774. By 1779, he had moved to CANADA to work as a fur trader and explore the largely uncharted land. He theorized that Cook's River in present-day ALASKA was the fabled Northwest Passage or "Western Sea," as he called it—a gateway from the Atlantic to the Pacific Ocean that would provide a shortcut to the spice-rich Orient.

"THE WESTERN SEA"

In 1788, Mackenzie served as director of the North West Company's operations in the Athabasca district of Canada. He succeeded explorer Peter Pond, who left behind a map he had drawn of a possible route to the Pacific Ocean. On it, Pond suggested it would take six days of paddling to the west from the Slave River and the icy GREAT SLAVE LAKE.

In 1789, Mackenzie led a crew that included his wife in several birch canoes from Fort Chipewyan in central Canada down the Slave River. Along the riverbanks, they introduced themselves to several Native American camps. Many of the Native Americans had never seen a white man, yet Mackenzie coerced some of them to join him as guides, interpreters, clothes menders, and hunters.

Mackenzie attempted to follow Pond's route, only to find that it was dangerous and incorrect, leading him toward what he called the "Northern Ocean" (modern Arctic Ocean). "I am much at a loss here how to act," Mackenzie wrote in his journal on July 10, explaining his decision to keep searching, "as it would satisfy people's curiosity tho' not their intentions."

Two days later, the canoes landed on Garry Island, near a delta where the river flows into the sea. Mackenzie climbed up a hill and saw the icy Arctic Ocean. More than 49 days and 1,200 miles (1,931 km) later, they arrived back at the fort with maps of northern Canada and a new route to the Arctic Ocean.

Still, Mackenzie wasn't ready to forget his theory. On May 9, 1793, he and nine others climbed into a 25-foot-long (7.6-m) canoe at Fort Fork along the PEACE RIVER for a second expedition to find the passage. While crossing the Peace, Mackenzie listened to the suggestions of Native American guides, who said he should continue his journey on land instead of trying to cross the rough and rocky Fraser River. Walking along the Blackwater River, a western tributary of the Fraser, the group crossed over to the Bella Coola River, and walked toward its mouth: a waterway to the Pacific.

As a result, Mackenzie became the first European north of MEXICO to reach the Pacific via an overland route—beating **Meriwether Lewis** and William Clark's Corps of Discovery, which arrived at the Pacific coast in 1805. On a rock near the ocean Mackenzie used a vermilion and grease mixture to paint the words: "Alexander Mackenzie, from Canada, by land, the twenty-second of July, one thousand seven hundred and ninety-nine."

Mackenzie returned to Great Britain to seek new opportunities for commercial ventures. Eighteen years later, the 48-year-old, who had been knighted by King George III in 1802, retired to Scotland. He later died of a degenerative kidney disease.

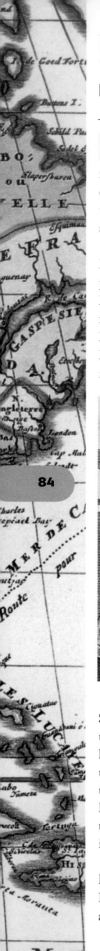

Ferdinand Magellan (1480–1521)

EXPLORER

Born Fernão de Magalhães (later known as Fernando de Magallanes to the Spanish) to a noble family in northern PORTUGAL, Magellan served as a court page in his youth. He later helped fight battles to defend Portuguese interests in India and was part of a crew that explored INDONESIA.

In 1513 he sailed to MOROCCO to help battle the Moors. Wounded in combat, Magellan developed a permanent limp. He returned home to face King Manuel of Portugal, who accused him of benefiting financially from the Moroccan trip. The king punished Magellan by denying his request to prove that the MOLUCCAS, also known as the "Spice Islands," (in modern Indonesia) could be reached by sailing west.

Magellan renounced his citizenship and sailed to SPAIN in 1517 to seek support for the expedition to the Moluccas from King Charles I. At this point in history, much of the world was divided between the two superpowers of Spain and Portugal. Magellan told the king that some of the Moluccas were probably located in the Spanish hemisphere—and the only way to prove it was to measure the earth's distance by sailing west to the Moluccas.

After he received the king's approval, Magellan led five ships with at least 250 men from Sanlúcar de Barrameda, Spain, on September 20, 1519. They sailed along the western coast of Africa, south to the equator,

and then turned southwest and crossed the Atlantic Ocean to reach the coastline of South America near RECIFE, BRAZIL, on December 6.

They continued sailing south, and spent the winter in PORT SAN JULIÁN (in modern ARGENTINA). In four months, Magellan suppressed a mutiny and lost a ship, but pressed onward. Eventually they came to a narrow, twisting strait.

PEACEFUL OCEAN

Magellan decided to sail through the strait. After passing through two bays connected by a narrow passage they reached a third bay. There, two more passages were sighted and Magellan again ordered ships to explore them. One ship's crew mutinied, but Magellan sailed on and found a land with many small fires. He named it TIERRA DEL FUEGO ("Land of Fire"), then continued on through a long channel which, on November 28, 1520, opened onto a large, seemingly calm ocean that Magellan named the Pacific. The route they traveled is now called the STRAIT OF MAGELLAN.

The ships continued sailing across the Pacific. Crew members who didn't die of scurvy, ran out of food and were forced to eat leather sail strips and rats. They finally reached an island—most likely Guam—and traded with the island inhabitants to get supplies.

Magellan then led the fleet southwest to the island of Mindanao in the PHILIPPINES. At the island of Zzubu (modern Cebu), he converted approximately 3,000 people to Christianity, including the ruler Humabon. Magellan and his crew helped Humabon battle Lapulapu, chief of the island of Mattan (modern Mactan in the Philippines). Magellan was killed when a lance pierced him in the face below his helmet.

Magellan's remaining ships sailed to the Moluccas and then returned home with a crew of only 18 on September 6, 1522. Though Magellan didn't complete the voyage, he is considered to have led the first voyage around the world because he had sailed to a point beyond the one he had reached earlier when sailing east. In doing this, Magellan confirmed the earth was round, measured its circumference, and proved that the world's oceans were connected.

Ella Katherine Maillart (1903–1997)

SPORTSWOMAN·TRAVELER

Born in Geneva, Switzerland, to a Swiss furrier and his Danish wife, Ella Katherine Maillart (nicknamed "Kini") spent her youth reading her older brother's adventure books, skiing in the ALPS, and sailing on Lake Geneva. At age 16, she formed an all-girls hockey club, but she did poorly in school. When Maillart failed the university entrance exam, she began to learn her father's business, only to find that her father was too bossy and the work was dull.

By age 19, Maillart lived in Wales, then in ENGLAND, working as a French teacher. A year later, she answered a newspaper ad seeking crew members for sailing expeditions and was hired. Soon after, Maillart joined three women on a voyage to GREECE. Once there, they sold their small boat and bought a 50-foot-long yacht, *Atalante*, in the hopes of sailing to the South Seas. The trip was cut short when one woman became sick. Maillart felt aimless. "I longed to work with people who shared a single aim," she later wrote, "and to feel the human warmth round me which created brave ideas, as well as the courage to realize them."

Maillart found excitement competing in the 1924 Paris Olympics in the single-handed women's sailing race. On behalf of SWITZERLAND, Maillart finished ninth, but she made a name for herself in the field of sports. She later founded Switzerland's first women's hockey team.

TRAVEL WRITER

In the late 1920s, Maillart spent time in PARIS and GERMANY in a variety of quick-money jobs, including actress and tour guide. By 1930, she had enough money to travel by train to MOSCOW, where she lived for five months before hiking with a group of students across the CAUCASUS MOUNTAINS. She later visited Kiev and Odessa on her own, and then sold a book about her travels to a French publisher. Though she admitted she wasn't a great writer—critics said her books were just detailed notes—from this time on, she decided to write about all of her travels.

Maillart returned to the Soviet Union (modern RUSSIA) for a six-month trip in 1932, visiting

KYRGYZSTAN and UZBEKISTAN. Alone, she climbed to the top of the mountain Sari Tor (approximately 16,000 feet [4,877 m]) and then skied down its slope. She traveled by train, bus, camel, horse, bicycle, paddle wheeler, wagon, kayak, plane, and skis, and was proud to have financed the trip with about $50.

Maillart next found work as a correspondent for the French publication *Petit Parisien*. In 1935, Maillart was in Peking (modern BEIJING), CHINA, and eager to cross Turkestan, then ruled by the Chinese, who prohibited foreigners to enter it. She joined with British newspaper correspondent Peter Fleming to make the 3,500-mile (5,633-km) journey, realizing solo travel would be difficult as the country was ruled by local warlords.

To gain entrance, Maillart bribed officials and falsified documents. She and Fleming traveled to ZHENGZHOU, XUZHOU, and XI'AN, and hopped on the back of a truck to LANZHOU. From there, they rode mules to XINING, where they traded the mules for horses. On the way, Maillart pitched the tent nightly, sewed, and cooked, while Fleming shot wild animals for food. Maillart remembered of the half-year trip, "…I should have liked the journey to continue the rest of my life."

After Maillart wrote her first English-translated book, *Forbidden Journey* (1937), she wrote articles and books about further travels to TURKEY and INDIA, and a journey from Switzerland to AFGHANISTAN. During World War II, Maillart traveled in India, TIBET, and later NEPAL. Her last trip, at 91, was to GOA, India.

Reinhold Messner (1944–)

MOUNTAIN CLIMBER·EXPLORER

The second-born in a family with eight brothers and one sister living in South Tyrol in northern Italy, Reinhold Messner grew up around mountains. His father taught him how to climb when he was just four. At age 25, Messner climbed Nanga Parbat (26,660 feet [8,125 m]) in the HIMALAYAS. On the way down, his younger brother Gunther was killed in an avalanche. Messner lost six toes to frostbite while searching, in vain, for his brother.

"ALPINE-STYLE" CLIMBER

In the early 1970s, Messner and climbing partner Peter Habeler of Austria began making climbs without supplemental canisters of oxygen. "I would rather cope...with my own abilities and not with the help of technology," he said. Also unique to Messner's climbs is that instead of moving up a series of camps to acclimatize to the thinning oxygen at higher altitudes, he generally prefers to use the "Alpine-style" method, which he developed. In it, the climber makes one stop at a camp half way up the mountain and then reaches the summit, thereafter making a quick descent.

After perfecting the technique in the ALPS, Messner decided to use it in the Himalayas on a climb of PAKISTAN's Gasherbrum I (26,470 feet [8,068 m]) in 1975. To condition himself, he used a strict schedule of distance running, weight training, and dieting, which reduced his pulse rate to 42 beats per minute (60 bpm is considered athletic). Messner and Habeler decided to

climb without the added weight of ropes tying them together, which would slow them down. "Climbing isn't interesting if we use all the technical aids available," explained Messner. The men dashed up and down the mountain in a record three days.

Three years later, Messner made a solo climb of Nanga Parbat. Then he and Habeler attempted to climb, MOUNT EVEREST (29,028 feet [8,848 m]), on the TIBET/NEPAL border. They decided not to use supplemental oxygen, but knew they would have to stop at a series of five camps. After arriving at base camp in March 1978, they spent a few weeks establishing a route and setting up other camps.

On May 6, Messner and Habeler reached the third camp at 23,616 feet (7,200 m). Exhausted, they agreed to carry oxygen cylinders to the next camp, in case of an emergency. They rested again at 26,194 feet (7,986 m), though both men frequently awoke from their naps gasping for air. On May 8, they reached Camp V 27,880 feet (8,500 m)—stopping to catch their breath every few steps—and rested for 30 minutes. Messner described feeling like he would "burst apart." By the time they reached 28,864 feet (8,800 m), the climbers were collapsing every 10 to 15 feet to lie in the snow. Then, around 2:00 PM, they reached the summit of Everest. "I no longer belong to myself and to my eyesight," Messner said into his tape recorder. "I am nothing more than a single narrow gasping lung, floating over the mists and summits."

Messner followed up his successful climb by making the first solo ascent of Mount Everest, again without the use of supplemental oxygen, on August 20, 1980. Ten years later he became the first to cross Antarctica on foot. He also began a 15-year study exploring the mountains of Central Asia—including a trek across eastern Tibet to BHUTAN, the HINDU KUSH, the PAMIRS, MONGOLIA, and Nepal—to dispel the legend of the Yeti, also known as the abominable snowman. In 2000, he published *The Crystal Horizon* claiming that Yeti is actually a rarely seen bear.

Messner now serves in European Parliament in Brussels. He has a castle in South Tyrol, which houses his collection of Tibetan art, and owns a yak farm as well as a small restaurant called the Yak & Yeti.

Tenzing Norgay (1914–1986)

MOUNTAIN CLIMBER

Born Namgyal Wangdi in Solo Khumbu, NEPAL, Tenzing Norgay was one of 13 children born to peasant Sherpas—a tribe who often work as porters for mountaineers because of their natural acclimation to great heights. He received the name by which he became famous, which translates to "wealthy-fortunate follower of religion," from a Buddhist holy man who believed Norgay was the reincarnation of a rich man who had died.

As a boy herding his family's yaks, Norgay often looked at the mountains and dreamt of climbing. At age 13, he ran away from home—walking for two weeks to reach the capital city, KATMANDU. Five years later, he left again, this time to live in DARJEELING, INDIA, so he could help with climbing expeditions.

MOUNT EVEREST

Though he never learned how to write, Norgay spoke five languages, including English and Tibetan. His first big break in climbing came in 1935 when he accompanied a British expedition to MOUNT EVEREST, the world's highest peak at 29,028 feet (8,848 m). The 5-foot, 3-inch (1.6-m) Sherpa continued to make climbs with British, French, and Swiss expeditions. By 1952, Norgay had been part of six trips up Everest.

In 1953, Colonel John Hunt, the leader of the British-sponsored Joint Himalayan Committee of the Royal Geographical Society and the Alpine Club, chose Norgay to make the climb with his team.

The team trained and acclimatized themselves in Nepal in March 1953. By April 12, they had reached base camp with 362 Nepalese porters, 35 Sherpa guides, and 10,000 pounds of baggage. As they climbed up and stopped at their nine camps, the party grew increasingly smaller. At the final camp, 1,100 feet (335 m) from the summit, Hunt sent two teams up. The first failed, but returned with advice for the second team, Norgay and **Edmund Hillary**.

On May 29, 1953, Norgay and Hillary set out for their final day of the seven-week climb, but were suffering from the lack of oxygen. "On the top of the rock cliff we rested again," Norgay later dictated for his autobiography "Certainly after the climb up the gap we were both a bit breathless, but after some slow pulls at the oxygen I am feeling fine. I look up; the top is very close now; and my heart thumps with excitement and joy."

Attached by a 30-foot (9-m) rope, much of which lay in loops in Norgay's hand, the men climbed with a six-foot space separating them. On Everest's summit, Norgay hugged Hillary and buried some candy in the snow as an offering to the Buddhist gods. Hillary took pictures to show proof of their feat.

Upon descending, both men were international celebrities. Norgay faced some controversy—both the Nepalese and Indian governments wanted to claim him as a citizen. The media also clamored to learn who reached the top first. "This is teamwork," Norgay answered. "Actually, we climbed together. Whatever Hillary say, I don't care, but I say, teamwork. There shouldn't be controversy there." Both men later noted that Hillary was actually the one in front.

Norgay never tried to climb Everest again. Instead, he lived quietly with his wife, children, and 25 dogs. In 1954 when the Himalayan Mountaineering Institute was established in Darjeeling, Norgay became its director of field training.

> **Tiger of the Snows was Norgay's nickname and the name of his 1955 autobiography.**

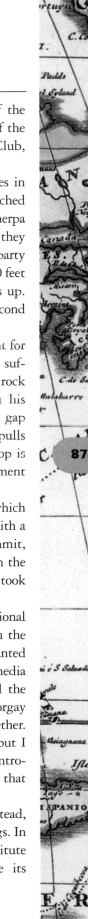

Francisco de Orellana (c. 1511–1546)

EXPLORER

Francisco de Orellana, born in the Spanish town of Trujillo, was related to explorers **Francisco** and Gonzalo **Pizarro**. At age 16, he traveled to PANAMA and NICARAGUA, and then he joined Francisco Pizarro in his conquest of PERU by fighting in battles at LIMA and CUZCO. Orellana lost an eye in a battle with the Incas, but was gifted with an estate at PUERTO VIEJO (in modern ECUADOR) for his valor.

When Orellana heard his cousin was having more problems in Lima with Native Americans in 1538, he led 80 men into battle to help. For his hard work, he was made lieutenant governor of Quayaquil.

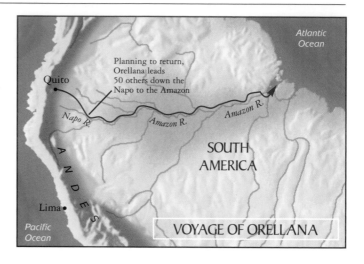

VOYAGE OF ORELLANA

IN SEARCH OF CINNAMON

In late 1540, Orellana resigned from his governorship and gathered 23 men to join Gonzalo Pizarro and a large group of Spaniards and Native Americans to search for cinnamon, a valuable spice that was rumored to grow on the eastern side of the Ecuadorian Andes. By March 1541, Orellana was named second in command on the expedition. Soon after, the men discovered eastern Ecuador's NAPO RIVER, which is a tributary of the AMAZON RIVER.

When food supplies were nearly exhausted, Gonzalo commanded that some party members head downstream to find food. With the agreement that he'd return, Orellana led at least 50 others, including Dominican friar/note-taker Gaspar de Carvajal, on a trip down the Napo on January 1, 1542.

It is unclear if Orellana intentionally never returned or if the force of the river made it too hard to turn back, but by February 2, Orellana and his men had sailed from the Napo into the Aguarico River. As they sailed down toward the Amazon, they stopped in Native American villages, where they were usually greeted warmly and given food. On February 11, they reached the main stream of the Amazon. They stayed in the town of Aparia to build a second, bigger boat.

After leaving Aparia on April 24, Orellana and his men fought many battles with Native Americans as they sailed down the river in their boats. At one point they were attacked by at least ten very tall, light-skinned women with bows and arrows. Carvajal called them "Amazons," in reference to the Amazons in Greek mythology. Spaniards reading Carvajal's notes later named the area and the river the Amazon.

In the meantime, Gonzalo and the men left behind by Orellana's expedition realized they were stranded and walked to QUITO. Gonzalo wrote a letter to the King of Spain, accusing Orellana of desertion.

Orellana's two boats reached the mouth of the Amazon at the Atlantic Ocean on August 26. It was the first expedition to sail down the entire Amazon. The boats sailed northwestward along the coast of present-day GUYANA and landed on the island of Cubagua near Margarita, off the coast of VENEZUELA. From there, Orellana made his way back to Spain in May 1543, where he defended himself against Gonzalo's charges and made a report of his journey for King Carlos I. Orellana also asked to be named governor of the territories he found along the banks of the Amazon.

He was granted the title of governor for the region, called *Nueva Andalucía*, and was authorized to lead another expedition to colonize lands south of the Amazon, though he had to finance it himself. On May 11, 1545, Orellana led four ships with 300 to 350 men to the Amazon. After stops in the CANARY and Cape Verde Islands and the deaths and desertion of many men, Orellana's fleet reached the Amazon by the end of December. He tried to sail upstream with a ship and boat, but died from fever before he made it.

Annie Smith Peck (1850–1935)

MOUNTAIN CLIMBER

Annie Peck was born in Providence, Rhode Island, to a wealthy family. She studied Greek at the University of Michigan, which had opened its doors to women only a few years before. After teaching in schools and colleges, in 1885 she became the first woman admitted to the American School of Classical Studies in Athens, GREECE.

To earn a living, Peck lectured on Greek and Roman archaeology, using photographs she had taken on travels in Europe. Mountains first peaked her interest while she was traveling through Switzerland and saw the ALPS. She particularly loved the MATTERHORN (14,700 feet [4,480 m]) on the SWITZERLAND/ITALY border. "On beholding this majestic, awe inspiring peak," she said, "I felt that I should never be happy until I, too, scale those frowning walls which have beckoned so many upwards, a few to their own destruction."

FEMINIST CLIMBER

After making a series of practice climbs in Switzerland and Greece, she made it to the summit of Mount Shasta (14,162 feet) in California's SIERRA NEVADA in 1888. Then, in 1895, Peck became the third woman to scale the Matterhorn. She became famous, not only because of the feat, but also because she made the climb in knickerbocker pants, a tunic, and a felt hat tied by a veil. Previous climbs by women were done in skirts, but ever the feminist, Peck wore pants to make a statement about her achievement. Later, Peck said that "any great achievement in any line of endeavor would be an advantage of my sex."

In 1927, Mount Huascarán's northern peak was named Cumbre Ana Peck.

Over the next two years, Peck climbed the volcano Popacatépetl (17,887 feet [4,318 m]) and Mount Orizaba (18,700 feet [5,701 m]) in Mexico, and then climbed a series of European mountains. She also began fundraising for a climb of Mount Sorata (21,283 feet [6,489 m]) in BOLIVA by increasing her number of lectures and courting advertisers for $100 donations. Finally, in 1904, Peck became the first person to climb Mount Sorata. It was her first (albeit unsuccessful) attempt at using oxygen canisters—something that is a given on most modern climbs.

Peck spent the next four years attempting to be the first to summit the southern peak of HUASCARÁN (22,205 feet [6,770 m]) in the Peruvian ANDES. The townspeople in Yungay, where the mountain was located, all recognized Peck as a determined American with gray hair and steel-rimmed glasses, and many helped her gather necessary items, including a kerosene lamp that she had lost on a previous attempt.

On August 31, 1909, Peck reached the top of Huascarán. Peck estimated that the mountain was (23,915 feet [7,291 m]), which, at that time, was the highest a female had ever climbed. Fellow climber Fanny Bullock Workman challenged Peck's claim and paid French engineers to triangulate the mountain's measurement. They corrected Peck's claimed height, but Peck still had a record climb for an American in the western hemisphere.

Peck was deeply concerned about women gaining the right to vote. At age 61, when she climbed Mount Coropuna (21,079 feet [6,455 m]) in Peru, she planted a "Votes for Women" sign at the summit—while wearing a wool facemask on which a long mustache was painted. Her final climb came at age 82 when she ascended the peak of Mount Madison (5,362 feet [1,635 m]) in New Hampshire.

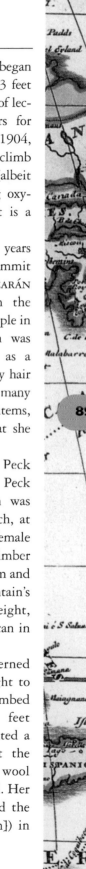

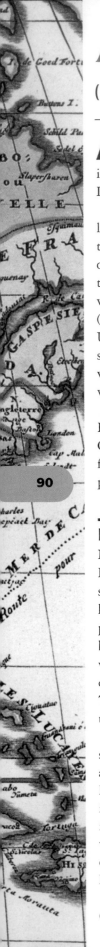

Auguste and Jacques Piccard

(1884–1962) (1922–) HOT AIR BALLOONISTS·DEEP SEA DIVERS

Auguste Piccard, born in Bassel, Switzerland, grew up with a strong interest in science. After receiving a doctorate in natural science from the Swiss Institute of Technology, he became a physicist.

By the 1920s, Auguste began flying hot-air balloons, believing they could help him gather information about stars' cosmic rays. A German firm developed a revolutionary balloon made of rubberized cotton for Auguste, and he designed and built an airtight vessel that could carry two people above 40,000 feet (12,192 m) without the need for pressurized suits. Using equipment and ideas developed for German submarines in World War I, Auguste planned for the vessel to enable the balloonists to breathe purified air, which would be constantly recycled.

On May 27, 1931, Auguste and his assistant, Paul Kipfer, lifted off in the balloon from Augsburg, GERMANY. They reached a record height of 51, 775 feet (15,781 m), and received attention from newspapers and radio stations around the world.

BATHYSCAPH: *TRIESTE*

Next, the Swiss scientist's interest turned to the ocean. In 1937, he completed work on a new vessel for deep-sea diving, called bathyscaph FNRS-2. Instead of keeping air pressure in, like his balloon vessel, it kept pressure out. The bathyscaph was like an underwater balloon that used gasoline—which is lighter than water—for lift. It made its first successful unmanned dive to a depth of 4,800 feet (1,463 m) in 1948. Though Auguste later took the vessel deeper, he sold it to the French Navy a few years later.

Auguste had already made an improved bathyscaph called *Trieste*. It used gasoline for buoyancy, but also iron pellets for balanced weight. *Trieste* could be lowered into the sea when those inside pumped water into its air tanks, or by outsiders using an inside line; it rose when water was pumped out and the pellets were released. Beneath the new bathyscaph was a long chain that was slowly lowered to hit the ocean bottom, helping the bathyscaph's steady descent.

Trieste made its first attempted dive into the Gulf of Naples in September 1953, with Auguste

and his 6-foot 7-inch son, a Brussels, Belgium-born scientist named Jacques, aboard. It was a dive of only 30 feet (9 m), but it proved the vessel worked. Auguste then dropped to 10,300 feet (3,139 m) later that year. In 1953, Auguste turned *Trieste* over to Jacques. With his father's assistance, Jacques made many dives for

scientific exploration. His work caught the attention of the U.S. Navy, who offered to buy the vessel for further explorations and allow Jacques to be its pilot.

On November 15, 1959, Jacques and oceanographer Andreas Rechnitzer dropped a record 18,150 feet (6,050 m) to the ocean floor. The U.S. Navy wanted to make an even deeper dive. On January 23, 1960, Jacques and Navy Lt. Don Walsh planned to take *Trieste* 35,810 feet (10,915 m) to the deepest ocean spot, the Pacific's Mariana Trench near Guam. To reach the seafloor, the vessel would have to withstand 3,000 tons of water pressure. The slightest leak would shoot water into the vessel with the force of a bullet. The men made a successful descent and remained on the seafloor for 20 minutes as they observed sea life.

In total, *Trieste* was sent on 128 dives before being retired. It is now on display at the Smithsonian Institution in Washington, D.C. Jacques Piccard continues his oceanographic studies from his laboratory in Lake Geneva, Switzerland.

Zebulon Pike (1779–1813)

ARMY OFFICER · EXPLORER

Zebulon Montgomery Pike was born in Trenton, NEW JERSEY. In his teens he began a military career as a cadet alongside his father, a U.S. Army officer. By 1799, 20-year-old Pike was a lieutenant, and began to travel to various camps in the West.

In 1805, General James Wilkinson, governor of the newly acquired LOUISIANA Territory, asked Pike to lead an expedition to find the source of the MISSISSIPPI RIVER. Pike and 20 others left ST. LOUIS, MISSOURI, in a keelboat. After spending part of winter at a camp below the Falls of St. Anthony (modern St. Paul, MINNESOTA), the group continued on in December. When they reached Leech Lake in northern Minnesota, Pike declared he found the Mississippi's source. (The source is actually farther west at Lake Itasca.)

The group explored Minnesota and met many British fur-traders, who were informed by Pike that they were trespassing on American territory. When Pike returned to St. Louis in 1806, General Wilkinson was pleased and gave him instructions for another mission. Pike was to return members of the Osage tribe, who had been taken captive, to their homeland to help bring peace between warring Osage and Kansas Native Americans. Pike was also told to explore the upper ARKANSAS and RED RIVERS, and—secretly—to find a route to Spanish settlements in SANTA FE, NEW MEXICO. Wilkinson also informed the Spanish that Pike would be snooping on their territory.

Pike left St. Louis on July 15, 1806, with 23 men, including the general's son, Lieutenant Wilkinson. They sailed up the MISSOURI and Osage Rivers in central Missouri through eastern Kansas, where they returned the Osages to their tribe. The party traveled through Pawnee villages in southern Nebraska before sailing south to the Arkansas River. On the way, the men became aware that a group of Spanish soldiers was following them. At the mouth of the Arkansas, the lieutenant and six others returned to St. Louis with news of the expedition.

COLORADO

The rest of the group traveled west, sighting the ROCKY MOUNTAINS on November 15. A week later they reached present-day Pueblo, COLORADO. The entire party sailed up the Arkansas to Royal Gorge, where they built a small fort.

Pike left the fort on January 14, 1807, with 13 men. They climbed through the Cristo Mountains in southern Colorado. Six of the men got gangrene from walking through the snow, and two of them had to have their feet amputated. Two weeks later the group built a fort on the Rio Conejos, which ran through New Mexico. A Spanish cavalry entered the fort on February 26 and arrested Pike and his men.

The Americans were taken to Chihuahua in present-day northern Mexico. There they met with the Spanish governor, who questioned them and took their documents. Pike had carefully memorized his expedition notes so he could give the general important military and geographical information when he returned home. He also managed to hide some notes in the barrel of his gun. Pike and the others were released in Louisiana in early July 1807, and returned to St. Louis.

Pike spent the next year writing about his expedition, and published a book in 1810. He noted that the GREAT PLAINS would never be suitable for settlement by American settlers, and he suggested several possible routes through the southwest to the Pacific Ocean, which encouraged westward expansion.

Pike was promoted to brigadier general after the start of the War of 1812 with Great Britain, and put in charge of the attack on York (modern TORONTO), CANADA. His orders were a success, but Pike was later killed in an explosion.

Francisco Pizarro (c. 1476–1541)

EXPLORER

Born in Trujillo, Spain, Francisco Pizarro was raised in poverty and never learned to read or write. In 1502 he sailed to HISPANIOLA (modern HAITI and the DOMINICAN REPUBLIC), where he lived for a few years. Pizarro joined a 1509 expedition, led by Alonso de Ojeda, to COLOMBIA before serving on an expedition led by **Vasco Nuñez de Balboa** in 1513 that claimed the Pacific Ocean for Spain.

Pizarro later sailed to PANAMA, where he served under Governor Pedrarias Dávila, who assigned Pizarro to arrest Balboa for treason. (Balboa was executed for his deeds in 1519.) While in Panama, Pizarro heard about a southern land full of gold and decided to explore it.

THE INCAN EMPIRE

He led two expeditions down the west coast of South America in November 1524 and November 1526 to locate gold. His second expedition was larger than the first, giving him command over 160 men and several horses in two ships. Expedition notes showed they met the Incas in PERU, and were impressed with the golden ornaments many of them wore. Meanwhile, Balboa returned to SPAIN to get the king's permission to conquer the Incan Empire, put it under Spanish control, and become the area's governor.

After building an army of approximately 200, Pizarro returned to Peru in 1532, and landed in San Mateo Bay. The Incan emperor, Atahualpa, was told of the arrival of Pizarro's fleet and—unaware of Pizarro's plan—allowed the men to pass freely on land to meet him in the town of CAJAMARCA. The Incas believed that the light-skinned men were gods whose coming they had been waiting for, and called the Spaniards *intip churin* ("children of the sun"). Pizarro's army, which included another famous explorer, **Hernando de Soto**, traveled through desert and snow-capped mountains to meet the emperor.

Pizarro's army and thousands of Incas, including leaders, feasted in the public square on November 16, 1532, to celebrate Pizarro's arrival. Suddenly Pizarro's army rushed toward the Incas with their swords. As cannons and horses were pulled into the square by the army, the Spaniards surrounded the shocked Incas and within a half hour killed all of the leaders, except Atahualpa, who they captured and held for ransom.

Much to Pizarro's delight, the emperor offered to fill a large room with gold and two smaller rooms with silver to gain his release. Couriers from around the empire brought gold and silver, giving Pizarro treasures worth at least $100 million in modern money. Still, Pizarro didn't free the emperor; he had him executed by strangulation on August 29, 1533.

CITY OF THE KINGS

Pizarro and his army then marched south to loot and take over the capital city of CUZCO. He established the *encomienda*, or forced labor, system on the Native Americans, who were frightened and offered little resistance. Pizarro founded *Ciudad de los Reyes* ("City of the Kings") in present-day LIMA, and governed Peru from there, beginning in 1535.

His position was short lived due to fighting among the Spaniards. Diego de Almagro, who governed present-day northern CHILE, brought an army into Cuzco and seized control of the city. The struggle for power between Pizarro and Almagro led to the War of Las Salinas in 1538. Though Almagro was killed, his son, Almagro the Lad, continued the war. Almagro's followers eventually killed Pizarro in his palace.

Marco Polo (1254–1324)

TRAVELER

Marco Polo was born into a family of merchants and raised in one of the most prominent trade centers in medieval Europe. Polo's family lived in Venice, ITALY, and his father and uncle, Niccoló and Maffeo Polo, were jewel merchants.

In 1260, the father and uncle sailed from Venice to the trading ports of CONSTANTINOPLE (modern ISTANBUL, TURKEY), Soldaia (modern Sudak, UKRAINE), and BUKHORO (in modern UZBEKISTAN). Then they joined a diplomatic mission to the Mongolian leader of CHINA, Kublai Khan. The leader was fascinated by his visitors' stories of Christianity and asked that the men return to Europe to ask the Pope for scholars to teach him more. The elder Polo brother returned home in 1269.

THE LONG MISSION

Two years later, a crew with two missionaries sent by the Pope, the brothers, and teenaged Marco Polo—whose mother had died years earlier—set sail to meet the khan. The missionaries, concerned about storms along the route, abandoned the mission. The others sailed to Acre (modern Akko, ISRAEL), and then traveled on horseback through ARMENIA and PERSIA (modern IRAN) to the Oxus River (now AMU DARYA) in Central Asia. From there, they sailed to the PAMIR MOUNTAINS, which they crossed on horseback. Finally, they journeyed around the southern edge of the TAKLA MAKAN DESERT to LOP NUR (in modern western China) and across the GOBI DESERT. Hunger and thirst were not their biggest concerns—ghosts were. They had heard stories of "whispering" spirits that make travelers stray from their paths. In reality, the "whispers" were most likely sand dunes shifting in the wind.

In 1275, they reached Shangdu (200 miles [300 km] north of modern BEIJING), the summer court of Kublai Khan. Polo and his uncle and father spent the next 17 years in China. The khan really enjoyed the company of the youngest Polo, who was an engaging speaker and storyteller, and sent him out on many diplomatic missions throughout China.

Polo reported back to the khan about his journeys, including those to SICHUAN PROVINCE in southern China and YUNNAN PROVINCE in the southwest.

In 1292, the men planned a return to Venice. The khan asked them to escort a Mongol princess to Persia, were she was set to marry that country's Mongolian ruler. Their ship sailed from China to SUMATRA, CEYLON (modern SRI LANKA), southern INDIA, and then into the Persian Gulf to drop off the princess. With the princess safely in Persia, the three men traveled on land to Trebizond (modern Trabzon, TURKEY), where they boarded a ship for Constantinople. They finally arrived home in Venice in 1295.

Young people from all over the city, according to Polo, visited him at his home upon his return. They were eager to hear stories about his travels, and gave Polo the nickname of *il milione* ("the man with a million stories").

While fighting in a naval conflict between Venice and commercial rival Genoa, Polo and 7,000 compatriots were captured and imprisoned. In prison, Polo told stories about his travels, which interested a romance writer from Pisa named Rustichello. The writer transcribed Polo's accounts and embellished some details to create an entertaining book. The book became very popular and was translated into Latin and English, among other languages. Merchants, cartographers, and explorers at the time used it as a guide for their future travels and map-making.

Juan Ponce de León (1460–1521)

EXPLORER

Born in San Servos, León, Spain, Juan Ponce de León served as a soldier fighting Muslims in southern Spain in the early 1490s. He then sailed on **Christopher Columbus**'s second expedition to the Americas in 1493. In HISPANIOLA (modern HAITI and the DOMINICAN REPUBLIC), Ponce de León was among those who captured and enslaved Native Americans rising up against Spanish rule. When Columbus made a return trip to Spain, Ponce de León stayed in Santo Domingo (modern Dominican Republic) and was appointed governor of the province of Higuey.

While serving as governor, Ponce de León heard tales of gold in the nearby island of Borinquén (modern PUERTO RICO) from Native Americans, and decided to check it out for himself. He sailed there with a crew, conquered the island, and claimed it for SPAIN. In return, the Spanish king made Ponce de León governor of Borinquén in 1510. Yet Ponce de León was removed from the position less than two years later when the king learned of his extreme brutality toward the Borinquén people under his control.

THE FOUNTAIN OF YOUTH

Ponce de León had a new expedition in mind anyway. He asked and was granted permission from the king to find, conquer, and colonize the island of Bimini (now in the BAHAMAS). The conquistador, by this time in his fifties, had heard from Native Americans that the island held the legendary fountain of youth, the spring that gave people eternal life and youth.

On March 3, 1513, Ponce de León sailed from Borinquén with 200 men on three ships—the *Santa Maria*, the *Santiago*, and the *San Cristobal*. After docking in Grand Turk Island and San Salvador, they reached the eastern coast of present-day ST. AUGUSTINE, FLORIDA, on April 2. To commemorate the fact that it was Easter Sunday, Ponce de León named the land *Pascua Florida* ("feast of the flowers") as he claimed it for Spain. He only ventured on land a few times, however, as the inhabitants were fierce and not quite as afraid of the Spaniards' guns as other Native Americans had been.

The fleet left Florida on April 8. Believing it was an island, they attempted to sail around it, by venturing south to present-day Key West. There, the crew fought with Native Americans before sailing up the west coast of Florida, and then south in the warm ocean current now called the Gulf Stream—which was a helpful key to future Spanish trips from Europe to America. They sailed to CUBA and then headed north, in another attempt to find Bimini. They were unsuccessful, but did find Andros Island.

Back in Puerto Rico in September, Ponce de León fought for years against the Carib tribe of Native Americans, who were rebelling against Spanish rule. For his efforts on behalf of Spain, the king named him Captain General in 1514 and encouraged him to search for Bimini again—though again he had no success.

In 1521 Ponce de León received permission to colonize Florida. He sailed with a crew of 200 people and 50 horses to the west coast of Florida. Upon landing, his crew was met by Native Americans who wounded many of them with poison-tipped arrows. One arrow pierced through Ponce de León's armor and hit his thigh. His men carried him back to the ship and sailed to Havana, Cuba, to find a doctor. Ponce de León died of his wounds in Havana, and was later buried in San Juan, Puerto Rico.

John Wesley Powell (1834–1902)

EXPLORER · ETHNOLOGIST · GEOLOGIST

John Wesley Powell developed an interest in nature at an early age. As a teen, he studied botany, zoology, and geology without the aid of a teacher and explored parts of WISCONSIN, ILLINOIS, IOWA, and MISSOURI. At age 22, Powell sailed down the MISSISSIPPI alone in a rowboat, collecting shells, minerals, and artifacts along the way. A year later he rowed down the OHIO RIVER, and explored the ILLINOIS RIVER the following year.

Powell then got caught up in the battles raging around him. He fought in America's Civil War on the Union side and lost his right arm at the Battle of Shiloh in 1862. He returned to fight in the battles of Champion Hill, Black River Bridge, and Franklin,

among others, before becoming a geology professor at Illinois Wesleyan University in Bloomington. In 1867, while a lecturer at what is now Illinois State University at Normal, he began a series of expeditions to the ROCKY MOUNTAINS and surrounding canyons.

GRIM DETERMINATION

On May 24, 1869, Powell led nine men in two boats on a treacherous 900-mile (1,450-km), three-month journey down the uncharted GREEN and COLORADO rivers and through the GRAND CANYON to the Virgin River (now submerged under Lake Mead). The ride, beginning at the mouth of the Green River in Wyoming, was rocky and full of surprises; one boat and its supplies had to be abandoned when it began to sink. At one point, Powell climbed a peak in the Rockies to prove that the rivers that drained into the Colorado River could provide a passage from the Rockies to the Pacific. Powell was awed by the journey, but some of his men didn't like the risk. A month into the trip, an Englishman named Frank Goodman told Powell, "I've had more excitement than a man deserves in a lifetime. I'm leaving."

Powell continued on into the muddy and rocky Colorado River, described by some people at the time as "too thick to drink and too thin to plow." In present-day Separation Canyon, three men complained to Powell "how we surely will all die if we continue on this journey." Powell insisted on finishing the exploration and the three men walked off.

From 1871 to 1879, Powell led a federally funded mapping survey of the Colorado Plateau (modern ARIZONA, NEW MEXICO, UTAH, and NEVADA) and promoted conservative land-utilization projects to the government. He theorized on how the plateau was created and made note of the fact that rivers in the Uinta Mountains maintained their water level throughout and cut through the mountains. Powell also conducted interviews with the Hopi, Shivwits, and other Native Americans, and studied their lands and migrations.

In 1879, Powell became the first director of the U.S. Bureau of Ethnology of the Smithsonian Institution in Washington, D.C. Within two years, he published the first complete classification and distribution map of 58 Native American languages of the UNITED STATES and CANADA.

From 1881–1892, Powell did double duty, also serving as director at the Bureau of Ethnology and U.S. Geological Survey (USGS). At USGS, he worked on mapping water sources and irrigation projects. Powell died from a cerebral hemorrhage at his summer home in Haven, MAINE, and was buried in Arlington National Cemetery.

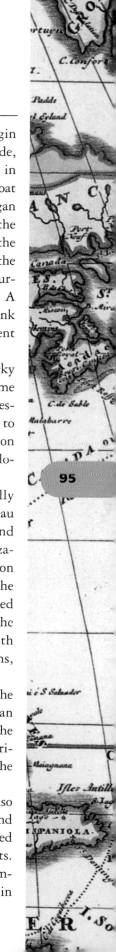

Pytheas (c. 300 BC)

EXPLORER

Greek astronomer and mathematician Pytheas lived in Massilia, a Greek colony on the northern shore of the MEDITERRANEAN SEA. Massilia was a center of trade, rivaling Carthage, the Phoenician colony off the coast of North Africa. For centuries the Greeks imported tin overland from a place called Europa (modern Cornwall, ENGLAND) to make bronze tools and weapons. The transportation of the needed material was very expensive, but no one dared to find a sea route for the tin because they would have to pass through the Pillars of Hercules (modern STRAITS OF GIBRALTAR) to get to the Atlantic Ocean. The Carthaginians controlled the Pillars of Hercules and warned the Greeks of dangerous whirlpools and monsters, which they said ruled the ocean.

In approximately 325 BC, Pytheas decided to become the first to sail through the Pillars of Hercules in order to find the source of tin. He made his way into the Atlantic, and sailed out of sight of land—a shocking deed then because many great minds of the time feared he could fall off the edge of the Earth.

Pytheas directed himself by measuring the shadow cast by the sun to determine his latitude. Doing so, he was able to sail along the western shore of present-day SPAIN, stop at the Phoenician city of Gades (modern CÁDIZ, SPAIN), and then sail east into the BAY OF BISCAY and north along the coast of FRANCE. He docked in what is now known as the Channel Islands, and learned from local people that the Tin Islands were actually one day's sail of about 100 miles (161 km) north.

THE COUNTRY OF TIN

Pytheas finally found what he called the "country of tin" and saw the underground tin mines. He learned that men normally carried the ore to an island from which European traders brought it home. Pytheas also met early British whom he called "the Keltic tribes" and noted their customs, wooded land, and cold, rainy weather. He felt they were primitive, eating simple foods and drinking curmi, a beer made from barley. As the first Greek to visit the British Isles, Pytheas explored most of Britain on foot and decided it was triangular in shape and measured its circumference at a close-to-accurate 4,000 miles (6,400 km).

The Keltics told Pytheas about Thule, which he believed was the "outermost of all countries." Pytheas sailed north for six days until he found a land where people ate grain and wild berries and drank an alcoholic beverage made from honey, called mead. Pytheas described long days with the sun up and a "sea of ice" that no one could sail or walk on (historians believe this was NORWAY or ICELAND.)

On his six-year, 7,000-mile (11,265-km) journey, Pytheas became the first European to reach the Arctic Circle and the first person to make factual claims that the world did not consist of an ocean around a central land mass. Upon his return, Pytheas sacrificed a bull to the god of the sea, Poseidon, to thank him for a safe trip, and wrote a book, *On the Ocean*. In it, he described his voyage and made the first observation that the moon affects tides. Still, few Greeks believed Pytheas's claims but no one would verify his findings by sailing through the Pillars of Hercules until Rome defeated

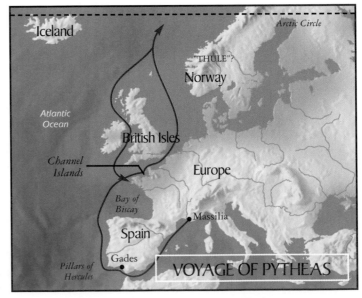

VOYAGE OF PYTHEAS

Carthage in 146 BC. The book was lost, but Greek historian Polybius's (c. 200 BC to 118 BC) later wrote an account of Pytheas's travels and observations.

Sir Walter Raleigh (c. 1554–1618)

EXPLORER

W alter Raleigh was born into a poor family related to British nobility and lived in a farmhouse in Hayes Barton, Devonshire, ENGLAND. His half brother, Humphrey Gilbert, was educated at Eton and Oxford and taught Raleigh how to read maps and charts. He also instructed Raleigh to use an astrolabe to measure the altitude of the sun to navigate a ship, and explained what he had heard about the New World (America) across the Atlantic Ocean. So influenced by Gilbert, the teenaged Raleigh joined him to fight on the Huguenot (French Protestant) side of France's Wars of Religion around 1569.

At the end of the war, Raleigh attended the University of Oxford and Middle Temple law college. He dropped out of school early, however, because he was so eager to travel. In 1578 Raleigh sailed to the New World with Gilbert on an exploratory trip that inspired him to later found an English empire there.

In 1580, Raleigh joined an effort to suppress a rebellion in Ireland. His good work caught the attention of Queen Elizabeth I, who took a liking to Raleigh. She knighted him in 1584, and granted him monopolies in wine and cloth trades as well as various government positions, all of which made him rich and powerful.

FIRST NEW WORLD COLONY

In 1584, Raleigh decided to set up the first English colony in the New World on Roanoke Island. Though the queen forbade him from traveling there, Raleigh sent four expeditions to Roanoke in the 1580s. The settlement at Roanoke failed, as did another colony Raleigh attempted to create two years later.

Feeling quite frustrated, Raleigh decided to concentrate his explorations on present-day South America. In 1595, he explored the coast of TRINIDAD and what is now GUYANA, captured the town of San Josef, and made an expedition up the ORINOCO RIVER searching for El Dorado, the fabled city of gold. Upon Sir Raleigh's return, the queen learned he had secretly married one of her maids of honor. In retaliation, she took away some of his special privileges.

The queen was succeeded by King James I, who disliked Raleigh for his bold ideas and proud nature. In 1603 Raleigh was accused and convicted of plotting against the king. Though Raleigh was sentenced to death, King James changed the sentence to life imprisonment. Raleigh spent the next 13 years in surprising comfort with his wife, son, and servants in the Tower of London. During this time, he worked on scientific experiments and wrote a volume of his *History of the World* (1614), which, along with his poems, helped him gain an importance among intellectuals.

Heir to the throne, Prince Henry, tried to secure Raleigh's release from prison, to no avail. When the prince died in 1612, Raleigh proposed to give King James a good deal of gold if he would allow him to lead an expedition from the Orinoco River to El Dorado to find gold. The king agreed on the condition that Raleigh didn't interfere with the Spanish. In 1616 Raleigh made the trip, but his son and an aide attacked the Spanish settlement of San Tomás. His son was killed in the battle. Raleigh returned to England to find that King James was angry that Raleigh's party had, in fact, made trouble with the Spanish. The king invoked the death sentence originally made in 1603 and in 1618 Raleigh was beheaded.

Johan Reinhard (1943–)

ANTHROPOLOGIST·MOUNTAIN CLIMBER

Born and raised in New Lenox, Illinois, Johan Reinhard took a summer job at age 16 digging telegraph line poles. At night, he and his fellow workers would challenge each other to boxing matches. "I learned I could put up with a hell of a lot," he later joked. "I thought I would make a good explorer." Reinhard studied anthropology and archaeology at the University of Arizona before leaving in his sophomore year to hitchhike through Europe. He learned German and was accepted into a Ph.D. program for anthropology at the University of Vienna, AUSTRIA.

While in Austria, Reinhard participated in the country's first underwater archaeological research and conducted research of Roman shipwrecks in the MEDITERRANEAN SEA. After three years, Reinhard moved to NEPAL to work on his thesis.

Reinhard learned the Nepali language, directed Peace Corps training projects, and climbed MOUNT EVEREST (29,028 feet [8,848 m]) as part of the 1976 American Everest Expedition. He also was part of a team to make one of the first rafting trips down Himalayan rivers, and assisted with anthropological research in Nepal, TIBET, BHUTAN, and Garwhal and Sikkim, INDIA. Reinhard's studies of the last remaining members of two hunter/gatherer societies in the HIMALAYAS—the Kusunda and Raute tribes—gained international attention as Reinhard managed to analyze texts in the Kusunda language, which at the time was spoken by only three people in the world.

INCAN MUMMIES

In the 1980s, Reinhard learned Spanish and changed the focus of his expeditions to South America. From 1989 to 1992, he led the first Andean underwater archaeological research project in LAKE TITICACA, the world's highest navigable lake. He also made more than 100 climbs in the ANDES, discovering numerous high-altitude Inca ritual sites complete with mummies—children sacrificed to the gods more than 500 years ago.

In 1995, Reinhard was climbing AMPATO, a 20,700-foot (6,309-km) snow covered volcano in PERU when he and his assistant saw an Incan mummy.

Nicknamed the "Ice Maiden," it was the first frozen female mummy found in South America. To keep it frozen, Reinhard attempted to carry it down the volcano wrapped in plastic and attached to his backpack as snow fell and a volcano erupted nearby. The experience was so dangerous that he finally had to leave the mummy at 19,900 feet (6,066 m) and climb into a tent 700 feet (213 m) below. He returned the next morning to retrieve it.

Reinhard uncovered 14 more Incan mummies on a 1996–1999 Andes expedition. At Mount Llullaillaco (22,000 feet [6,706 m]) in Argentina, his six-person team carried more than a ton of supplies to base camp and spent five days adjusting to the altitude and

bringing supplies to a higher camp. They used their fingers to uncover three fragile, but well-preserved mummies on the world's highest archaeological site. To keep the bodies frozen, they buried them in snow until dry ice could be brought. Only then did Reinhard make a descent to Catholic University in AREQUIPA, Peru, where the mummies were studied.

Reinhard's research continues to focus on the sacred beliefs and cultural practices of mountain peoples, especially in the Andes and the Himalayas. "People look at what I've done and make the comparison to Indiana Jones," said Reinhard. "I don't really like that because what they are thinking about is the adventure.... I think about it more as delving into the mystery and the knowledge I can find."

Sally Ride (1951–)

ASTRONAUT

Sally Kristen Ride was the eldest of two daughters born to a political science professor and a teacher in Los Angeles, California. Though she was quiet and shy, Ride loved sports, especially softball and tennis. In fact, as a teen, she ranked nationally as an amateur. In high school, Ride found an interest in science, specifically physiology and problem solving. She went to Stanford University, obtaining degrees in physics and English in 1973 and five years later a Ph.D. in astrophysics.

While finishing her Ph.D. dissertation and serving as a research assistant, Ride applied to NASA's astronaut training program. After a series of interviews and physical and mental tests, she was accepted on January 16, 1978. Ride's acceptance into the program was mainly due to her strong research projects, including an in-depth study on X-rays given off by stars, which NASA hoped would help make it possible to one day send energy to Earth from space stations. During training at Johnson Space Center in Houston, Texas, Ride obtained her pilot's license and studied math, computers, and how to operate every wire and circuit on the shuttle. She began weightlifting and ran 4 miles (6 km) a day during the week and 8 to 10 miles (13 to 16 km) on weekends.

For two years, she studied her assignment: the Remote Manipulator System (RMS), a 50-foot (15-m) mechanical arm that moves objects, such as satellites, around the payload bay. She also served as the first female capsule communicator, the only person at Mission Control who can speak to the astronauts in space, on two *Columbia* missions.

FIRST TIME IN SPACE

On June 18, 1983, aboard the shuttle *Challenger*, Ride became the first American woman in space. "I did not come to NASA to make history," she said. "It's important to me that people don't think I was picked for this flight because I am a woman." As a flight engineer/mission specialist, Ride used her RMS skills to launch two communications satellites and launch and retrieve a test satellite with astronaut John Fabian. During the shuttle's 98 orbits around Earth, Ride was also responsible for seven experiments, including those on ants, glassmaking, and plant and crystal growth.

She later took part in the 100th space flight from October 5–13, 1984. This time a crew of seven, including Kathryn Sullivan, the first American woman to walk in space and, coincidentally, Ride's second grade classmate, accompanied her. The trip had many mechanical difficulties. Chief among these was when Ride had to use the robotic arm to fold a large radar panel that wouldn't close.

As Ride was preparing for a third flight, a *Challenger* mission with seven astronauts aboard—including the first civilian in space, teacher Christa McAuliffe—exploded 3 minutes after take-off on January 28, 1986. Ride served on the commission investigating the cause of the accident, which killed everyone aboard. She decided she would never fly into space again.

She resigned from NASA on her birthday in 1987 and began work at Stanford University's Center for International Security and Arms Control. Two years later, Ride became director of the California Space Institute at the Scripps Institution of Oceanography and professor of physics at the University of California at San Diego. She continues to research at the University of California at San Diego, focusing on the theory of free electron lasers.

Sacagawea (c. 1786–1812)

EXPLORER·TRANSLATOR

Sacagawea was born into the Lemhi Shoshone tribe (also called Snake), who lived in present-day southeastern IDAHO and southwest MONTANA. Around 1800, the young girl was captured by a tribe of Hidatsa at Three Forks, where three rivers join to form the MISSOURI RIVER. Four years later, Sacagawea was purchased by and married to French-Canadian fur trapper Toussaint Charbonneau.

Meriwether Lewis and William Clark's Corps of Discovery, an expedition to take notes on and map the UNITED STATES to the Pacific Ocean, spent a winter in present-day NORTH DAKOTA at Fort Mandan in November 1804. They hired Charbonneau as a translator and Sacagawea came along to interpret the Shoshone language. By then, she was about 16 and pregnant. Early in the expedition Sacagawea gave birth to her first child, a son named Jean Baptiste, who was nicknamed "Pomp." Though the birth was difficult and she almost died, Sacagawea continued to travel with the Corps—numbering 23 men and Lewis and Clark—and carried her son in a cradleboard.

DEDICATED FRIEND

Sacagawea not only helped the Corps relate to Native Americans, but also aided with knowledge of local geography, edible plants, and cooking. She showed her support for the mission when the boat she was riding in almost capsized during a storm. She sat in the stern and grabbed the most valuable supplies and surveying instruments that were being swept overboard into the water, later diving in to grab more supplies. Sacagawea's dedication earned her the reverence of many of the men, especially Clark, who nicknamed her "Janey."

On July 27, 1805, the Corps reached Three Forks. Sacagawea assured them that the Shoshones, whom they hoped would give them horses, were nearby. When the Corps reached the Shoshone camp, they were met by Chief Cameahwait and 60 warriors. Sacagawea ran to the chief and hugged him—he was her brother.

At the end of August, the Corps continued westward with Shoshone guides and horses. The next month they crossed the ROCKY MOUNTAINS, battling snow and a low food supply. Sacagawea was not familiar with the land, but still traveled with the men because, as Clark said, she "reconstitutes all the Indians as to our friendly intentions—a woman with a party of men is a token of peace." They reached the Pacific by mid-November.

On the return trip, the Corps settled for the winter near the mouth of the COLUMBIA RIVER. Everyone was hungry, so Sacagawea, Clark, and others took meat from a beached whale. The men, unaware at how the concentrated fats would affect their malnourished bodies, overate and became sick. Sacagawea spent days searching for fennel roots, knowing their aromatic seeds would cure them.

They continued traveling east on March 23, and Lewis and Clark parted company to cover more ground. With Clark, Sacagawea led the men to the Yellowstone River. When they returned to Fort Mandan, Charbonneau was paid $500 for his services, and he returned with Sacagawea and their son to the Hidatsa village at the mouth of the Knife River.

Though there is some disagreement among scholars as to where and when Sacagawea died, it is largely believed she had about four more children before dying in 1812 at Fort Manuel on the Missouri River in present-day northern SOUTH DAKOTA.

Father Junipero Serra (1713–1784)

MISSIONARY

Miguel José Serra was one of five children born to two farmers in the small Spanish island town of Petra, Majorca, but only one of two to survive to adulthood. Serra was considered a frail child, so weak that he was unable to participate in many games. Instead, he mainly spent time studying religion. His family was very religious, and regularly attended the Franciscan church of San Bernadino, where Serra also studied with friars.

Though Serra was initially rejected because of his unhealthy appearance, he entered the Franciscan Order in 1730. While serving to become a Brother, Serra spent seven hours a day in prayer and used the rest of his time to maintain the monastery. During this period, he decided that he wanted to travel to the New World (America) to work as a missionary, to help Native Americans and convert them to Catholicism. In 1731, Serra became a Brother in the Franciscan Order, and took the name Junipero.

During the next 18 years, Serra continued to study and preach in Majorca. He developed a reputation as the best speaker on the island. Yet, he was unhappy with his work.

In 1748, Father Rafael Verger decided to travel to MEXICO to work at missions there. Serra and his friend, Francisco Palou, volunteered to serve as his assistants. Three days after Easter in 1749, the three men set sail for Mexico. They spent 99 days at sea before arriving at VERACRUZ on the eastern coast. The men then walked to mission college of San Fernando in MEXICO CITY.

Serra did not like the wealth-oriented atmosphere of Mexico City. After only five months, he traveled to the Sierra Gorda, where the Mexicans were said to be unruly. Serra enjoyed his time teaching them Spanish farming techniques and weaving, and converting many to Catholicism. He soon became president of all of the areas' missions, but he yearned for more demanding, hands-on work.

CALIFORNIA MISSIONS

Finally, in 1767, Serra traveled to California. He entered California with 16 other monks, and took office in Loreto as president of all the lower-California missions. In 1769, Serra traveled to SAN DIEGO to establish a mission. Though troubled by recurring conflicts with Native Americans there, that sometimes turned deadly, Serra managed to maintain the mission. His success encouraged him to establish the Mission San Carlos in Monterey the following year.

Over the next two years, Serra opened three more missions—San Antonio, San Carlos, and San Gabriel—in California. Then, in 1772, Serra established San Luis Obispo, which became one of the most prosperous missions. Still, he had a desire to build San Buenaventura Mission in the Santa Barbara Channel. While military leaders refused to send him more supplies, Serra would not back down. He spoke directly to the viceroy in Mexico, who was worried that the colonization of CALIFORNIA was failing. Assured by Serra that stronger missions would help the colony, the viceroy approved the supplies Serra needed. Serra, in return, later gained a reputation of saving California.

After he established San Buenaventura in 1782, Serra fell ill. By 1784, he was bedridden. Realizing he was near death, Serra requested that the mission carpenter make him a simple redwood coffin. After his death, Serra grew even more popular. A large funeral was held in Monterey, as clergymen and followers begged for his possessions.

Sir Ernest Henry Shackleton

(1874–1922) EXPLORER

Ernest Henry Shackleton was the second of ten children born to a Quaker doctor and his wife in Kilkee, County Kildare, Ireland. He studied at Dulwich College in LONDON, ENGLAND, for three years before becoming a merchant marine at age 16.

In 1901 he joined the British National Antarctic Expedition led by British naval officer Robert Falcon Scott. Aboard the ship *Discovery*, Scott and his crew sailed to a base on Ross Island in hopes of reaching the SOUTH POLE. From there, Shackleton, Scott, and zoologist Edward Wilson rode horses to latitude 82° 17' south on December 30, 1902—it was the farthest south anyone had ever reached. When they returned to base, Shackleton was sent home by ship to recuperate from scurvy while the others continued their explorations.

Shackleton attempted to reach the South Pole again between 1907 and 1909 by leading the British Antarctic Expedition. After sailing to a base on Ross Island, Shackleton and three others traveled over the TRANSANTARCTIC MOUNTAINS and through the Beardmore Glacier to the pole. On January 9, 1909, they determined that they were at latitude 88° 23' south, just 111 miles (178 km) from the pole. Low food supplies forced them to turn back. "I thought you'd rather have a live donkey than a dead lion," he wrote to his wife. Upon his return, he was knighted by British king Edward VII for again setting the record for traveling the farthest south.

By late 1911, Norwegian explorer **Roald Amundsen** had reached the South Pole. Shackleton's new focus became crossing Antarctica. In 1914 he set sail with a crew of 27 from ENGLAND as leader of the British Imperial Trans-Antarctic Expedition.

> **The Shackleton family motto was *Fortitudine Vinicimus* (Latin for "endurance we conquer").**

ENDURANCE

Before reaching Antarctica, Shackleton's ship, the *Endurance*, was trapped in ice on the WEDDELL SEA on January 18, 1915. After nine months on board the ship, which was beginning to crush under the strain of the ice, Shackleton ordered his men to abandon it.

They lived for six months by floating on a pack of ice that was drifting north. When the ice broke apart, Shackleton and his crew attempted to sail for seven days in three small boats salvaged from the *Endurance*. They finally reached the uninhabited Elephant Island, where they were greeted by a blizzard.

Leaving 22 crew members behind to eat penguin meat, Shackleton and five others left to find help in one of the boats, the 23-foot-long (7-m) *James Caird*. After 16 days of sailing across the icy South Atlantic Ocean, they reached the island of SOUTH GEORGIA. Shackleton knew a whaling station was set up there, but unfortunately the men found that they landed on an uninhabited side of the island. Shackleton and two others walked nonstop for 36 hours—making the first crossing of the island's icy mountain interior—to reach the whaling station on May 20, 1916.

Shackleton did not forget the crew he left behind. After three attempts in four months, he finally reached the rest of his men at Elephant Island on August 30, sailing in a tugboat he borrowed from the Chilean government.

In 1921, while leading another expedition to Antarctica, Shackleton suffered a heart attack aboard his ship near Grytviken, South Georgia. At least ten geographical features near Antarctica, including a mountain range and coast, bear Shackleton's name.

Alan Shepard (1923–1998)

ASTRONAUT

Alan Shepard, born in East Derry, New Hampshire, was the son of a retired army colonel. Though his mother wouldn't allow him to play sports, he'd sneak off after school to ride horses and play tennis. After riding on a plane for the first time at age 14, Shepard decided he wanted to be a pilot. He attended the U.S. Naval Academy in Annapolis, Maryland, and was assigned to the destroyer *Cogswell* in the Pacific Ocean at age 21.

By 1947, Shepard had spent enough time in naval flight training to realize his dream. He attended test pilot school at Patuxent River Naval Station in Maryland, but was almost kicked out for bad behavior. In June 1952, he looped around the Chesapeake Bay Bridge while testing a jet. He later flew so low over an Ocean City, Maryland, beach that he blew the bikini tops off girls who didn't have them fastened (the act was caught on film by a newspaper photographer). Shepard received warnings both times, but took them seriously only when he was threatened with dismissal after he attempted another low-flying act over the Naval Air Station in Chincoteague, Virginia.

Shepard was sent to the Pacific twice during the Korean War. One rainy night with his navigation equipment not working, he landed his plane on a destroyer with less than five minutes of fuel remaining. His courage, quick thinking, and articulate nature were well known in the military and he was recommended to NASA.

FIRST AMERICAN IN SPACE

After being selected as one of NASA's first seven astronauts in April 1959, Shepard trained for more than a year before learning on January 19, 1961, that he would make the first flight. NASA, still unsure how a living thing would fare with weightlessness and high G-forces, sent two chimpanzees into space early in the year. "I protested again and again," said Shepard, "but NASA insisted the little ape go first." The Soviet Union (modern RUSSIA) sent the first man in space on April 12, frustrating Shepard who dreamed of being the first man in space. Instead he had to settle for being the first American.

On May 2, just hours before lift-off, Shepard's launch aboard Mercury capsule *Freedom 7* was announced publicly. His flight at Cape Canaveral, Florida, was cancelled due to low cloud cover, but on May 5 fellow astronaut John Glenn helped him lay on his back in the 10-foot-high (3-m) by 6-foot-wide (1.8-m) capsule. Shepard tested the radios and switch settings and then tried to relax for almost three hours as the launch was delayed by technical problems. At one point, he told ground control, "Why don't you fix your little problems and light this candle." Finally, Shepard shot 116 miles (187 km) up on a 15-minute sub-orbit above Earth. The capsule splashed down in the Atlantic Ocean and was picked up by a helicopter.

Shepard took a break from flying in 1963 when NASA flight surgeons found he had an inner ear disorder. During that time, he helped monitor the training of other astronauts and flight experiments. After surgery, Shepard was ready to fly again in 1969. Two years later, he launched into space aboard *Apollo 14* (January 13–February 9) as commander with astronauts Stuart Roosa and Edgar Mitchell. They spent 9 hours and 17 minutes making observations on the moon and carried more than 100 pounds (45 kg) of moon rock back to Earth. "The tears just rolled down my cheeks," he said later of the landing. "Every time I look back at the moon, I think of being there." During a live television transmission, Shepard celebrated by hitting two golf balls into a meteor crater with a six-iron club he had snuck aboard the craft.

Shepard retired from NASA and the Navy on August 1, 1974, and became a businessman in Houston, Texas.

Jedediah Strong Smith (1798–1831)

EXPLORER·TRADER

Jedediah Strong Smith was born in Bainbridge, NEW YORK, and made his first trip west to trap furs while he was in his teens. In 1822 he joined the Rocky Mountain Fur Company on a fur trading expedition along the Snake River to the ROCKY MOUNTAINS. He continued to trade for the remainder of the decade.

THE GREAT SALT LAKE

Smith was on a trading expedition in 1824 when his party rediscovered the South Pass, a passage from WYOMING to the Northwest. He became friendly with fur trader/explorer William Henry Ashley, and took over Ashley's business with two other men in 1826. Smith's first goal was to lead a party of 17 from the GREAT SALT LAKE across the Mojave Desert to Mission San Gabriel (near modern LOS ANGELES), CALIFORNIA, to find trade routes and gain fur-trapping rights. The desert crossing was an especially grueling 15-day trek made difficult by a blazing sun and food and water shortages. Yet they made it to their destination and became the first Americans to enter California from the east.

Smith had hoped to travel through California north into OREGON. Yet California was under Mexican rule, and the state's governor, suspicious of Smith's actions, would not allow his trading party to travel freely. Thus, Smith decided in 1827 to instead travel to the American River near Sacramento, cross the SIERRA NEVADA and the desert, and return to the Great Salt Lake. Again Smith made a name for himself, this time by becoming the first American to return from California on an overland route and the first European to cross the GREAT SALT LAKE DESERT.

Later in the year, Smith led 18 men overland in an attempt to make the same trips backwards, traveling from Great Salt Lake to southern California. On the way, his party was met by a tribe of Mojave who killed ten of his men. Smith and the others managed to reach California, only to be jailed by Mexican authorities who were unhappy Smith had returned.

DANGEROUS JOURNEY

In 1828, Smith's party was set free and proceeded north through the Sacramento Valley. When they couldn't find a path through the Sierras, they crossed the COAST RANGE MOUNTAINS and crossed and/or followed the Klamath, Umpqua, and Willamette Rivers before reaching Oregon. On the journey Native Americans—this time from the Umpqua tribe—attacked them again. Only two of Smith's men survived.

A shaken Smith retired from Rocky Mountain trade in 1830, after he had successfully opened the coastal route from California to Fort Vancouver (modern Vancouver, Washington) on the COLUMBIA RIVER. The following year, Smith began trading in SANTA FE. He was attempting to reach Santa Fe via the Santa Fe Trail when a tribe of Comanche at a water hole near the Cimarron River killed him.

Hernando de Soto (c. 1500–1542)

EXPLORER

Hernando de Soto was born in Jérez de los Caballeros, Spain, near the Portuguese border. He received an education at the University of Salamanaca, and in about 1519 traveled to DARIEN in present-day PANAMA as an aide to the governor. Five years later, de Soto joined Francisco Hernandez de Córdoba on an expedition to NICARAGUA, where they founded the city of Granada. De Soto stayed there and became wealthy, due in part to his work in slave trading.

In 1530 explorer **Francisco Pizarro** asked de Soto to help in his third expedition to PERU, where he hoped to take over the Inca Empire. By December 1531, the men were in Peru and had traveled into the ANDES to the city of CAJAMARCA, where Inca ruler Atahualpa lived. Once in the city, on November 15, 1532, Pizarro sent de Soto to meet the leader—and he became the first European to do so.

At a dinner the next night, Pizarro took Atahualpa prisoner. Though de Soto argued against it, Pizarro later killed the Inca leader. Still, de Soto accepted his share of Inca gold when Pizarro took over the Empire.

De Soto returned to Spain in 1536 as a rich man. King Charles V of Spain named him governor of the newly conquered areas in the Americas: CUBA and FLORIDA. De Soto had heard **Álvar Núñez Cabeza de Vaca**'s stories of the "Seven Cities of Cíbola," and was eager to colonize the mostly uncharted land in Florida and take its gold.

IN SEARCH OF THE SEVEN CITIES

On April 7, 1538, de Soto left Spain with about 600 men and 200 horses. After sailing to Havana, Cuba, to pick up supplies, they sailed on to Florida. They docked at TAMPA BAY on May 27, 1539, and traveled north along the coast of the GULF OF MEXICO.

The Spaniards settled in the town of Apalachen, near present-day Tallahassee, on October 6, 1539. Though they fought with local Native Americans, they spent the winter there before heading to Cofitachequi, an area 75 miles from the mouth of the Savannah River in eastern GEORGIA. They had heard that a rich queen lived there, but upon their arrival they found that her only treasures were a few salt-water pearls.

Following other reports of gold, the Spaniards crossed the APPALACHIANS and traveled to Burns Island in the Tennessee River. Again, they found no gold. Undaunted, the men traveled south and met with Native American chiefs, including Tuscaloosa, on the shores of the Alabama River. Yet, de Soto made many enemies of other Native Americans by taking their grain, burning villages, and enslaving them. After battling Native Americans, the Spaniards headed northwest to set up a winter camp approximately 125 miles (201 km) east of the MISSISSIPPI RIVER.

An attack by the Chickasaw tribe on March 4, 1541, resulted in the death of 12 Spaniards. Yet, de Soto and his men continued. Finally, they became the first Europeans to see the Mississippi River, most likely near present-day Memphis, Tennessee, on May 8, 1541. They built rafts and crossed the river on June 18 so they could reach the Ozark Mountains, another area where de Soto believed gold would be found.

By the time they reached ARKANSAS, the Spaniards had explored at least 350,000 square miles (906,000 sq km) in the southeastern UNITED STATES. Still having found no gold, but having lost many men, de Soto decided to go back to the Mississippi and sail down to the sea. At the river, de Soto developed a fever and died. The 311 surviving expedition members sailed down the Mississippi and continued along the Gulf Coast before reaching a settlement in Pánuco, MEXICO, in September 1543.

Sir Henry Morton Stanley

(1841–1904) SOLDIER·JOURNALIST·EXPLORER

Born John Rowlands in Denbigh, Wales, Henry Morton Stanley's parents abandoned him before his first birthday and left him in the care of poor relatives. As a youth he worked odd jobs before sailing to NEW ORLEANS, LOUISIANA, at age 18 while serving as a cabin boy. There, he met a merchant named Henry Stanley, who found him a job and made him part of his family. As a sign of respect, Rowlands changed his name to Henry Morton Stanley.

Two years later, when the American Civil War began, 21-year-old Stanley joined the Confederate army but was soon captured. Upon release, Stanley joined the U.S. Navy on trading expeditions. In 1867, he moved to New York City and worked as a reporter for the *New York Herald*.

IN SEARCH OF LIVINGSTONE

In the next few years, Stanley reported on the opening of the SUEZ CANAL in EGYPT, as well as other stories in Crimea (in modern UKRAINE), PERSIA (modern IRAN), and INDIA. Yet his most famous assignment was to find Scottish missionary David Livingstone, whose whereabouts were unknown—he had not been heard from by anyone outside Central Africa for five years.

In March 1781, Stanley guided 192 men eastward from ZANZIBAR toward LAKE TANGANYIKA, where Livingstone was last seen. After eight months, Stanley entered the town of Ujiji, and on November 10, spotted a sick-looking 58-year-old Livingstone. He greeted him by saying, "Dr. Livingstone, I presume?"—a phrase that became famous around the world when the story was picked up by newspapers. "Yes," answered Livingstone, "You have brought me new life."

Stanley and his team gave Livingstone much-needed supplies, nursed him back to health, and then joined him as he explored the northern end of Lake Tanganyika. At the end of the journey, Stanley wrote *How I Found Livingstone* (1872), which became a best seller in Britain.

After Livingstone's death in 1873, the *New York Herald* and *London Daily Telegraph* cosponsored Stanley on an expedition to answer questions about Central Africa that remained from Livingstone's notes. In

October 1874, Stanley left Zanzibar with 359 others and headed toward LAKE VICTORIA. While on the lake, Stanley and his party were involved in several battles with African tribes, killing dozens of tribesmen.

After circumnavigating the lake, Stanley traveled south to explore Lake Tanganyika, and then led his party down the LUALABA and CONGO RIVERS to the Atlantic Ocean, maneuvering through thick forests and uncharted waters. Water-born diseases and attacks by more African tribes further hindered the approximately 2,000-mile (3,000-km) journey. Only 108 of the 359 people in Stanley's party finished the trek. Yet, Stanley proudly offered up a great deal of information, including the size of Lake Victoria and Lake Tanganyika and the fact that the Congo River was a navigable waterway for commercial ventures to reach Central Africa.

Belgian King Leopold II hired Stanley to help him open the lower Congo to commerce. Between 1879 and 1884, Stanley aided in constructing a road from the lower river to present-day Pool Malebo, where the river was navigable.

Stanley's next adventure was to help Great Britain keep its hold on East Africa. While trying to find Mehmed Emin Pasha, a governor in the Egyptian Sudan, and remove him from power, Stanley discovered that the Semliki River linked LAKE ALBERT and LAKE EDWARD. This fact later helped further trade in the area.

Stanley won a seat in the British Parliament from 1895 to 1900, and was knighted by Queen Victoria in 1899. The *London Times* later reported his death with the headline: "Stanley is Dead, One Presumes."

Junko Tabei (1939–)

MOUNTAIN CLIMBER

Junko Ishibashi was the fifth of six children born to a family in the Japanese town of Miharumachi. At age ten she took part in a class trip to climb Mount Asahi (6,233 feet [1,900 m]) and Mount Chausu (6,365 feet [1,941 m]) in Nasu, and she became hooked on climbing. "It wasn't like a competition," she said in Sports Illustrated in 1996. "Even if you go slow, you can make it to the top. Or, if you must, you can quit in the middle."

The 4-foot 9-inch (1.4-m) Ishibashi climbed in high school, but in 1958 she enrolled in Tokyo's Showa Women's University to become a teacher. After graduation, she joined local climbing clubs.

THE JOSHI-TOHAN CLUB

In the early 1960s, Ishibashi climbed all of JAPAN's major peaks, including Mount Fuji (12,388 feet [3,776 m]). While scaling a mountain near Tokyo, she met Masanobu Tabei, a well-known Japanese mountaineer. After they married, the couple climbed together until 1969, when the new Mrs. Tabei decided to form Japan's first climbing club for women, the Joshi-Tohan Club. The following year the team scaled ANNAPURNA (26,500 feet [8,077 m]) in NEPAL.

By 1971, Tabei decided her team was ready to attempt MOUNT EVEREST, the world's highest mountain at 29,028 feet (8,848 m) tall. She applied for a permit to make the first all-female climb, but was told the mountain's schedule was full until late 1974. Tabei spent much of the next three years finding financial sponsorship for the climb and editing the Physical Society of Japan's journal. Finding funding was difficult, so Tabei and her teammates took second jobs, Tabei as a piano teacher. The Tokyo newspaper *Yomiuri Shimbun* as well as Nihon Television later added funding.

In mid-December 1974, Tabei arrived in KATMANDU to

supervise the hundreds of porters she hired to carry the women's 15 tons of supplies to the Everest Base Camp. By mid-March the team was at Base Camp. They spent the next two months climbing up and down from Camp I to VI to adjust to the lack of oxygen.

At about 12:30 AM on May 4, 1975, Tabei and 14 other Japanese female climbers were asleep at Camp II, when they were awakened by a thunderous sound. Tabei knew it was an avalanche. She and the four teammates in her tent, still in their sleeping bags, were thrown around as a wave of snow and ice pounded down. Their tent tangled around them, slamming them into each other and the mountain terrain. Tabei had a vision of her two-and-a-half-year-old daughter and then blacked out.

She awoke in great pain to find that her team's six Sherpas had dragged her out of the snow by her ankles. Her body was covered with bruises and the pain was so great in her lower back and legs that she could hardly stand. Yet she was insistent on remaining team leader. Within two days, Tabei stood in front as the women continued their climb up Everest.

On May 16 at 12:30 PM, Tabei became the first woman to summit Everest. After the climb down, she made personal appearances around Japan. Tabei tried to play down the fact that she was the first woman to make the climb, pointing out that she was the 36th person to reach the summit.

After having another child, Tabei climbed many of the world's tallest peaks: MOUNT KILIMANJARO in Tanzania, Argentina's ACONCAGUA, the U.S.'s MOUNT MCKINLEY, Russia's EL'BRUS, Antarctica's VINSON MASSIF, Indonesia's Carstensz Pyramid, and Mexico's Pico de Orizaba, among others. In 1992, Tabei became the first woman to climb the tallest peak on every continent. Her goal since then has been to climb the highest peak in every country.

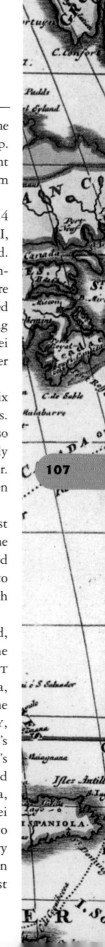

Abel Tasman (c. 1603–c. 1659)

EXPLORER

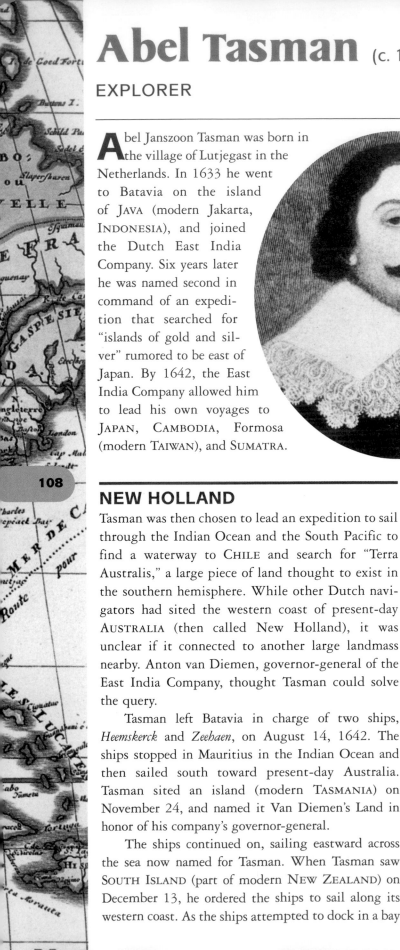

Abel Janszoon Tasman was born in the village of Lutjegast in the Netherlands. In 1633 he went to Batavia on the island of JAVA (modern Jakarta, INDONESIA), and joined the Dutch East India Company. Six years later he was named second in command of an expedition that searched for "islands of gold and silver" rumored to be east of Japan. By 1642, the East India Company allowed him to lead his own voyages to JAPAN, CAMBODIA, Formosa (modern TAIWAN), and SUMATRA.

NEW HOLLAND

Tasman was then chosen to lead an expedition to sail through the Indian Ocean and the South Pacific to find a waterway to CHILE and search for "Terra Australis," a large piece of land thought to exist in the southern hemisphere. While other Dutch navigators had sited the western coast of present-day AUSTRALIA (then called New Holland), it was unclear if it connected to another large landmass nearby. Anton van Diemen, governor-general of the East India Company, thought Tasman could solve the query.

Tasman left Batavia in charge of two ships, *Heemskerck* and *Zeehaen*, on August 14, 1642. The ships stopped in Mauritius in the Indian Ocean and then sailed south toward present-day Australia. Tasman sited an island (modern TASMANIA) on November 24, and named it Van Diemen's Land in honor of his company's governor-general.

The ships continued on, sailing eastward across the sea now named for Tasman. When Tasman saw SOUTH ISLAND (part of modern NEW ZEALAND) on December 13, he ordered the ships to sail along its western coast. As the ships attempted to dock in a bay

to come ashore six days later, island inhabitants killed four crew members. Tasman decided it would be fitting to name the body of water, Massacre Bay (modern GOLDEN BAY).

SOUTH PACIFIC

Next, Tasman ordered his ships to continue along the west coast of NORTH ISLAND (part of modern New Zealand). He named the islands of New Zealand, Staten Land, referring to the States of Holland. Continuing north, Tasman discovered TONGA on January 21 and the FIJI ISLANDS on February 6. The ships then turned northwest and stopped in New Guinea, before returning to Batavia on June 15, 1643. Although ten men died from illness while on the journey, it was considered a success. Tasman reported that he didn't see mainland Australia, but he had sailed between it and ANTARCTICA, proving that Australia was a separate continent.

Tasman led a 1644 expedition to the southwest coast of PAPUA NEW GUINEA and Australia's northern coast, during which he mapped the GULF OF CARPENTARIA. He went on to guide trading voyages to Sumatra and Siam (modern THAILAND), as well as lead a fleet against the Spaniards in the PHILIPPINES.

Mutiny on the Bounty

ALTHOUGH TASMAN discovered Fiji, and British Captain James Cook explored the islands about 130 years later, credit for mapping the islands goes to British explorer William Bligh. He sailed around Fiji in a small boat after being thrown off his ship, the *Bounty*, by his mutinous crew.

Valentina Tereshkova (1937–)

COSMONAUT·PARACHUTIST

Born the second of three children to a tractor driver and textile plant worker in the rural village of Maslennikovo, Yaroslavl, United Soviet Socialist Republic (modern RUSSIA), Valentina Vladimirovna Tereshkova began school at age eight. At 16, after her father died, Tereshkova quit school to work in a textile factory. She took correspondence classes to finish her schooling. Always fascinated with skydiving, Tereshkova made her first jump at age 22, after training with a local aviation club. Soon after, she founded the Textile Mill Workers Parachute Club.

PARACHUTING TO PILOTING

Parachuting brought Tereshkova to the attention of the Soviet space agency. In the early days of space travel, the Soviets were in a "space race" with the UNITED STATES, wherein each country attempted to claim "firsts" thereby showing the superiority of their

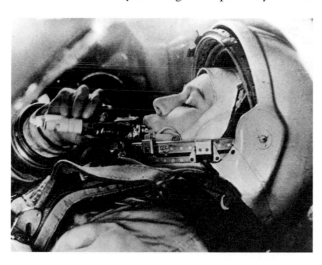

space program. In 1961 the Soviets became the first to recruit women. Because few Soviet women were pilots, the members of the selection committee, led by the first man in space **Yuri Gagarin**, looked to parachutists. Tereshova was among four female parachutists and a pilot chosen to train.

The women went through 15 months of intense training, including classroom study, more than 120 parachute jumps, and jet pilot training. They endured at least two flight simulations inside a grounded capsule for six, and later, twelve days. During training, the Soviets insisted that the women—like their male cosmonauts—not tell anyone about their participation in the space program, to ensure the news didn't leak to the United States. As a result, Tereshkova told her family she was at a training camp for an elite skydiving team.

Tereshkova's mother finally learned the truth about her daughter's space program plans when Radio Moscow announced a few days before her June 16, 1963, flight that Tereshkova would be the first woman in space. Tereshkova herself had learned only days earlier that she had been chosen to make the historic flight in *Vostok 6*.

The Soviets planned that Tereshkova's first flight would be their second dual flight—in which two crafts would be in orbit at the same time, and ground control would have them fly within 3 miles (5 km) of each other. On June 14, *Vostok 5* launched with cosmonaut Valeriy Bykovsky on board. Tereshkova lifted off two days later, flying with the call name *Chaika* ("Seagull"). The cosmonauts briefly exchanged communications while in space, and although Tereshkova was trained to be the first cosmonaut to work her capsule's controls, she did not. Those in charge decided she wasn't mentally prepared for the challenge.

After 48 orbits totaling 70 hours and 50 minutes in space, Tereshkova ejected from her capsule as planned, and parachuted down about 20,000 feet (6,000 m) to Earth. She landed near Karaganda, KAZAKHSTAN, on June 19.

In November of that same year she married fellow cosmonaut Andrian Nikolayev. Their child, Elena, was the first to be born to two parents who had been in space.

Tereshkova later enrolled in a Soviet Military Air Academy, from which she graduated in 1969. She reportedly trained for another flight that was to include a space walk, but Tereshkova never again went to space. Instead she served as a Communist in the Supreme Soviet, the USSR's national parliament, among other government positions. She lost her position with the fall of Communism in Russia, and is believed to have retired to Moscow.

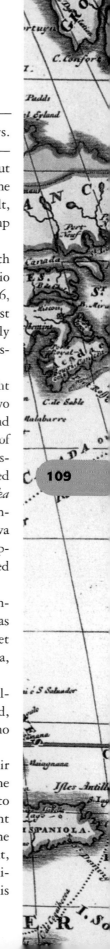

Naomi Uemura (1941–1984)

MOUNTAIN CLIMBER

Naomi Uemura was born to a farming family in the Tajima region of JAPAN. He began mountain climbing while studying agriculture at Tokyo's Meiji University. The diminutive 5-foot 3-inch (1.6-m), 135-pound (61-kg) adventurer preferred climbing alone. "It is a test of myself," he explained, "and one thing I loathe is to have to test myself in front of other people."

In 1966, Uemura made a solo climb of MONT BLANC (15,771 feet [4,807 m]) in FRANCE. At one point he fell into a crevasse that was covered by snow. He managed to climb out of the icy crack, and on future climbs decided to carry a pair of 17-foot-long (5-m) bamboo poles to test the snow in front of him as he walked.

NATIONAL HERO

By 1970 Uemura was a national hero in Japan, after being a member of the first Japanese team to successfully climb the world's tallest mountain, MOUNT EVEREST (29,028 feet [8,848 m]). He received special attention because he was the first in the team to actually reach the peak and the first person to reach the highest peak on five continents.

Other expeditions were more dangerous. In 1978, Uemura became the first man to reach the NORTH POLE alone by traveling across the Arctic Ocean—a 450-mile (724-km) trip. One night while Uemura was sleeping, a polar bear invaded his camp and attacked him in his sleeping bag. Uemura escaped, killed the bear the next day when it returned, and finally completed the journey.

Soon after, he made an 18-month journey from GREENLAND to ALASKA by dogsled. During the trip his hunger grew so great that he had to kill several sled dogs for food. He also rafted 3,700 miles (5,955 km) down the AMAZON RIVER and walked the 1,750-mile (2,816-km) length of his native country.

MISSING

Though he climbed North America's highest peak, MOUNT McKINLEY in Alaska (20,320 feet [6,194 m]) in the summer of 1970, Uemura decided to do it again in 1984. This time, he attempted a solo climb up the western side, in the hopes of making the first solo ascent of the ice-filled mountain in mid-winter. On February 13, he contacted support personnel on his Citizen's Band (CB) radio to tell them he made it to the top of McKinley and was on his way down.

The next day those monitoring Uemura's progress found that his CB was not working. They assumed the subzero temperatures had weakened its batteries, and they were probably correct because a pilot made a pre-planned flight over the mountain and spotted Uemura descending at 16,400 feet (5,000 m). Uemura waved, offering the pre-arranged signal that he was fine.

No sign of Uemura was reported by February 19, days after he should have reached the bottom of McKinley. Friends worried that the mountaineer did not have a tent with him, and his supplies of raw caribou meat, fruit, sea oil, and fuel to melt snow for water would have run out two days earlier.

Rescue workers from the U.S. National Park Service were called to the scene, but their efforts were hindered by eight days of high winds and snowstorms. Two of Uemura's friends, climbers Eiho Otani and Jim Wickwire volunteered to drop by helicopter onto the mountain to help search. "The only thing I can do now is pray for his safety," his wife Kimiko said from Tokyo. "It's been so often like this with my husband."

In late February searches for Uemura were called off and he was presumed dead. Searchers had found his snowshoes, a diary, and his two 17-foot-long bamboo poles.

George Vancouver (1757–1798)

EXPLORER · CARTOGRAPHER

George Vancouver spent many childhood days walking alone along the seaport near his home in King's Lynn, ENGLAND. He liked to talk to the fishermen and impress them with his knowledge of the ships in the harbor. At 13, Vancouver announced that he wanted to join the British Navy.

In July 1771, Captain **James Cook** returned to England after a trip to the South Pacific. The men in the seaport openly discussed Cook's next trip, one in search of a continent that supposedly lay between NEW ZEALAND and SOUTH AFRICA. Vancouver spoke to his parents about joining Cook. His mother disapproved, but his father, who knew Cook's crew members, sent a letter to Cook asking for an introduction.

FIRST EXPEDITION

By June 1772, 15-year-old Vancouver was on board Cook's boat, *Resolution*. Compared to the other young men on board for their first expedition, Vancouver stuck out as short, pudgy, and very obedient. The ship sailed around South Africa, into the Antarctic Circle, and toward SOUTH ISLAND (modern NEW ZEALAND). On January 13, 1774, the ship began sailing through icy Antarctic seas when Vancouver ran to the bow of the ship and shouted, *Ne plus ultra!* ("the utmost point"). His action made Cook change the direction of the ship, and made Vancouver proud to be the crew member to come closest to the SOUTH POLE. The ship returned to ENGLAND in August 1775. Vancouver's parents were dismayed to see that the 18-year-old was ready to be part of Cook's next voyage.

The *Resolution*, and the smaller *Adventure*, which held Vancouver, set out to find the fabled Northwest Passage through a western entrance in 1776. After discovering the Sandwich Islands (modern HAWAII) in 1778, Cook decided the crew would winter there. Cook

and five others died while fighting with Hawaiians who had stolen supplies. The ships continued on, but found no passage.

Five years later Vancouver was serving as part of a crew in JAMAICA when Commodore Sir Alan Gardner began looking for someone to map all of the bays and harbors there. Once Gardner heard Vancouver was the best cartographer available, he offered him the job.

VANCOUVER ISLAND

When British naval officers decided to send ships to the Pacific coast of North America in an effort to carry on Cook's quest for the Northwest Passage, Gardner suggested Vancouver lead the expedition. He was given his own ship, the 79-foot-long (24-m) *Discovery*, with 101 men, and the smaller ship, *Chatham*.

In April 1791 Vancouver led the ships toward CAPE TOWN, SOUTH AFRICA, crossed the Indian Ocean, mapped the southern coast of Australia, and sailed to TAHITI. After spending a month restocking the ships with meat and vegetables, Vancouver led the ships to the Sandwich Islands and on to New Albion (modern CALIFORNIA) in mid-April 1792.

The crew continued mapping the coast up to ALASKA for three years, becoming the first Europeans to sail around present-day VANCOUVER, a large island off the coast of BRITISH COLUMBIA. Their greatly detailed charts enhanced Europe's knowledge of geography. "I trust that the survey will remove any doubt and set aside every opinion of a Northwest Passage," Vancouver said proudly. The ships returned to England in 1795.

After the four-year, six-month journey, in which six men died in various accidents, Vancouver ended his explorations. His health was poor, but he wrote an account of his travels with his brother Charles's help.

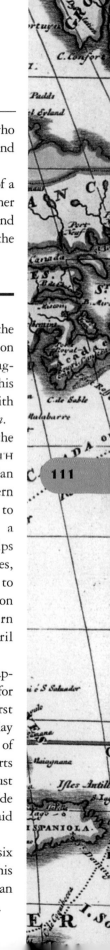

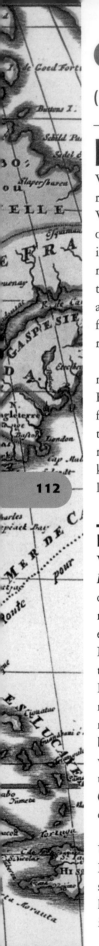

Giovanni da Verrazano

(c. 1485–1528) EXPLORER • NAVIGATOR

Born in the Chianti region of Tuscany, Italy, Giovanni de Verrazano (sometimes spelled Verrazzano) was part of a wealthy family. After he received an education in Florence, Verrazano moved to Dieppe, a port on the northwest coast of FRANCE, in the hopes of becoming a mariner. He sailed on expeditions to the eastern MEDITERRANEAN and NEWFOUNDLAND, but became famous as a *corsair* (pirate) who raided Spanish ships.

In 1523 a group of Italian merchants asked French King François I to sponsor an expedition from present-day FLORIDA to Newfoundland to find the legendary passage to Asia from the west. They requested that Verrazano serve as commander. The king ordered Verrazano to also attempt to claim new lands for France.

EAST COAST EXPLORATION

Verrazano left Dieppe in early 1524 on the ship *La Dauphine* and another vessel, both of which held a large crew that included his younger brother, Girolamo, a mapmaker. They crossed the Atlantic Ocean and sighted land near the present-day coast of CAPE FEAR, NORTH CAROLINA. After sailing south along the coast, the ships turned north and docked at present-day CAPE HATTERAS, located on a sandbar separated from the mainland by Pamlico Sound. Verrazano did not see the mainland. Thus, he incorrectly suggested that the body of water was actually the Pacific Ocean, which would lead to CHINA. Girolamo even prepared maps that showed the large continent of the New World (North America) tapering off at the North Carolina coast.

On April 17, Verrazano continued north into the Upper Bay of New York Harbor, becoming the first European to do so. "We found a very pleasant place, situated amongst certain little steep hills," he wrote in his journal. "From amidst which hills there ran down into the sea a great stream of water (the HUDSON RIVER), which within the mouth was very deep, and from the sea to the mouth of same, with the tide, which we found to rise eight foot, any great vessel laden may pass up."

Next, Verrazano sailed to the entrance of Narragansett Bay. He named one of the islands he saw "Rhode Island" because it resembled the shape of a Greek island in the eastern Mediterranean. The ship anchored in Newport Harbor for a few weeks as exploring parties walked inland as far as Pawtucket.

The expedition continued up the coast of MAINE, around NOVA SCOTIA, and northward to Newfoundland before returning to France on July 8. Upon his return, Verrazano wrote a report for the king. It offered the first personal account of the eastern coast of North America and the Native Americans who lived there.

Verrazano led another expedition in 1527. It was sponsored in part by Philippe de Chabot, admiral of France, because King François I was busy preparing for a war against Italy and could not offer any ships. This time, Verrazano traveled along the coast of BRAZIL. He returned with a large load of logwood, a valuable commodity used in making textile dyes.

On a second expedition to North America, Verrazano was to again find the passage to the Pacific near North Carolina. He left France with two ships in the spring of 1528, and stopped at an island (most likely Guadeloupe) in the Lesser Antilles. There members of a native tribe of cannibals killed and ate him. His crew sailed south to Brazil, where they picked up another cargo of logwood to bring home to France.

Bridging the Gap

THE VERRAZANO-NARROWS Bridge spans New York Harbor between Brooklyn and Staten Island. Built between 1959 and 1964 and named in the explorer's honor, it was once the world's longest suspension bridge.

Amerigo Vespucci (1454–1512)

EXPLORER·CARTOGRAPHER

Amerigo Vespucci grew up in the right place at the right time—Florence, ITALY—during the Renaissance. His parents, Stagio and Elizabetta, belonged to a large family who were friendly with the city-state's wealthy ruling family, the Medici. Vespucci did poorly in school, but fortunately found work through his family connections. In 1479, the 24-year-old traveled to PARIS as secretary to his uncle, who served as Florence's ambassador to France.

Upon his return home, Vespucci spent several years working for Lorenzo di Pier Francesco Medici. In the fall of 1489, Vespucci was sent to Seville, SPAIN, on business. He met many men who shared a passion for his hobby—mapmaking and collecting—and was awed by the country's unity (Italy was a disjointed group of city-states then) and allegiance to King Ferdinand and Queen Isabella.

In early 1492, Vespucci moved to Seville. There, he entered a business partnership with banker Gianetto Berardi. One of their clients was **Christopher Columbus**, who came to the men seeking funds for his first voyage across the Atlantic Ocean.

DREAMS OF EXPLORATION

When Columbus returned to Spain in the spring of 1493, he brought news of a group of islands lying in the present-day CARIBBEAN SEA. Vespucci dreamed of making a similar trip.

Columbus's second trip brought him back to Spain in 1496, but this time he was scolded by the king and queen for his mismanagement of HISPANIOLA (modern HAITI and the DOMINICAN REPUBLIC), and for possibly taking too much gold for himself. King Ferdinand was so unhappy with Columbus that he asked Vespucci, among others, to sail toward the newly discovered islands to check on Columbus's claims. Vespucci eagerly accepted the invitation to travel.

Vespucci served as a mapmaker and observer along with a crew, led by Spanish soldier Alonso de Ojeda. The expedition left from CÁDIZ on May 10, 1497. They sailed around CUBA and along the shores of present-day COSTA RICA, NICARAGUA, HONDURAS, and MEXICO. Vespucci returned to Spain on October 15,

1498, and gave a favorable report to the king. In return, Vespucci was rewarded with another expedition, on which he served as leader of at least three ships. During this two-year trip, Vespucci mapped large sections of the Atlantic's South American shores and discovered BRAZIL. A recently drawn treaty that divided the world into Portuguese and Spanish rule showed that Brazil was under King Manuel of PORTUGAL's control. Vespucci moved to Portugal and sailed on two more voyages for his new homeland.

On his first expedition for Portugal, Vespucci sailed along South America and realized that another landmass, which he called the "New World," was attached to it. He wrote about his findings in a letter to his old boss Piero Solderini. The letter was published by printers who exaggerated Vespucci's words, and distributed across Europe.

A copy of the letter was sent to German cartographer Martin Waldseemüller, who drew a map of the present-day South American coast and a few Caribbean islands. His map noted the location of Brazil and America (on present-day South America). "I see no reason why we should not call it 'America,'" Waldseemuller wrote, "that is to say, land of Americus, for Americus its discoverer, man of sagacious wit." A book, which included the map, was printed in 1507. The name "America" stuck, and future maps used the name though Vespucci was not the first person to discover the lands named after him.

By 1505, Vespucci was finished with explorations. He returned to Seville, where he established a naval academy.

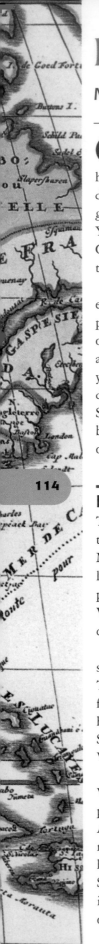

Erik Weihenmayer (1968–)

MOUNTAIN CLIMBER

Connecticut-raised Erik Weihenmayer was not born blind, but in his youth doctors found that he was suffering from retinoschisis, a disease in which the retinas detach and gradually split, leading to blindness. Yet, his father, Ed, a former Marine Corps pilot, encouraged his son "...to take reasonable risks."

As a result, while Weihenmayer's eyesight was deteriorating, he continued playing basketball and ramp jumping on his bike with his two brothers. By age 13, he was legally blind, but three years later he found a sport for which he didn't need sight. At Weston High School in Connecticut, Weihenmayer became team captain and the state's second-ranked wrestler in his weight class.

LOVE OF CLIMBING

Then at age 16, Weihenmayer learned to rock climb at the Carroll Center for the Blind in Newton, Massachusetts. He loved the freedom it gave him, and later attended a wrestling camp where climbing was part of the training. While away that summer, Weihenmayer learned that his mother was killed in a car accident. He was devastated.

To keep the family busy, Weihenmayer's father suggested they hike on the 27-mile (43 km) Inca Trail in PERU. Weihenmayer used a cane and let his father and brothers steer him by holding the back of his neck. The family took similar treks through SPAIN, PAKISTAN, and PAPUA NEW GUINEA before Weihenmayer began his studies at Boston College.

Blindness made finding a job difficult, but Weihenmayer finally found a fifth-grade teaching position at Phoenix Country Day School in ARIZONA. His move there enabled him to continue rock climbing. After several climbs, he told friends he wanted to climb the highest peak in the UNITED STATES, MOUNT MCKINLEY (20,320 feet [6,194 m]) in ALASKA. To prepare, he ran up and down the stairs of a 50-story building wearing a 70-pound (32-kg) backpack and practiced pitching tents wearing heavy mittens. He also discovered that using trekking poles helped him stumble less and enabled him to test for crevasses in the snow.

On the climb, Weihenmayer's five partners—sponsored by the American Foundation for the Blind—gave him oral clues to navigate the uneven rock and ice mountain. To gain firm footing, Weihenmayer tried to step in his partner's footprints during the 19-day climb. They made the summit on June 27, 1995—coincidentally, Helen Keller's birthday.

Weihenmayer decided to make it his life's work to become the first blind person to climb the highest peaks on all seven continents. After climbing MOUNT ACONCAGUA (22,934 feet, [6,990 m]) in ARGENTINA, Weihenmayer climbed Africa's highest peak, MOUNT KILIMANJARO (19,340 feet [5,895 m]) in 1997. Halfway up he married fellow schoolteacher/climber Ellie Reeve. He had proposed to her atop Arizona's 2,700-foot (823-m) Camelback Mountain.

Weihenmayer knows being a blind climber is hard for some people to understand. "I like the spiritual feeling of being on a mountain," he told Sports Illustrated in 2001. "You don't climb for a view.... The real beauty of life happens on the side of the mountain."

In June 2000 he and his wife had a baby, but Weihenmayer continued climbing. He left his home in Golden, COLORADO, in late March 2001 with the hopes of summiting EVEREST by mid-May. His ten-man expedition was underwritten by $250,000 from the National Federation of the Blind. At the end of his ten-day trek to base camp, Weihenmayer was dehydrated and bloody, after falling into a crevasse and being hit by another climber's pole.

Still, he continued climbing. On May 24, 2001, Kevin Cherilla, the manager of the expedition's base camp called Ellie with the latest news. "They're standing on top of the world!"

Edward White (1930–1967)

ASTRONAUT

Born in San Antonio, Texas, Edward Higgins White, Jr., attended Western High School in Washington, D.C. There he excelled in track, particularly hurdling. Upon graduation from the U.S. Military Academy at West Point in 1952, White had set the 400-meter hurdles record and nearly made the 1952 Olympics team. Still, he was drawn to flying. He served as an Air Force test pilot in Florida and Texas, and then began studying toward a Master of Science degree from the University of Michigan, before being called to active duty for three and a half years as a U.S. fighter pilot in Germany.

In 1959 he began three years of test pilot work at the Air Force Test Pilot School at Edwards Air Force Base in California and Ohio's Wright-Patterson Air Force Base. The lieutenant colonel was selected as one of NASA's second group of astronauts in 1962.

SPACE WALK

During White's first space flight, he served as pilot of the *Gemini 4* capsule. The *Gemini 4* blasted off on June 3, 1965, and was commanded by James A. McDivitt. On day one of the four-day flight, White stepped out of the craft attached only to a 25-foot-

long (7-m) cord, through which flowed oxygen and communication signals. As the capsule flew over the Pacific Ocean and North America, White peered back at McDivitt through the craft's windshield and moved around space by shooting a gun that fired small bursts of compressed oxygen.

Solemn Reminder

WHEN NEIL ARMSTRONG and "Buzz" Aldrin finally landed their capsule on the moon in July 1969, they left behind a shoulder patch that was said to have been worn by the *Apollo 1* crew on their flight.

"I can sit out here and see the whole California coast," White told McDivitt. White was the first American to walk in space and the first person to propel himself in space on his own accord. After 22 minutes he reentered the capsule, where he and McDivitt completed 12 scientific and medical experiments.

The 62-orbit flight and space walk made White a national hero. "I think the entire world is grateful for what you have done…" President Lyndon B. Johnson told the men in a phone call, before inviting them to his ranch. "You have written your names in history and in our hearts." White was given an honorary Doctorate in Astronautics from the University of Michigan after his flight.

He trained as a backup commander on *Gemini 7*, and was chosen as senior pilot on the three-man *Apollo 1* flight, set to be the first manned orbital spacecraft to reach the moon. *Apollo 1* was scheduled to launch in February 1967.

On January 27, 1967, astronauts White, **Virgil "Gus" Grissom,** and rookie Roger Chaffee were inside the capsule at Cape Kennedy (modern Kennedy Space Center) in Florida on a daylong training simulation, practicing countdown and launch. There were technical problems all day, but at 6:31 PM a camera focused on the capsule's hatch recorded a huge flash. Seconds later the entire capsule was in flames. Apparently, the fire started from a bundle of wires in front of Grissom's chair. The men were the first Americans to be killed in the space program.

The disaster made NASA halt its flight schedule for almost two years while spacecrafts were redesigned. Future crafts were designed to be less flammable, filled with flame-resistant materials, and topped by an escape hatch that was easier to open.

Charles Wilkes (1798–1877)

EXPLORER·NAVAL OFFICER

Born in New York City, Charles Wilkes joined the U.S. Navy as a midshipman at age 20. He sailed on expeditions to the MEDITERRANEAN SEA and Pacific Ocean performing surveying work before being made a lieutenant in 1826. He then became head of the newly established Depot of Charts and Instruments (modern Naval Observatory).

On May 18, 1836, Congress authorized a survey and exploration expedition to the Pacific Ocean and the South Seas on a four-year round-the-world trip. The expedition was meant to promote trade, "extend the bounds of science, and promote knowledge."

In April 1838, four ships were assigned to the expedition—*Vincennes* (on which Wilkes would mainly sail), *Peacock*, *Porpoise*, and *Relief*. Two smaller boats, *Sea Gull* and *Flying Fish* were to be used as survey vessels close to shore. Wilkes's crew consisted of 82 officers, 9 scientists and artists, as well as 342 sailors.

They set sail from NEW YORK on August 18, 1838, venturing down the South American coast to the southern tip of TIERRA DEL FUEGO, where they stopped so Wilkes could split the expedition into three teams of two boats each. Wilkes boarded the *Porpoise* and attempted to sail as far south as possible. The other groups were sent to explore **James Cook**'s findings to the southwest and survey the Tierra del Fuego and STRAITS OF MAGELLAN.

After ten days, the *Porpoise* and the *Seagull* were surrounded by fog and ice. Deciding going further south would be dangerous, Wilkes turned back; along the way the *Seagull* sank off the coast of CHILE. The remaining ships sailed along the coastlines of the Paumoto Islands, TAHITI, Samoa, the Marshall Islands, and HAWAII and dropped off scientists and chart makers to collect botanical and geological specimens and map the lands.

AROUND THE WORLD

They docked again in Sydney, AUSTRALIA, and Wilkes boarded the *Vincennes* for the trip to Macquarie Island, near TASMANIA, on December 26, 1839. As the fleet sailed north toward NEW ZEALAND, an officer captured an emperor penguin with 30 pebbles in its stomach. This convinced Wilkes that there was more land in the south. He declared that he discovered the Antarctic continent on January 19, 1840.

By this time the fleet had charted almost 300 islands in the Pacific, and Wilkes was ready to move on to the western coast of the UNITED STATES. Wilkes sent some members of the expedition ashore to explore and survey the land between present-day OREGON and WASHINGTON states. After sailing back along the coast, the PHILIPPINES, and around the CAPE OF GOOD HOPE, the boats finally docked in NEW YORK with 223 of the original sailors.

Wilkes wrote a five-volume book about his travels, *Narrative of the United States Exploring Expedition* (1844). He also edited and drew atlases for 20 volumes of scientific data collected on the trip.

Early in the Civil War, Wilkes commanded the *U.S.S. San Jacinto*. On November 8, 1861, he ordered his men to stop the British mail steamer *Trent* in the CARIBBEAN, and remove James Murray Mason and John Slidell, the Confederate commissioners sailing to BRITAIN and FRANCE. The act, called the Trent Affair, almost caused a war between the Union and Britain.

To keep the peace with Britain, President Lincoln demoted Wilkes for his actions, and sent him to South America to protect interests there. Wilkes again made impulsive decisions that angered several foreign governments. He was court-martialed for insubordination and conduct unbecoming an officer. Wilkes retired with the rank of rear admiral on July 25, 1866.

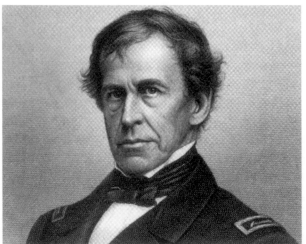

Bibliography

Assad, Thomas. *Three Victorian Travelers: Burton, Blunt, and Doughty*. New York: Routledge & Kegan Paul, 1964.

Baker, Daniel S. (ed.). *Explorers and Discoverers of the World*. Detroit: Gale Research Inc., 1993.

Bergman, Brian. "A River of Destiny," *Maclean's*, July 1992: p. 44+.

Blum, Arlene. *Annapurna: A Woman's Place*, San Francisco: Sierra Club, 1998.

Boyle, Alan. "Women Break the Last Space Barrier," MSNBC.com, July 23, 1999.

Brothers, Barbara and Julia M. Gergits. *Dictionary of Literary Biography, Vol. 159: British Travel Writers*, Detroit: Gale Research, 1998.

Camp, Carole Ann. *Sally Ride: First American Woman in Space*, Springfield, NJ: Enslow Publishers Inc., 1997.

Cardee, Marjorie Dent. *Current Biography*, Bronx, NY: The HW Wilson, 1954.

Chaundry, Bob. "Sir Ranulph Fiennes: Up to the Pole," BBC News online (www.news.bbc.co.uk), February 11, 2000.

Cole, Michael D. *Vostok 1: First Human in Space*, Springfield, NJ: Enslow Publishers, Inc., 1995.

Commire, Anne (ed.). *Women in World History (Vol. 4)*, Detroit: Gale Group, 1999.

Craig, Simon. "Passage to Disaster," *Geographical Magazine*, June 1997: p. 64+.

Deegan, Paul. "Friends in High Places," *Geographical Magazine*, Dec 2000: p. 38+.

Deplar, Helen (ed.). *The Discoverers*, New York: McGraw-Hill, 1980.

Dictionary of American Biography. Detroit, MI: Biography Resource Center/The Gale Group, 2001.

Edwards, Ron. "Bessie Coleman...," *Aviation History*, Nov 1998: p. 8+.

Events & People of the American Frontier. Great Neck, NY: Great Neck Publishing, 2000. {no editor noted}

Explorers and Discoverers of the World. Detroit, MI: Biography Resource Center/The Gale Group, 2001.

Fagg Olds, Elizabeth. *Women of the Four Winds*, Boston: Houghton Mifflin Co., 1985.

"Fears for an Intrepid Explorer (Naomi Uemura)," *Time*, March 5, 1984: p. 47.

Fecher, Constance. *The Last Elizabethan: A Portrait of Sir Walter Ralegh*, New York: Farrar, Straus & Giroux, 1972.

Fiennes, Ranulph. *Mind Over Matter: The Epic Crossing of the Antarctic Continent*, New York: Delacorte Press, 1994.

Gentleman, Amelia. "My Life on Mir (Sergei Avdeyev)," www.guardian.co.uk, March 14, 2001.

Gilmartin, Pat. "Fish and Fetishes: A Victorian Woman on African Rivers," *Women & Environments*, Spring 1990: p. 10+.

Hutton, Paul Andrew. "Frontier Hero Davy Crockett," *Wild West*, Feb 1999: p. 38+.

Jenson, Malcolm C. *Leif Erikson the Lucky*, Danbury, CT: Franklin Watts, 1979.

Keerdoja, Eileen and Bernard Krisher. "Why? Because It's There (Naomi Uemura)," *Newsweek*, March 10, 1980: p. 16+.

Kim, Albert. "Vision Quest (Erik Weihenmayer)," *Sports Illustrated*, June 4, 2001: p. 36+.

Kunitz, Stanley J. and Howard Haycraft. *American Authors 1600–1900: A Biographical Dictionary of American Literature*, Bronx, NY: H.W. Wilson, 1938.

Lacouture, John. "You Can Be Good and Colorful (Alan Shepard)," *Naval History*, June 2001: p. 41+.

Lavendel, Brian. "Her Royal Deepness," *Animals*, March/April 1999: p. 36+.

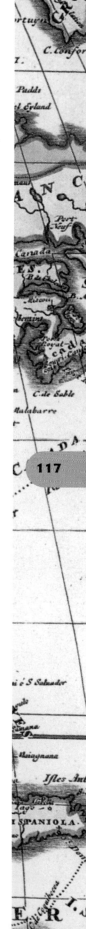

Lehrer, Eli. "Deep-Sea Explorer Brings History to Life," *Insight on the News*, Detroit: Gale Group, 2000.

Levathes, Louise. *When China Ruled the Seas*, New York: Simon & Schuster, 1994.

Lindbergh, Reeve. "The Flyer: Charles Lindbergh," *Time*, June 14, 1999: p. 50+.

Lomask, Milton. *Great Lives: Exploration*, New York: Charles Scribner's Sons, 1988.

Mcgill, Frank N. (ed.). *Encyclopedia of World Authors, Third Edition*, Englewood Cliffs, NJ: Salem Press, 1997.

Millman, Lawrence. "Looking for Henry Hudson," *Smithsonian*, Oct. 99: p. 100+

The New York Times Biographical Service, New York: Associated Press, 1986, 1997. [No editor given]

Nielson, Quig. "Sacagawea of the Lewis and Clark Expedition," *Wild West*, Dec 1999: p. 36+.

O'Leary, Jim. "Jacques Cousteau," *Odyssey*, Dec 1998: p. 6+.

Olney, Ross R. *Men Against the Sea*, New York: Grosset and Dunlap, 1969.

Pollard, Jean Ann. "Beebe Takes the Bathysphere," *Sea Frontiers*, August 1994: p. 40+.

Roberts, Jack. *The Importance of Dian Fossey*, San Diego: Lucent Books, 1995.

Roisman-Cooper. "Polar Dreams, Polar Disappointments," *British Heritage*, Oct/Nov 1999: p. 52+.

Schefter, Jim. "When Yuri Took Flight," *Astronomy*, April 2001: p.36+.

Scheller, William G. "Race to the End of the Earth," *National Geographic World*, Feb 2000: p. 22+.

Slung, Michele. "Living with Cannibals and Other Women's Adventures," *National Geographic Society*, 2000.

Smith, Carter III. *One Giant Leap for Mankind*, Englewood Cliffs, NJ: Silver Burdett Company, 1985.

Stefoff, Rebecca. *Marco Polo and the Medieval Explorers,* New York: Chelsea House Publishers, 1992.

Swift, E.M. "Blind Ambition (Erik Weihenmayer)," *Sports Illustrated*, April 23, 2001: p. 16+.

Syme, Ronald. *Vancouver: Explorer of the Pacific Coast*, New York: Morrow Junior Books, 1970.

Thomas, Dana. "Solo Survivor: Isabelle Autissier," *Women's Sports & Fitness*, Nov/Dec 1999: p. 122+.

Waldman, Carl and Alan Wexler (eds.). *Who Was Who in World Exploration*, New York: Facts on File, 1992.

Wallach, Janet. "Daughter of the Desert: Gertrude Bell," *Smithsonian*, April 1998: p. 33+.

Wexler, Mark. "Sylvia Earle's Excellent Adventure," *National Wildlife*, April/May 1999: p. 32+.

Winters, Christopher (ed.). *International Dictionary of Anthropologists*, New York: Garland Publishing, 1991.

BIOGRAPHY MAGAZINE

Eskes, David. "Aiming High (Erik Weihenmayer)," Aug 1997: p. 54+.

"John Glenn," Dec 1998, p. 66+.

Mura, Laura. "Revered and Reviled: Charles Lindbergh," Dec 1998, p. 96+.

Schleier, Curt. "Jane of the Jungle (Jane Goodall)," May 2000, p. 88+.

ONLINE RESOURCES

Amelia Earhart: www.ameliaearhart.com

American Academy of Achievement: www.achievement.org

Arlene Blum: www.arleneblum.com

Astronaut Hall of Fame: www.astronauts.org

Biography Magazine: www.biography.com

Buzz Aldrin: www.buzzaldrin.com

Encarta Online: www.encarta.com

Enchanted Learning: www.enchantedlearning.com

The Field Museum's Women in Science:
www.fmnh.org

Gale Group Biography Resource Center Online:
www.galenet.com

Iceland: www.iceland.org

James Beckwourth: www.beckwourth.org

Jane Goodall: www.janegoodall.org

The Jason Project: www.jason.org

John Wesley Powell: www.powellmuseum.org

Johnson Space Center, NASA: www.jsc.nasa.gov

Leakey Foundation: www.leakeyfoundation.org

The Mariners' Museum: www.mariner.org

Matthew Henson: www.matthewhenson.com

The Mountain Institute: www.mountain.org

National Geograhic: www.nationalgeographic.org

National Women's Hall of Fame:
www.greatwomen.org

Solo Spirit Balloon Flight: www.solospirit.wustl.edu

Space.com: www.space.com

Women in Aviation History: www.ninety-nines.org

PBS.ORG ARTICLES

"Alexander the Great"

"The Conquest of the Incas"

"Empire of the Bay"

"Everest"

"Into the Abyss

"New Perspectives on the West"

119

ACKNOWLEDGMENTS

Library of Congress: 8, 9, 11, 19, 20, 21, 23, 25, 27, 28, 30, 31, 32, 36, 39, 42, 44, 47, 49, 52, 56, 60, 61, 63, 68, 70, 72, 75, 77, 78, 89, 90, 91, 92, 93, 94, 97, 100, 101, 102, 104, 105, 107. **Corbis:** 15, 16, 18, 24, 33, 45, 46, 54, 55, 57, 58, 59, 62, 65, 71, 86, 87, 108, 111, 114. **Media Projects Archives:** 12, 17, 34, 43, 83 112, 113, 116. **NASA:** 14, 41, 64, 66, 82, 99, 103, 115. **The London Illustrated News:** 13, 53, 80, 81, 106. **The Granger Collection, New York:** (Image Number: 0022861) 50, (Image Number 0007398) 69, (Image Number 0041922) 76. **Hulton Getty:** 22, 74, 109. **Superstock:** 26, 84. **Courtesy of the Dept. of Library Services, American Museum of Natural History** (Neg. No. 46353): 10. *Forbidden Journey: From Peking to Kashmir* by Ella K. Maillart. W. Heinemann, Ltd: London, 1937: 85. Eakins, Thomas / *Frank Hamilton Cushing* / Oil on canvas / 0126.2315, From the collection of Gilcrease Museum, Tulsa: 48. Photo by Motohisa Ando, courtesy of Bungei Shunju Ltd: 110. Riss, Francois / National Archives of Canada / C-011226: 35. **National Museum of American History:** 95. **National Park Service, Independence National Historical Park:** 79. Tu, Shen / *The Tribute of Giraffe with Attendant* / Philadelphia Museum of Art: Given John T. Dorrance: 38. Photo courtesy of Johan Reinhard: 98. **The United States Postal Service:** 40. *Wanderings in Arabia* by Charles M. Doughty. Duckworth: London, 1908: 51. **Wyoming State Archives:** 29. All Maps designed by Ron Toelke Associates. Cover Design by Oxygen Design.

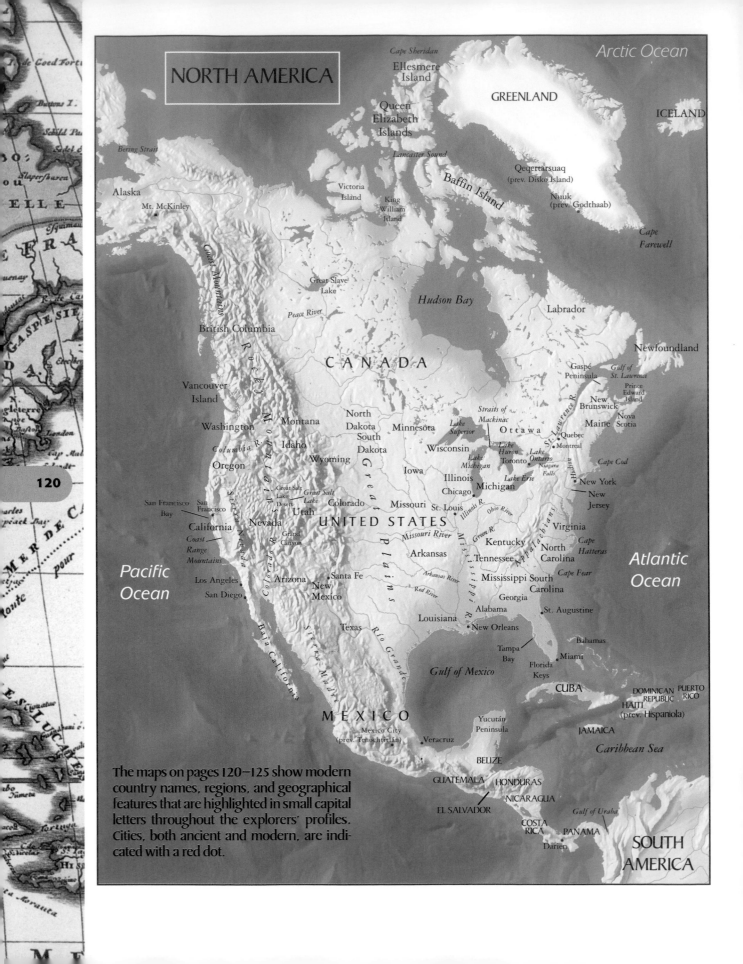

NORTH AMERICA

Arctic Ocean

Cape Sheridan
Ellesmere
Island

GREENLAND

ICELAND

Queen
Elizabeth
Islands

Bering Strait

Lancaster Sound

Qeqertarsuaq
(prev. Disko Island)

Alaska

Victoria
Island

Nuuk
(prev. Godthaab)

Mt. McKinley

King
William
Island

Baffin Island

Cape
Farewell

Coast Mountains

Great Slave
Lake

Hudson Bay

Labrador

Peace River

Newfoundland

British Columbia

CANADA

Gaspé
Peninsula

Gulf of
St. Lawrence

Rocky

Vancouver
Island

Prince
Edward
Island

St. Lawrence R.

New
Brunswick

Nova
Scotia

Washington

Montana

North
Dakota

Minnesota

Straits of
Mackinac

Ottawa

Maine

South
Dakota

Lake
Superior

Quebec

Columbia R.

Mountains

Idaho

Wisconsin

Lake
Huron

Lake
Ontario

Montreal

Oregon

Wyoming

Lake
Michigan

Toronto

Niagara
Falls

Cape Cod

Sierra Nevada

Great Salt
Lake
Desert

Great Salt
Lake

Iowa

Illinois

Lake Erie

Hudson R.

New York

San Francisco
Bay

San
Francisco

Colorado

Missouri

Chicago

Michigan

New
Jersey

California

Nevada

Utah

St. Louis

Illinois R.

Ohio River

Coast
Range
Mountains

Grand
Canyon

UNITED STATES

Missouri River

Green R.

Virginia

Los Angeles

Colorado R.

Arizona

Santa Fe

Kentucky

North
Carolina

Cape
Hatteras

Atlantic
Ocean

San Diego

New
Mexico

Arkansas

Tennessee

Mississippi

Cape Fear

Arkansas River

South
Carolina

Pacific
Ocean

Red River

Georgia

Texas

Rio Grande

Louisiana

Alabama

St. Augustine

New Orleans

Bahamas

Baja California

Sierra Madre

Gulf of Mexico

Tampa
Bay

Florida
Keys

Miami

CUBA

DOMINICAN
REPUBLIC

PUERTO
RICO

M E X I C O

Yucatán
Peninsula

HAITI
(prev. Hispaniola)

Mexico City
(prev. Tenochtitlán)

Veracruz

JAMAICA

Caribbean Sea

BELIZE

The maps on pages 120–125 show modern
country names, regions, and geographical
features that are highlighted in small capital
letters throughout the explorers' profiles.
Cities, both ancient and modern, are indicated with a red dot.

GUATEMALA

HONDURAS

NICARAGUA

EL SALVADOR

Gulf of Uraba

COSTA
RICA

PANAMA

SOUTH
AMERICA

Darién

SOUTH AMERICA

Caribbean Sea

Gulf of Uraba

Panama

TRINIDAD & TOBAGO

Caracas

VENEZUELA

Orinoco R.

Ciudad Bolivar (prev. Angostura)

GUYANA

FRENCH GUIANA

COLOMBIA

Quito

ECUADOR

Puerto Viejo

Napo R.

Amazon River

Amazon Rainforest

Cajamarca

Recife

Mt. Huascarán

PERU

BRAZIL

Andes

Lima

Machu Picchu

Cuzco

Mt. Ampato

Lake Titicaca

BOLIVIA

El Misti

Arequipa

Pacific Ocean

Paraná River

PARAGUAY

Uruguay R.

CHILE

ARGENTINA

URUGUAY

Mt. Aconcagua

Río de la Plata

Mendoza

Buenos Aires

Punta del Este

Atlantic Ocean

Port San Juan Julián

Strait of Magellan

Falkland Islands

Tierra del Fuego

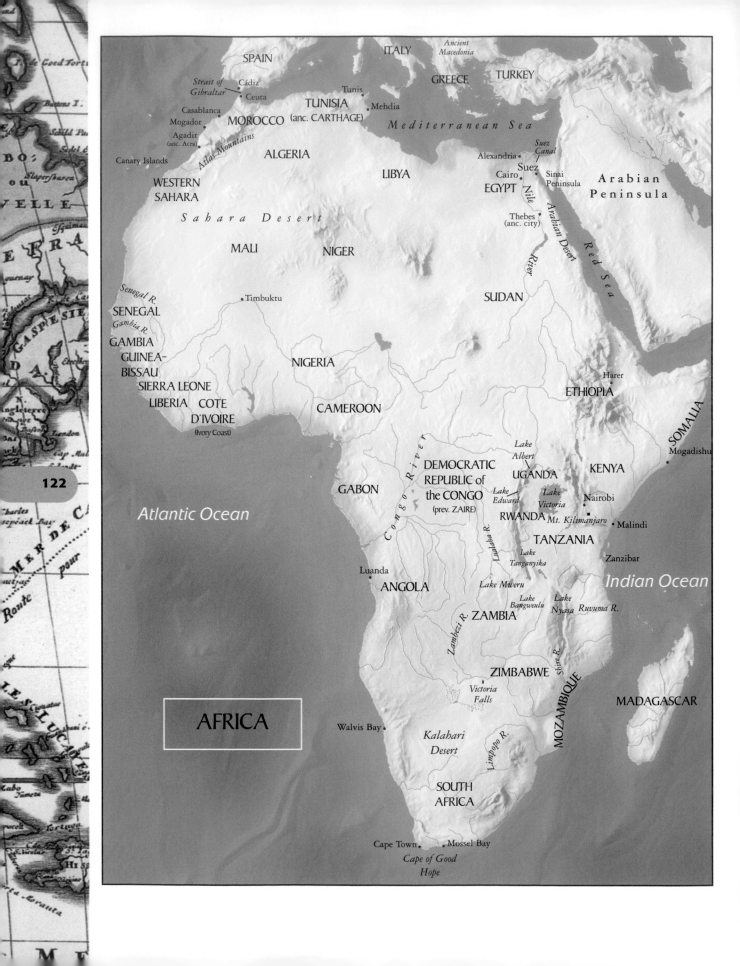

SPAIN

Strait of
Gibraltar
Cádiz
Ceuta

ITALY

Ancient
Macedonia

GREECE   TURKEY

Tunis

Casablanca   TUNISIA   Mehdia
Mogador   MOROCCO   (anc. CARTHAGE)
Agadir
(anc. Acra)   Atlas Mountains   Mediterranean Sea

Canary Islands   ALGERIA   Alexandria   Suez Canal

WESTERN   LIBYA   Cairo   Suez   Sinai   Arabian
SAHARA   EGYPT   Peninsula

Sahara Desert   Thebes   Peninsula
(anc. city)

Arabian Desert

MALI   NIGER   SUDAN

Red Sea

Senegal R.

SENEGAL   Timbuktu

Gambia R.

GAMBIA
GUINEA-
BISSAU   NIGERIA   Harer

SIERRA LEONE   ETHIOPIA

LIBERIA   COTE   CAMEROON
D'IVOIRE   SOMALIA

(Ivory Coast)

Lake   Mogadishu
Albert

DEMOCRATIC   UGANDA   KENYA
REPUBLIC of
GABON   the CONGO   Lake
(prev. ZAIRE)   Edward   Lake   Nairobi
Victoria

Atlantic Ocean   RWANDA   Mt. Kilimanjaro   Malindi

Lualaba R.   TANZANIA   Zanzibar

Lake
Tanganyika

Luanda   Lake Mweru   Indian Ocean

ANGOLA   Lake
Bangweulu   Lake
Nyasa   Ruvuma R.

ZAMBIA

ZIMBABWE

Victoria
Falls   MADAGASCAR

AFRICA   Walvis Bay

Kalahari
Desert   Limpopo R.

SOUTH
AFRICA

Cape Town   Mossel Bay

Cape of Good
Hope

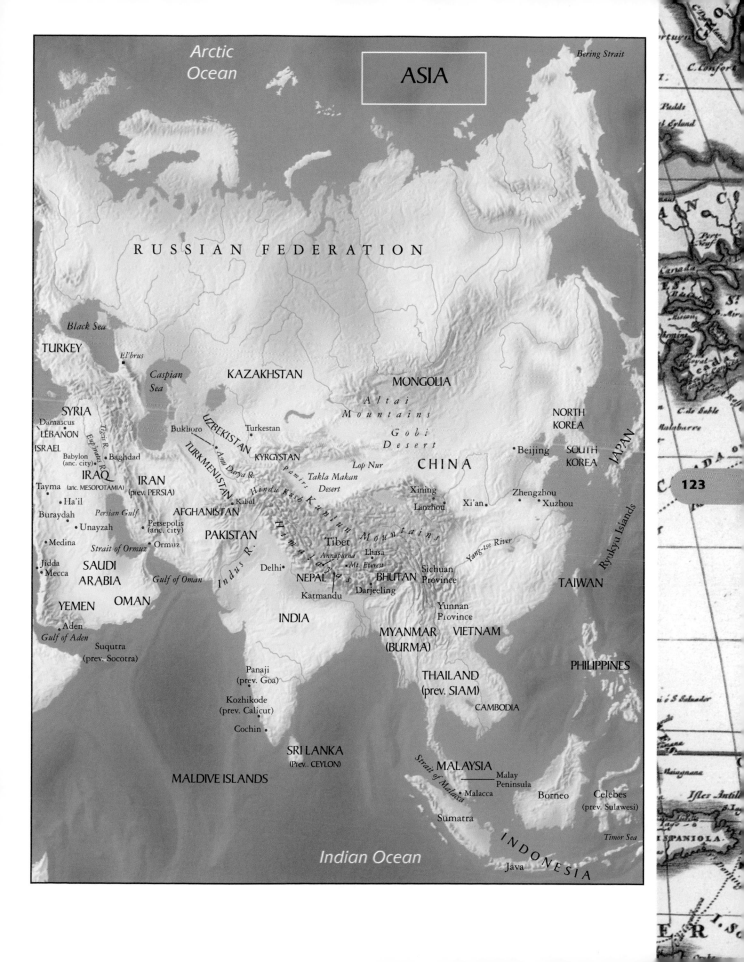

EUROPE

Snaefellsnes
Peninsula
ICELAND

FINLAND

Ural Mountains

NORWAY

SWEDEN

Scotland

Baltic
Sea

Moscow

RUSSIAN FEDERATION

REPUBLIC OF
IRELAND

GREAT
BRITAIN

England

Bristol

London

Aral
Sea

Atlantic
Ocean

English Channel

GERMANY

POLAND

Saint-Malo

Paris

Bay of Biscay

FRANCE

SWITZERLAND

UKRAINE

Mt. Blanc

Alps

AUSTRIA

Caucasus
Mountains

Matterhorn

Trieste

Caspian
Sea

SPAIN

PORTUGAL

ITALY

Adriatic

Black Sea

Lisbon

Rome

Sea

Istanbul

ARMENIA

Cádiz

Granada

(prev. Constantinople)

Strait of
Gibraltar

Mediterranean Sea

TURKEY

GREECE

ASIA

AFRICA

124

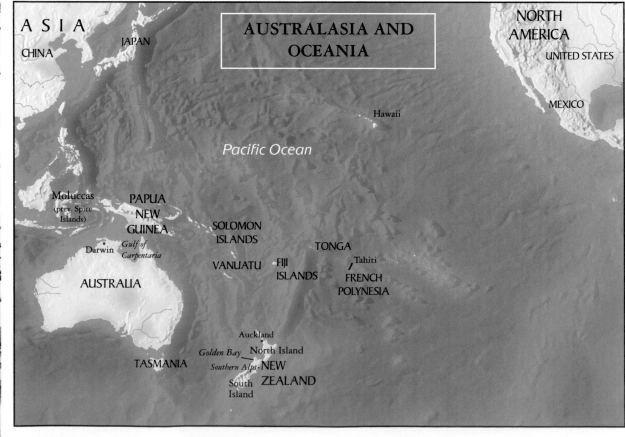

ASIA

JAPAN

AUSTRALASIA AND
OCEANIA

NORTH
AMERICA

CHINA

UNITED STATES

MEXICO

Hawaii

Pacific Ocean

Moluccas
(prev. Spice
Islands)

PAPUA
NEW
GUINEA

SOLOMON
ISLANDS

TONGA

Darwin

Gulf of
Carpentaria

VANUATU

FIJI
ISLANDS

Tahiti

FRENCH
POLYNESIA

AUSTRALIA

Auckland

TASMANIA

Golden Bay

North Island

Southern Alps

NEW

South
Island

ZEALAND

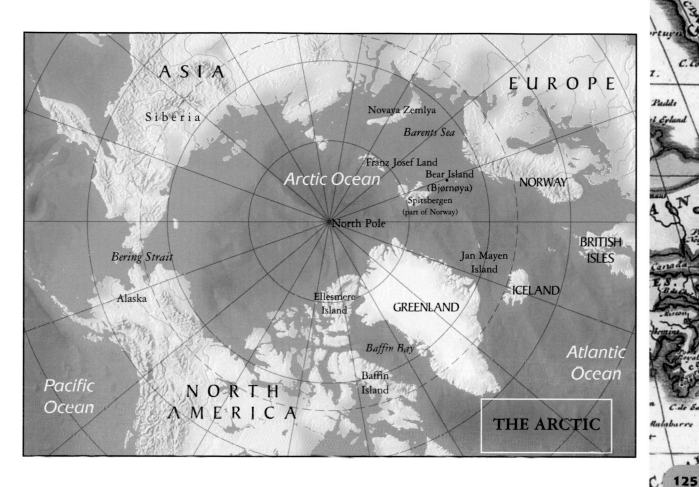

A S I A

Siberia

Novaya Zemlya

Barents Sea

Franz Josef Land

Bear Island
(Bjørnøya)

Spitsbergen
(part of Norway)

E U R O P E

NORWAY

Arctic Ocean

North Pole

BRITISH
ISLES

Bering Strait

Jan Mayen
Island

ICELAND

Alaska

Ellesmere
Island

GREENLAND

*Atlantic
Ocean*

Baffin Bay

*Pacific
Ocean*

N O R T H
A M E R I C A

Baffin
Island

THE ARCTIC

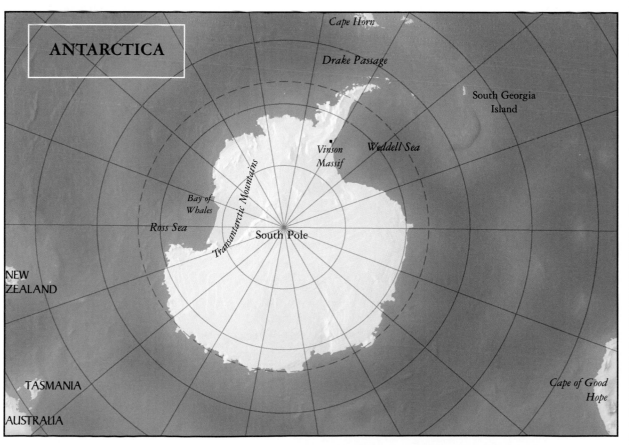

ANTARCTICA

Cape Horn

Drake Passage

South Georgia
Island

Weddell Sea

Vinson
Massif

*Bay of
Whales*

Transantarctic Mountains

Ross Sea

South Pole

NEW
ZEALAND

TASMANIA

AUSTRALIA

*Cape of Good
Hope*

Index